AI-Proof Career: Thrive in the Future of Work & Stay Ahead of Automation

How to Stay Competitive, Adapt, and Succeed

in the Age of Artificial Intelligence

Bradford M. Smith

Dedication

This book is dedicated to the countless individuals who are bravely navigating the ever-evolving landscape of the modern workplace. It's for the entrepreneurs, the innovators, and the lifelong learners who embrace change not with fear, but with a spirit of possibility and determination. It's for those who understand that the future of work is not a destination but a journey of continuous growth, adaptation, and collaboration – a journey where human ingenuity and artificial intelligence work in harmony. This work is a testament to their unwavering dedication to their careers and their commitment to shaping a future where technology and humanity thrive together, creating a more equitable and prosperous world for all. This is for those who see AI not as a threat, but as an opportunity; not as an ending, but as a beginning.

Table of Contents

Introduction

The rapid advancement of artificial intelligence is reshaping our world at an unprecedented pace. Its impact extends far beyond the headlines about factory closures and self-driving cars; it's quietly transforming the very fabric of the modern workplace. This book is not about fear-mongering or predicting a dystopian future where robots have taken all our jobs. Rather, it's a proactive guide designed to empower you to navigate this transformation and not just survive, but thrive in the age of AI. Within these pages, you'll find a realistic assessment of how AI is evolving and the profound impact it will have on various industries and professions. We'll dispel common myths and anxieties, providing a data-driven understanding of the opportunities and challenges that lie ahead. Most importantly, this book offers a practical, three-step strategy to future-proof your career: embrace AI tools, cultivate uniquely human skills, and position yourself as an AI-literate leader. The future of work is not predetermined. By understanding the forces at play and actively shaping your own trajectory, you can secure your place among the leaders and innovators of tomorrow.

Artificial intelligence is no longer a futuristic fantasy; it's a present-day reality reshaping the global economy and the way we work. While some foresee a bleak future of widespread job displacement, a more nuanced perspective reveals a complex interplay of disruption and opportunity. This book delves into the heart of this transformative period, providing a clear, concise, and accessible exploration of AI's impact on the modern workplace. We will examine its penetration into diverse sectors, from marketing and finance to sales and leadership, debunking common myths and providing a realistic assessment of how AI will reshape the jobs market over the next decade and beyond. However, this is not a narrative of impending doom. Instead, we focus on equipping you with the knowledge and actionable steps to navigate this evolving landscape successfully. We will present a comprehensive three-pronged approach to career resilience in the age of AI, encompassing the strategic adoption of AI tools, the cultivation of uniquely human skills irreplaceable by machines (such as emotional intelligence and critical thinking), and the development of your own expertise as an AI-literate leader. This book will provide you with practical strategies, real-world examples, and actionable steps to not just survive but thrive in a future defined by collaboration between human intelligence and artificial intelligence. Prepare to embrace the transformative power of AI and forge a future where your career is not only secure but exceptionally rewarding. The journey begins now.

Chapter 1: The AI Revolution: Reshaping the Modern Workplace

The Inevitable Rise of AI in the Workplace

The relentless march of artificial intelligence (AI) is reshaping the very fabric of the modern workplace, a transformation that's not confined to the realm of science fiction but is unfolding right now, in real time. While anxieties around AI often focus on the potential displacement of low-skill jobs, the reality is far more nuanced and pervasive. AI's impact extends across all levels, from entry-level positions to executive suites, demanding a reassessment of traditional career paths and skillsets. This isn't a distant threat; it's a present reality demanding proactive adaptation.

The misconception that AI only affects low-skilled jobs is a dangerous oversimplification. While repetitive, manual tasks are indeed prime candidates for automation, AI's capabilities are rapidly advancing to encompass more complex cognitive functions.

Consider the field of finance, where AI-powered algorithms are already analyzing vast datasets to predict market trends, assess risk, and even execute trades with greater speed and accuracy than human analysts. This doesn't imply that financial analysts are rendered obsolete; rather, the nature of their roles is evolving. The focus is shifting from manual data crunching to strategic interpretation of AI-generated insights, requiring a new set of analytical and decision-making skills. Similarly, in marketing, AI-powered tools are automating tasks like targeted advertising, content creation, and customer segmentation, leading to increased efficiency and personalization. Marketers, however, need to adapt by mastering these tools and focusing on more strategic, creative aspects of their roles, such as developing brand narratives and understanding consumer behavior at a deeper level.

The transformative power of AI is evident across diverse industries.

In healthcare, AI is assisting in diagnosis, drug discovery, and personalized treatment plans, leading to improved patient outcomes. In manufacturing, AI-powered robots are automating assembly lines, increasing productivity, and improving precision. In transportation, self-driving vehicles are poised to revolutionize logistics and transportation systems, creating new opportunities while simultaneously disrupting existing ones. The common thread in all these examples is the need for human adaptation. The jobs themselves may be redefined, but the need for human intelligence, creativity, and strategic thinking remains crucial.

Let's explore some specific examples to further illustrate this point. Consider the rise of AI-powered chatbots in customer service. These chatbots can handle routine inquiries, freeing up human agents to focus on more complex issues requiring empathy and nuanced problem-solving. This shift, while potentially leading to job displacement for some customer service representatives, creates new opportunities for those with the skills to manage and refine these AI systems, ensuring smooth operation and addressing exceptions. Similarly, in the legal field, AI is being used to analyze vast amounts of legal documents, identifying relevant precedents and streamlining the research process. Lawyers now need to be adept at utilizing these tools and focusing on the strategic aspects of legal practice, such as client interaction, negotiation, and courtroom advocacy – skills that require emotional intelligence and sophisticated reasoning, abilities that AI currently lacks.

The speed of AI integration into the workplace is accelerating, making proactive adaptation paramount. Consider the rapid advancements in machine learning, natural language processing, and computer vision. These advancements are not only enhancing the capabilities of existing AI systems, but also creating entirely new applications with the potential to transform industries and job markets. Companies are rapidly adopting AI-powered solutions to enhance efficiency, reduce costs, and gain a competitive edge. This adoption rate means the window for professionals to adapt and upskill is rapidly closing. The longer we wait, the greater the risk of being left behind.

The evolving workplace isn't just about adapting to new technologies; it's also about the evolving nature of work itself. The traditional hierarchical structures are becoming increasingly fluid, with project-based teams and remote collaborations becoming more common. This requires a shift in mindset, embracing flexibility and the ability to work effectively in dynamic and diverse teams. The ability to quickly adapt to new tools and technologies, collaborate effectively, and continuously learn new skills becomes crucial in this volatile environment.

Furthermore, the ethical considerations surrounding AI deployment in the workplace are increasingly important. Issues such as bias in algorithms, data privacy, and job displacement must be addressed responsibly. Professionals need to be not only technically proficient but also ethically aware, understanding the potential implications of AI and advocating for responsible implementation. This requires a broader understanding of societal implications and the potential impact on individuals and communities.

The shift towards an AI-powered workplace is not solely about technological advancement; it's a fundamental change in the way work is organized, performed, and managed. It demands a shift in mindset, from passively reacting to change to proactively shaping one's career in light of this evolving landscape. It's a call to action, urging us to embrace the transformative potential of AI while simultaneously safeguarding our human skills and values. The future of work is not about human versus machine; it's about human and machine, working together in a dynamic and symbiotic relationship. The key to success lies in proactively adapting to this new reality, mastering the tools of the future, and cultivating the uniquely human qualities that will continue to be highly valued in an increasingly automated world. This requires a lifelong commitment to learning, adaptability, and a forward-looking vision of the future of work, a future that demands our active participation and shaping. The challenge is clear: to not simply survive, but to thrive in the age of AI. This requires embracing the changes, understanding the implications, and proactively positioning ourselves for success in a world increasingly shaped by artificial intelligence.

AIs Impact on Different Industries

The pervasive influence of AI extends far beyond generalized observations; its impact is profoundly reshaping individual industries, demanding a granular understanding of its effects on specific roles and processes. Let's examine several key sectors to illustrate this transformative power.

In marketing, the integration of AI has revolutionized how businesses connect with consumers. Gone are the days of broad, untargeted campaigns. AI algorithms now analyze vast datasets of consumer behavior, preferences, and demographics, enabling hyper-personalized advertising. This targeted approach maximizes campaign effectiveness, leading to improved return on investment (ROI) and a more streamlined marketing spend. For example, companies like Netflix utilize AI to personalize movie recommendations, significantly increasing user engagement and retention. Similarly, social media platforms leverage AI to curate newsfeeds, showing users content tailored to their interests, optimizing ad delivery and boosting revenue. However, this sophistication presents challenges. Marketers must now be proficient in using AI-powered tools, interpreting data insights, and adapting campaigns in real-time based on algorithmic feedback. The creative aspects of marketing remain crucial, but they are now augmented by data-driven precision. The role of the marketer is shifting from simply executing campaigns to strategizing, interpreting complex data, and overseeing AI systems. The human element – creativity, understanding nuances of brand messaging, and crafting compelling narratives – remains irreplaceable, even in this increasingly automated landscape.

The finance industry is undergoing a dramatic metamorphosis thanks to AI. Algorithmic trading is rapidly replacing traditional human-driven trading strategies. AI-powered systems can analyze market data at speeds and scales unimaginable to human analysts, identifying profitable trading opportunities with remarkable efficiency. This doesn't mean human traders are obsolete; rather, their roles are evolving. They are now focusing on developing, overseeing, and refining these algorithmic systems, ensuring their integrity and mitigating potential risks. Furthermore, AI is proving invaluable in fraud detection. Sophisticated algorithms can identify anomalous transactions and patterns indicative of fraudulent activity, protecting financial institutions and consumers alike.

Consider the example of credit card companies using AI to detect fraudulent transactions in real-time, preventing significant financial losses. While AI significantly improves efficiency and security, it also introduces complexities. Financial professionals must now be well-versed in data science, algorithmic trading, and the ethical implications of AI-driven decisions. The need for regulatory oversight and understanding the limitations of AI in this high-stakes industry is paramount. The future of finance will rely heavily on a symbiotic relationship between human expertise and AI capabilities.

In the sales sector, AI is streamlining processes and enhancing efficiency across the board. AI-powered lead generation tools analyze customer data to identify potential clients, improving sales teams' focus and productivity. Customer service is another area significantly impacted by AI, with chatbots handling routine inquiries, freeing up human representatives to address more complex customer issues. Companies like Amazon utilize chatbots extensively to manage customer queries, resolving common problems quickly and efficiently. This improvement reduces response times and allows human agents to focus on situations requiring empathy and problem-solving skills. However, the implementation of AI in sales isn't without its challenges. Sales professionals need to adapt to working alongside AI tools, understanding their limitations and leveraging their strengths to improve their performance. The emphasis will be on relationship building, high-level negotiation, and handling complex sales cycles– tasks where human intuition and empathy still hold a significant advantage.

The impact of AI extends to the very top of organizational hierarchies, revolutionizing leadership styles and decision-making processes. AI-powered analytics provide leaders with data-driven insights, enabling them to make more informed decisions based on objective metrics. For example, companies can use AI to analyze employee performance data, identify areas for improvement, and personalize training programs to optimize overall productivity.

Leaders must embrace these analytical tools, interpreting the information to guide strategic planning and team management. Furthermore, AI tools can assist with talent acquisition, analyzing candidate profiles to identify top talent, streamlining the hiring process. While AI assists in these tasks, the role of human leadership remains critical. The ability to guide and motivate teams, foster collaboration, and make ethical and empathetic decisions are qualities that remain uniquely human. The integration of AI in leadership necessitates a new skillset, a blend of technical proficiency and emotional intelligence. Leaders need to understand how to utilize AI insights to inform decisions while maintaining their role as motivators, mentors, and strategic thinkers.

The successful integration of AI across all these industries relies on a crucial element: a skilled workforce capable of both utilizing and managing these systems. This requires substantial investments in education and reskilling initiatives, providing employees with the necessary skills to navigate the changing landscape. Furthermore, ethical considerations are paramount. The potential for algorithmic bias, data privacy concerns, and job displacement necessitates responsible implementation and rigorous oversight. Companies need to proactively address these concerns, ensuring fair and ethical use of AI technology while mitigating potential negative consequences. The future of work is not a zero-sum game of humans versus machines; it's a collaboration, requiring a workforce adept at adapting to the transformative power of AI, leveraging its strengths while embracing the uniquely human skills that will continue to be highly valued. The transition requires strategic planning, ethical considerations, and a continuous commitment to learning and adaptation. This ongoing evolution demands a proactive approach to reskilling, upskilling, and embracing the evolving nature of work in an AI-driven world.

Debunking Myths and Addressing Concerns

The rapid advancements in artificial intelligence (AI) have understandably sparked anxieties about job security and the future of work. Fear-mongering headlines often paint a dystopian picture of widespread unemployment, fueled by the misconception that AI will simply replace human workers wholesale. This, however, is a significant oversimplification. While AI undoubtedly automates certain tasks, its impact is far more nuanced, creating new opportunities even as it transforms existing roles. Let's dissect some common myths and concerns to build a more realistic and informed perspective.

One of the most pervasive myths is that AI will only impact low-skill jobs. This couldn't be further from the truth. AI is already making inroads into highly skilled professions, from financial analysts using AI-powered trading algorithms to doctors using AI for diagnostic assistance. The automation of routine tasks, even in complex fields, is accelerating. Consider the legal profession, where AI is being used to review contracts, research case law, and even predict case outcomes. This doesn't necessarily mean that lawyers are becoming obsolete; instead, their roles are evolving, requiring a greater emphasis on strategic thinking, client communication, and the application of legal expertise in more complex and nuanced situations where human judgment is paramount. The same principle applies to numerous other professions. Doctors, for instance, are increasingly leveraging AI for image analysis and diagnostic support, but the human element of patient care, empathy, and clinical judgment remains essential. The role shifts from purely diagnostic to one that incorporates AI assistance, allowing doctors to focus more on patient interaction and complex case management.

Another common concern is the speed of AI adoption and the resulting potential for large-scale job displacement. The truth is, the pace of technological change varies significantly across different industries and sectors. While some industries are experiencing rapid transformation, others are adapting more gradually. The "AI replacement timeline" is not linear; it's a complex and evolving process influenced by numerous factors, including technological advancements, regulatory frameworks, and economic conditions. Furthermore, the introduction of AI often creates new jobs in areas like AI development, data science, AI ethics, and AI system management. The net effect on employment is therefore not a simple equation of job losses versus job gains, but rather a complex interplay of transformation, creation, and adaptation.

The question, "Will AI replace my job?" is therefore not easily answered with a simple yes or no. A more accurate response would be: "Will AI change my job?" The answer to that is almost certainly yes, for most roles. The nature of work will evolve significantly as AI becomes more integrated into various industries. Instead of focusing on anxieties around replacement, it's far more productive to assess how AI might transform one's specific role and proactively develop the necessary skills to adapt and thrive in this new landscape.

What skills will become obsolete? This is another frequently asked question. While rote, repetitive tasks are most susceptible to automation, uniquely human skills will remain in high demand. These include critical thinking, complex problem-solving, creativity, emotional intelligence, adaptability, and strong communication skills. These skills are difficult, if not impossible, to replicate with current AI technology. For instance, negotiation, empathy, and the ability to understand subtle emotional cues are all crucial in many professions, particularly those involving human interaction. While AI can analyze large datasets to identify patterns and make predictions, it struggles to understand the nuances of human behavior and emotion. In marketing, the ability to create compelling brand narratives, understand consumer psychology, and build relationships remains critical, even as AI handles data analysis and targeted advertising. In leadership, emotional intelligence, strategic thinking, and the ability to motivate and inspire teams continue to be invaluable assets. Focusing on developing and honing these uniquely human capabilities is essential for future-proofing one's career.

The fear of obsolescence should be replaced with a proactive approach to continuous learning and skill development. The workforce needs to adapt to the evolving demands of the AI-driven workplace through targeted upskilling and reskilling initiatives.

This requires a multi-faceted approach, involving collaborations between educational institutions, businesses, and governments to ensure that individuals have access to the necessary training and resources. This includes investing in STEM education, promoting digital literacy, and providing opportunities for employees to acquire skills in data analysis, AI ethics, and other AI-related fields.

Furthermore, companies have a responsibility to invest in their employees' development, offering training programs and opportunities for skill enhancement. A collaborative approach, involving proactive workforce development strategies and a willingness to embrace continuous learning, will be crucial in navigating the transition to an AI-driven future.

Another major concern surrounding AI is the potential for bias and discrimination. AI algorithms are trained on data, and if that data reflects existing societal biases, the algorithms will perpetuate and even amplify those biases. This is particularly problematic in areas like hiring, loan applications, and even criminal justice, where biased algorithms can lead to unfair and discriminatory outcomes.

Addressing this requires careful attention to data quality and algorithm design, ensuring that algorithms are fair, transparent, and accountable. This includes rigorous testing and auditing to detect and mitigate bias, as well as the development of ethical guidelines and regulations governing the use of AI. The focus should be on creating AI systems that are not only efficient but also equitable and just. This is a complex challenge requiring collaboration between technologists, ethicists, policymakers, and the broader community.

Finally, the discussion of AI's impact on the workplace must also include the critical aspect of job displacement. While the creation of new roles will undoubtedly occur, there will be jobs lost due to automation. Proactive mitigation strategies must be employed to address this challenge. This includes government-led initiatives such as unemployment benefits, job retraining programs, and investment in social safety nets to support workers transitioning to new roles.

Companies also bear a responsibility to ensure a fair and ethical transition, potentially providing support and retraining opportunities for employees whose roles are affected by AI. This requires a societal commitment to managing the transition in a way that balances economic efficiency with social justice.

In conclusion, the AI revolution is not a simple narrative of replacement but rather a complex process of transformation. By understanding the nuances of AI's impact, dispelling common myths, and actively developing uniquely human skills, individuals and organizations can navigate the evolving landscape successfully. A proactive, multi-faceted approach, combining individual initiative with collective action, will be crucial in shaping a future where humans and AI collaborate to create a more productive, equitable, and prosperous world. The future of work isn't a battle between humans and machines; it's a partnership, requiring adaptability, continuous learning, and a commitment to responsible innovation. The key is not to fear the change, but to embrace it and shape it for the betterment of all.

The AI Replacement Timeline: A Realistic Assessment

Predicting the future is inherently uncertain, but by analyzing current trends and the pace of technological advancements, we can construct a plausible, albeit imperfect, timeline for AI's impact on the workplace over the next five, ten, and twenty years. This timeline won't offer definitive dates for specific job losses, but rather a range of possibilities and potential shifts across various sectors. Remember, the actual timeline will be influenced by numerous factors – technological breakthroughs, regulatory landscapes, economic conditions, and societal adaptation.

The Five-Year Outlook (2024-2029): Automation Accelerates

Over the next five years, we can expect to see a significant acceleration in the automation of routine, repetitive tasks across numerous industries. This will be most noticeable in sectors heavily reliant on data processing, such as customer service, data entry, and basic accounting functions. AI-powered chatbots will become even more sophisticated, handling a larger percentage of customer interactions, freeing up human agents to focus on more complex issues. Similarly, AI-driven software will further automate financial transactions and streamline accounting processes. While these changes won't necessarily lead to massive job losses overnight, they will undoubtedly reshape job roles, demanding increased proficiency in digital tools and a focus on higher-level skills.

Manufacturing will also see significant changes. Robots and automated systems, guided by increasingly sophisticated AI, will handle more assembly line tasks and other repetitive jobs, increasing efficiency and potentially reducing the need for human intervention in certain areas. However, this will also create opportunities in areas like robotics maintenance, programming, and AI system oversight. The demand for skilled technicians and engineers capable of managing and maintaining these advanced systems will rise. It's not a matter of robots replacing human workers completely, but rather a shift toward human-robot collaboration, requiring upskilling and reskilling initiatives to prepare the workforce for these new roles.

In the healthcare sector, we'll see a continued integration of AI-powered diagnostic tools, leading to improved efficiency and accuracy. However, the human element of patient care – empathy, emotional intelligence, and complex decision-making in ambiguous situations – will remain irreplaceable. The role of medical professionals will evolve, requiring them to become adept at collaborating with AI systems while maintaining the core values of compassionate and personalized care.

The Ten-Year Outlook (2029-2039): The Rise of Intelligent Automation

By 2039, we'll likely see a more profound transformation driven by "intelligent automation" – systems capable of performing more complex tasks, requiring less direct human supervision. This will impact a broader range of professions, including some currently considered highly skilled. For instance, AI-powered legal research tools will become increasingly sophisticated, allowing lawyers to process significantly more information in less time. This doesn't mean lawyers will become obsolete, but it will alter the nature of their work, demanding higher levels of strategic thinking, client communication, and nuanced legal analysis. Similar shifts can be anticipated in other professions, such as financial analysis, where

AI-driven algorithms will further automate portfolio management and risk assessment.

The transportation sector will undergo a significant shift, with autonomous vehicles becoming more prevalent, impacting the roles of truck drivers, taxi drivers, and delivery personnel. While this could lead to job displacement in some areas, it will also create new job opportunities in areas such as autonomous vehicle maintenance, software development, and system management. The societal impact will be significant, requiring careful planning and policy interventions to ensure a smooth transition and mitigate potential job losses.

The creative industries will also experience changes. AI tools will become increasingly sophisticated in generating various forms of content, including text, images, and music. However, the uniquely human aspects of creativity – originality, emotional depth, and the ability to connect with audiences on an emotional level – will continue to be highly valued. The role of creative professionals will likely shift toward collaboration with AI tools, utilizing these technologies to enhance their creative process and reach wider audiences, rather than being replaced entirely.

The Twenty-Year Outlook (2039-2059): The AI-Augmented Workplace

Looking further ahead, to 2059, the workplace will be significantly different. AI will be deeply integrated into nearly every aspect of professional life, augmenting human capabilities and transforming the nature of work. The distinction between human and AI tasks may become increasingly blurred, with a focus on collaborative systems where humans and AI work together to achieve common goals. This could involve humans focusing on complex problem-solving, strategic planning, and creative endeavors, while AI handles routine tasks, data analysis, and other repetitive functions.

The concept of a traditional "job" might even evolve. We may see a shift toward more project-based work and flexible employment arrangements, enabling greater autonomy and potentially blurring the lines between professional and personal life. The demand for skills in AI development, data science, AI ethics, and human-computer interaction will be significantly higher. This will require ongoing investment in education and training to equip the workforce with the necessary skills to navigate this transformed landscape. It's critical to emphasize that this longer-term vision is not about a fully automated world but rather a workplace where humans and AI collaborate, augmenting each other's strengths and creating a more productive and efficient work environment. The challenge will be to ensure a just and equitable transition, addressing potential job displacement and ensuring access to appropriate training and retraining opportunities for all members of the workforce.

This realistic assessment of the AI replacement timeline highlights the need for proactive adaptation. The future of work will not be solely defined by technological advancements, but also by how we, as individuals and as a society, choose to respond to them. This calls for a multifaceted approach, encompassing individual skills development, institutional support for education and retraining, and strategic government policies designed to mitigate potential disruptions and create a more equitable and inclusive future of work. The focus should be on harnessing the power of AI to enhance human potential, rather than succumbing to fears of replacement. The key is not just survival, but thriving in this evolving landscape.

Understanding the Shifting Skills Landscape

Understanding the shifting skills landscape in the age of AI requires a nuanced perspective. While the fear of widespread job displacement is understandable, the reality is more complex. AI won't simply replace humans; it will transform the nature of work, demanding a new set of skills and competencies. This transformation necessitates a proactive approach to continuous learning and upskilling, focusing on uniquely human capabilities that complement AI's strengths.

The most immediate impact is the automation of routine and repetitive tasks. Jobs heavily reliant on data processing, data entry, basic accounting, and even some aspects of customer service are already experiencing this shift. While these changes will lead to job role evolution, it's not a simple case of "humans versus machines." Instead, it creates opportunities for human workers to focus on more complex and strategic tasks, requiring higher-level skills and abilities. This transition demands a shift in mindset – from executing routine procedures to analyzing data, identifying patterns, and making informed decisions based on that analysis. This means increased reliance on analytical skills, critical thinking, and problem-solving abilities.

The skills that will become increasingly valuable in this new landscape are those that leverage uniquely human capabilities. Critical thinking, the ability to analyze information objectively and make reasoned judgments, will become paramount. AI can process vast amounts of data, but it currently lacks the capacity for truly independent, nuanced critical analysis. Humans will be needed to interpret data, identify biases, and formulate strategic decisions based on incomplete or contradictory information. This necessitates honing one's analytical skills through dedicated practice and continuous learning, including engaging with critical thinking frameworks and methodologies. Formal courses in critical thinking, coupled with real-world application and reflection, can significantly enhance this crucial skill.

Complex problem-solving, another critical skill set, will be in high demand. AI excels at solving well-defined problems with clear parameters, but struggles with ambiguous, ill-defined situations requiring creative solutions and adaptable approaches. Humans will be needed to tackle complex, multi-faceted problems requiring innovative solutions and the ability to adapt to changing circumstances. Practicing problem-solving through case studies, simulations, and real-world projects, coupled with seeking out mentorship and collaborative problem-solving opportunities, will prove invaluable.

Creativity and innovation, often considered uniquely human traits, will only grow in importance. While AI can generate creative outputs (such as text or images), it lacks the capacity for truly original, groundbreaking thought. The ability to think outside the box, develop novel ideas, and push creative boundaries will continue to be highly valued. Creative professionals can enhance their skills by actively engaging in creative projects, collaborating with others, seeking feedback and actively engaging in continuing education focused on fostering innovative thinking and problem-solving strategies. This could include design thinking workshops, brainstorming sessions and mentorship from established creatives.

Emotional intelligence, the ability to understand and manage one's own emotions and the emotions of others, will be a vital differentiator in the age of AI. While AI can process and analyze vast amounts of data, it currently lacks the capacity for genuine empathy, compassion, and nuanced interpersonal understanding. In roles involving direct human interaction, such as healthcare, education, and social work, these skills will remain irreplaceable. Improving emotional intelligence requires self-reflection, active listening, empathy exercises, and seeking feedback on one's emotional interactions. Professional development opportunities focused on emotional intelligence can offer structured guidance in enhancing these capabilities.

Conversely, some skills may become less relevant as AI automates routine tasks. These include basic data entry, repetitive manual tasks, and certain aspects of customer service that can be handled by AI chatbots. However, this is not necessarily a negative development. It allows workers to focus on higher-value tasks requiring critical thinking, creativity, and emotional intelligence. The key is to anticipate these shifts and proactively develop skills that are complementary to, rather than competitive with, AI.

The adaptation required isn't just about acquiring new technical skills; it also involves embracing a mindset of continuous learning. The fast pace of technological advancements means that acquiring new skills is not a one-time event but an ongoing process.

Individuals must cultivate a lifelong learning attitude, actively seeking out new knowledge and staying abreast of the latest developments in their fields. This could involve pursuing online courses, attending workshops and conferences, engaging in professional development programs, and actively participating in peer-to-peer learning communities.

This necessitates a collaborative approach between individuals, educational institutions, and employers. Educational institutions must adapt their curricula to reflect the evolving skills landscape, offering programs and courses focused on developing the skills needed for the future of work. Employers need to invest in upskilling and reskilling initiatives for their employees, providing opportunities for professional development and creating a workplace culture that values continuous learning. Furthermore, governments play a crucial role in fostering a supportive ecosystem for continuous learning, investing in education and training initiatives and implementing policies that promote lifelong learning.

The successful navigation of the AI revolution in the workplace requires a multifaceted approach. It necessitates a proactive mindset, focused on acquiring and enhancing uniquely human skills while adapting to the changing demands of the job market.

Individuals must take responsibility for their own professional development, seeking out opportunities to acquire new skills and embrace a lifelong learning approach. Educational institutions, employers, and governments all play crucial roles in creating a supportive ecosystem for this transition, investing in education, reskilling initiatives, and policies that encourage continuous learning and adaptability. The future of work isn't about human versus AI; it's about human *with* AI, leveraging the strengths of both to create a more efficient, productive, and equitable work environment. This requires proactive planning, continuous learning, and a collaborative effort across all stakeholders. The future is not predetermined; it is shaped by the choices we make today.

Chapter 2: Embracing AI Tools: A Practical Guide

Identifying and Leveraging Relevant AI Tools

Identifying and leveraging the power of AI tools is no longer a futuristic concept; it's a present-day necessity for professionals across various sectors. The sheer volume of available AI tools can be overwhelming, but a strategic approach, focusing on relevance and practical application, can unlock significant productivity gains and competitive advantages. This section provides a framework for identifying and effectively utilizing AI tools tailored to your specific profession.

First, it's crucial to understand your current workflow and identify areas ripe for automation or enhancement. What tasks are repetitive and time-consuming? Where do bottlenecks occur? Analyzing your daily activities will reveal areas where AI could significantly improve efficiency. For instance, a marketing professional might spend hours manually analyzing social media analytics. An AI-powered tool could automate this process, providing comprehensive reports and insightful visualizations in a fraction of the time.

Similarly, a financial analyst might spend considerable effort on data entry and reconciliation. AI-driven solutions can streamline these tasks, freeing up time for more strategic analysis and decision-making.

Once you've identified key areas for improvement, the next step involves researching and evaluating relevant AI tools. This research should be tailored to your specific needs and the nature of your work. There's a broad spectrum of AI tools available, ranging from simple automation software to sophisticated machine learning platforms. The optimal choice will depend on factors like the complexity of the task, your technical expertise, and your budget. For example, a basic project management team might benefit from AI-powered scheduling tools, while a data scientist would need access to more advanced machine learning libraries and platforms.

Exploring these tools requires a combination of online research and networking. Start by searching for AI solutions specifically designed for your industry or profession. Review online resources, such as industry publications, technology blogs, and review sites, to gather information on available tools and compare their functionalities and capabilities. Attend industry conferences and webinars to learn about the latest developments and engage with vendors and experts. Professional networking also plays a crucial role. Engage with colleagues, peers, and mentors to learn about their experiences with AI tools and gather recommendations based on their firsthand knowledge and experience.

Furthermore, consider the scalability and integration capabilities of any tool under consideration. Will it seamlessly integrate with your existing systems and workflows? Can it adapt to your evolving needs as your business grows and changes? These are critical factors to evaluate, ensuring that the chosen AI tool becomes a long-term asset, not a short-term solution that quickly becomes obsolete or incompatible with your operational environment.

Let's explore some specific examples. For marketing professionals, tools like HubSpot and SEMrush offer AI-powered features for SEO optimization, content creation, and social media management.

These tools leverage machine learning to analyze data, identify trends, and optimize marketing campaigns. For financial analysts, platforms like Bloomberg Terminal and Refinitiv Eikon integrate AI-powered tools for financial modeling, risk management, and algorithmic trading. These sophisticated platforms provide real-time market data and analytical capabilities to support informed decision-making. In sales, tools like Salesforce Einstein and Microsoft Dynamics 365 utilize AI for lead scoring, sales forecasting, and customer relationship management. These AI functionalities help to personalize customer interactions, optimize sales processes and improve sales team efficiency.

In the realm of human resources, AI is transforming recruitment and employee management. AI-powered recruitment tools automate tasks such as candidate screening, resume parsing, and interview scheduling, significantly improving the efficiency of the hiring process. Furthermore, AI-driven employee engagement platforms can analyze employee data to identify potential issues and proactively address them. For customer service representatives, AI-powered chatbots automate responses to common inquiries, freeing up human agents to address more complex issues. This leads to faster response times, improved customer satisfaction, and increased overall efficiency.

The selection process shouldn't solely focus on features; consider factors like user-friendliness, technical support, and cost-effectiveness. A powerful tool that's difficult to use or requires extensive technical expertise may not be the most efficient option. Equally important is the availability of robust technical support and comprehensive documentation to troubleshoot problems and ensure smooth operation. Cost-effectiveness is a critical consideration, balancing the potential return on investment against the initial and ongoing expenses.

Beyond individual tools, there is also the opportunity to build custom AI solutions. This approach requires more technical expertise, often involving data scientists and software engineers.

However, this approach offers the potential to create highly specialized solutions tailored precisely to the specific needs of the organization. This approach demands a considerable upfront investment, but it can yield long-term benefits in terms of efficiency, innovation and competitive advantage. The decision to develop a custom AI solution versus using off-the-shelf tools hinges on factors such as budget, technical capabilities, and the complexity of the task at hand.

Once an AI tool is selected and implemented, continuous monitoring and evaluation are essential. Track its performance, measure its impact on productivity and efficiency, and gather feedback from users. This ongoing evaluation will help to identify areas for improvement and ensure that the tool continues to deliver optimal results. Regular training and ongoing support for users are critical to ensure the effective and efficient utilization of the AI tools. This training should focus on practical application and problem-solving, empowering users to confidently leverage the tool's capabilities. It should also equip users with the skills to interpret the outputs of the AI tools and make informed decisions based on the insights provided.

It is important to remember that AI tools are not replacements for human judgment and expertise. They are designed to augment human capabilities, not replace them. AI tools should be viewed as powerful instruments to enhance productivity and efficiency, but they are most effective when integrated with human insight and critical thinking. The successful integration of AI in the workplace involves a shift in mindset, from viewing AI as a threat to recognizing it as a valuable ally in achieving business objectives and personal career advancement.

The process of identifying and leveraging relevant AI tools is iterative. Start with a clear understanding of your needs, conduct thorough research, evaluate potential tools based on a holistic set of criteria, and then implement and continuously monitor the chosen tools. Remember that the landscape of AI is constantly evolving. Continuous learning and adaptation are essential to stay abreast of the latest developments and effectively utilize the most advanced AI tools available.

This commitment to ongoing professional development is critical for navigating the ever-changing dynamics of the workplace in the age of AI. Embracing this mindset will not only enhance your productivity and efficiency but will also position you for long-term success and advancement in your chosen field. The future of work isn't just about surviving the AI revolution; it's about thriving by intelligently leveraging its transformative power.

Mastering AI-Powered Software and Platforms

Having established the importance of identifying and evaluating AI tools relevant to your profession, let's now delve into the practical application of these tools. This section offers a more hands-on approach, providing specific examples and step-by-step guidance on utilizing AI-powered software and platforms effectively.

Mastering AI-powered tools requires a combination of understanding their functionalities and developing a strategic approach to their implementation. It's not just about knowing *what* a tool can do, but *how* to integrate it seamlessly into your existing workflows to maximize its potential. Let's explore this through various professional contexts.

Data Analysis with AI: For data analysts, the ability to extract meaningful insights from large datasets is paramount. AI significantly accelerates this process. Tools like Python libraries (Pandas, NumPy, Scikit-learn) combined with AI-powered data visualization platforms like Tableau and Power BI revolutionize data analysis.

Imagine you're analyzing sales data for a retail company. Manually sifting through thousands of records to identify trends would be immensely time-consuming. With AI, you can automate this process. First, you'd import the data into Python, using Pandas to clean and structure it. NumPy would then facilitate efficient numerical computations. Scikit-learn's machine learning algorithms can identify patterns and predict future sales. For example, a clustering algorithm might group customers into segments based on purchasing behavior, allowing for targeted marketing campaigns. Finally, Tableau or Power BI would translate the complex data into easily understandable visualizations—charts, graphs, and dashboards—presenting clear insights to stakeholders. This entire process, from data acquisition to insightful presentation, is significantly faster and more accurate with the strategic use of AI.

AI in Marketing Automation: Marketing professionals face the challenge of managing multiple channels, analyzing campaign performance, and personalizing customer experiences. AI-powered marketing automation platforms streamline these processes.

HubSpot, for instance, offers features like AI-driven lead scoring, where AI algorithms analyze customer behavior to predict the likelihood of conversion. This allows marketers to prioritize leads and allocate resources effectively. Similar AI-powered tools facilitate automated email marketing, social media scheduling, and A/B testing of different marketing materials.

Let's consider a hypothetical scenario: a company launching a new product. Using AI, the marketing team can segment their audience based on demographics, interests, and online behavior. AI-powered tools then automate the creation of targeted email campaigns, social media posts, and even personalized website content for each segment. They can also automatically analyze the performance of each campaign, providing real-time data on open rates, click-through rates, and conversions. This real-time feedback loop enables marketers to constantly optimize their campaigns for maximum impact, a task impossible to manage manually at scale.

AI in Project Management: Efficient project management is critical for success in any organization. AI tools are transforming this field by automating task assignments, predicting project delays, and optimizing resource allocation. Tools like Asana and Monday.com utilize AI to analyze project data and identify potential bottlenecks. They can automatically flag tasks that are falling behind schedule, suggest optimal resource allocation, and even predict potential project delays based on historical data.

Consider a software development project with numerous tasks and deadlines. Manually tracking progress, identifying potential issues, and reassigning resources would be a complex and time-consuming endeavor. AI-powered project management tools can automatically track task completion, identify dependencies between tasks, and alert the project manager to any potential delays. This allows for proactive intervention, preventing minor issues from escalating into major problems, ultimately ensuring on-time and within-budget project completion.

AI in Sales and Customer Relationship Management (CRM): Salesforce Einstein is a prime example of AI revolutionizing sales. It leverages AI for lead scoring, sales forecasting, and customer relationship management. Imagine a sales team struggling to prioritize leads. Salesforce Einstein uses AI to analyze customer data, predict the likelihood of closing a deal, and automatically prioritize high-potential leads. This enables sales representatives to focus their efforts on the most promising opportunities, leading to increased sales conversion rates. Furthermore, AI can personalize customer interactions by providing relevant product recommendations and anticipating customer needs based on past behavior. This leads to improved customer satisfaction and stronger customer relationships.

Beyond these specific examples, the applications of AI are virtually limitless. In finance, AI powers algorithmic trading, fraud detection, and risk assessment. In healthcare, AI aids in disease diagnosis, drug discovery, and personalized medicine. In education, AI personalizes learning experiences and provides adaptive feedback to students.

Successfully integrating AI tools demands more than simply purchasing software. It requires a strategic approach. This involves:

Defining clear objectives: Before choosing any tool, identify what specific problem you are trying to solve or what task you want to automate. This clarity guides the selection process.

Data preparation: Many AI tools require clean and structured data. This often necessitates data cleaning, transformation, and preprocessing.

Continuous learning and adaptation: The field of AI is constantly evolving. Stay updated on new tools and techniques through continuous learning.

Ethical considerations: Be mindful of potential biases in AI algorithms and ensure data privacy.

Mastering AI-powered tools is not a one-time achievement; it's an ongoing process of learning, adaptation, and refinement. By embracing a strategic approach and continuously expanding your knowledge, you can leverage the immense potential of AI to enhance productivity, improve decision-making, and ultimately, thrive in the rapidly evolving landscape of the modern workplace.

The key is not to fear AI, but to understand it, adapt to it, and harness its transformative power for your professional advantage.

Developing AI Literacy A Foundational Skill

Developing a robust understanding of AI is no longer a luxury; it's a necessity for navigating the modern workplace. AI literacy isn't about becoming a data scientist or programmer; rather, it's about developing a fundamental comprehension of how AI systems function, their capabilities, and their limitations. This understanding empowers you to effectively utilize AI tools, interpret their output, and critically assess their implications for your work and the broader society.

The core components of AI literacy involve grasping the basic concepts of artificial intelligence and machine learning. Artificial intelligence, at its heart, aims to create systems that can mimic human intelligence—learning, reasoning, problem-solving, and decision-making. Machine learning, a subset of AI, focuses on enabling computer systems to learn from data without explicit programming. Instead of being explicitly programmed with rules, machine learning algorithms identify patterns, make predictions, and improve their performance over time based on the data they are exposed to. Understanding this distinction—between explicitly programmed rules and learning from data—is crucial for understanding the capabilities and limitations of different AI systems.

Several common machine learning techniques underpin many AI applications. Supervised learning, for instance, involves training an algorithm on a labeled dataset – data where the desired output is already known. This allows the algorithm to learn the relationship between the input data and the output, and subsequently predict outputs for new, unseen data. Think of training a system to identify spam emails: you would feed it a dataset of emails labeled as "spam" or "not spam," allowing it to learn the characteristics that differentiate them. Unsupervised learning, on the other hand, works with unlabeled data. The algorithm's task is to discover inherent structures or patterns in the data without any prior knowledge of the desired outcome. This technique is often used for clustering similar data points or identifying anomalies. Imagine analyzing customer purchase history to identify distinct customer segments based on buying patterns – unsupervised learning can achieve this without pre-defined categories. Reinforcement learning, a third significant approach, involves an agent learning through trial and error by interacting with an environment. The agent receives rewards or penalties based on its actions, guiding it to learn optimal strategies for achieving a specific goal. This method is frequently applied in robotics and game playing, where the agent learns to navigate complex situations through repeated interactions.

Understanding these fundamental concepts is only the first step. AI literacy also necessitates an awareness of the different types of AI systems and their applications. From simple rule-based systems to complex deep learning models, the diversity of AI technologies is vast. Rule-based systems, the simplest form, operate on a set of predefined rules to make decisions. These systems are effective for tasks with clearly defined rules and limited variability, such as basic chatbots or simple diagnostic tools. In contrast, deep learning models, a more advanced form, utilize artificial neural networks with multiple layers to analyze complex data. These models are powerful tools for image recognition, natural language processing, and other complex tasks. Familiarizing oneself with these different architectures allows one to better understand the suitability of specific AI systems for various tasks and applications.

Furthermore, AI literacy extends beyond technical understanding to incorporate ethical considerations. AI systems, especially those based on machine learning, can inherit biases present in the data they are trained on. This can lead to unfair or discriminatory outcomes, highlighting the critical need for careful data selection and algorithm design. For instance, an AI system trained on biased data could perpetuate gender or racial biases in hiring decisions or loan applications. Understanding these potential biases is paramount in ensuring the responsible and ethical development and deployment of AI systems. The importance of data privacy is equally crucial. AI systems often rely on large amounts of data, and ensuring the responsible handling and protection of this data is fundamental to maintaining user trust and complying with relevant regulations. Understanding data privacy principles and regulations, such as GDPR (General Data Protection Regulation) or CCPA (California Consumer Privacy Act), is therefore a vital aspect of AI literacy.

Beyond these fundamental concepts, AI literacy also involves the ability to critically evaluate the output of AI systems. AI systems are tools, and like any tool, their output requires careful interpretation and validation. Understanding the limitations of AI systems is crucial to avoid over-reliance or misinterpretation of their results.

AI systems are not infallible; they can make mistakes, produce unexpected results, or be vulnerable to manipulation. Therefore, critical evaluation of AI output, coupled with human oversight and judgment, is essential for responsible decision-making. The ability to effectively communicate about AI, both its capabilities and limitations, is equally crucial. Effectively conveying the implications of AI to colleagues, clients, or the public requires clear and concise communication that avoids technical jargon and emphasizes the practical consequences of AI technologies.

To enhance your AI literacy, consider engaging in practical exercises. Experiment with readily available AI tools and platforms, such as online machine learning platforms or AI-powered writing assistants. This hands-on experience will reinforce theoretical concepts and provide a clearer understanding of how AI systems work in practice. Explore online courses and resources: many reputable organizations offer courses on AI and machine learning, catering to various skill levels. These resources can provide a structured learning path and deepen your understanding of AI concepts. Staying informed about recent advancements in AI is also crucial. Read industry publications, follow leading researchers on social media, and attend conferences and workshops to stay abreast of the latest developments and best practices in the field.

Participating in discussions and sharing your learnings with peers can further solidify your understanding and provide opportunities for collaborative growth.

Finally, remember that AI literacy is an ongoing journey, not a destination. The field of AI is rapidly evolving, and continuous learning and adaptation are essential for staying ahead of the curve.

Embrace this evolving landscape with curiosity and a proactive approach to learning, and you will equip yourself with a crucial skillset for thriving in the AI-driven future. By embracing AI literacy, you're not just enhancing your career prospects; you're positioning yourself as a responsible and effective participant in shaping the future of work and society.

Building an AI-Powered Workflow

Building an AI-powered workflow isn't about wholesale replacement of human effort; it's about intelligent augmentation. It's about leveraging AI's strengths to amplify human capabilities, freeing us from tedious tasks and empowering us to focus on higher-level strategic thinking and creative problem-solving. This requires a strategic approach, a careful consideration of your existing workflow, and a willingness to experiment and adapt.

The first step is identifying tasks ripe for automation. These are typically repetitive, data-heavy processes that can be easily defined algorithmically. Consider tasks such as data entry, email filtering, scheduling appointments, or generating basic reports. In marketing, for instance, AI can automate social media posting, analyze campaign performance, and even personalize marketing messages based on customer profiles. In finance, AI can automate invoice processing, fraud detection, and risk assessment. In sales, AI-powered tools can automate lead generation, qualify leads, and even engage in initial customer conversations through chatbots.

Even in seemingly creative fields like writing, AI can assist with research, editing, and even generating initial drafts, leaving the writer to focus on refining the narrative and imbuing it with unique human perspectives.

Once you've identified these automatable tasks, the next step is selecting the appropriate AI tools. The market is flooded with AI-powered solutions, ranging from standalone applications to integrated platforms. It's crucial to carefully assess your specific needs and choose tools that seamlessly integrate with your existing workflow. Consider factors such as ease of use, integration capabilities, data security, and cost. Many free or low-cost options exist for smaller businesses or individuals, while enterprise-grade solutions offer more advanced features and support. For instance, a small business might use a free CRM with integrated AI for lead management, while a large corporation might invest in a custom-built AI system for complex data analysis and predictive modeling.

The integration process itself requires careful planning and execution. This involves configuring the AI tools to interface with your existing systems, ensuring data flow and compatibility. It might involve training the AI system on relevant data, adjusting parameters for optimal performance, and establishing clear protocols for human oversight and intervention. This process is often iterative, requiring continuous monitoring and adjustment to fine-tune the system's performance and address any unforeseen challenges. The goal isn't simply to automate tasks; it's to optimize the entire workflow for maximum efficiency and accuracy.

For example, a financial analyst might integrate an AI-powered tool for analyzing market trends and identifying investment opportunities. The AI system could sift through vast amounts of data, identifying patterns and anomalies that might be missed by a human analyst. This doesn't replace the analyst's role; instead, it empowers them to make more informed decisions by providing them with a clearer picture of the market. The analyst can then use their expertise to interpret the AI's findings, validate the results, and formulate investment strategies.

Similarly, a marketing professional might use an AI-powered tool for managing social media campaigns. The AI can automate posting schedules, analyze engagement metrics, and even suggest optimal content based on audience preferences. This frees the marketing professional from mundane tasks, allowing them to focus on developing creative campaigns, building brand relationships, and engaging with their audience on a more personal level.

A key aspect of building an AI-powered workflow is understanding the limitations of AI. AI systems are not infallible; they can be prone to errors, biases, and unexpected behavior. Therefore, it's crucial to establish robust processes for monitoring the AI's performance, validating its output, and providing human oversight.

This might involve regularly reviewing the AI's decisions, implementing quality control checks, and incorporating human feedback loops to improve the system's accuracy and reliability.

Furthermore, the ethical implications of using AI in the workplace must be considered. AI systems can perpetuate biases present in the data they are trained on, leading to unfair or discriminatory outcomes. It's crucial to ensure that AI tools are used responsibly and ethically, minimizing bias and promoting fairness and inclusivity. This might involve carefully selecting the data used to train AI systems, implementing algorithms designed to mitigate bias, and establishing clear ethical guidelines for the use of AI in the workplace.

Building an AI-powered workflow is not a one-time event but an ongoing process of refinement and adaptation. As AI technologies evolve, new tools and techniques will emerge, necessitating continuous learning and adaptation. It's crucial to stay updated on the latest advancements in AI and adapt your workflow accordingly. This might involve adopting new AI tools, refining existing processes, and retraining employees to work effectively with AI systems.

Consider the case study of a project manager who successfully integrated an AI-powered scheduling tool into their workflow. Previously, scheduling meetings and managing projects involved numerous emails, spreadsheets, and manual adjustments. The AI tool automatically schedules meetings based on participant availability, manages project timelines, and provides real-time updates on project progress. This significantly reduced the project manager's workload, allowing them to focus on strategic planning and problem-solving. The initial integration process required some time and effort to train the AI system and configure it to integrate with existing systems, but the long-term benefits far outweighed the initial investment.

Another example is a customer service representative who integrated an AI-powered chatbot into their workflow. The chatbot handles routine inquiries, providing immediate responses to common questions. This frees the representative to focus on more complex issues and provide personalized service to customers requiring more attention. The chatbot continuously learns from its interactions with customers, improving its responses and efficiency over time. This integration not only increased efficiency but also enhanced the customer experience by providing quicker and more consistent service.

In summary, building an AI-powered workflow is a strategic investment that requires careful planning, execution, and ongoing adaptation. It involves identifying tasks ripe for automation, selecting appropriate AI tools, ensuring seamless integration, establishing protocols for human oversight, and addressing ethical considerations. By strategically integrating AI into their workflows, individuals and organizations can significantly enhance their productivity, efficiency, and overall competitiveness in the rapidly evolving landscape of the modern workplace. The key is not to fear AI but to embrace it as a powerful tool for augmenting human capabilities and driving innovation. The future of work is not about humans versus AI, but about humans *with* AI, creating a synergistic partnership that unleashes unprecedented potential.

Staying Updated on AI Advancements

Staying abreast of the relentless pace of AI advancement is crucial for anyone seeking to leverage its power in their career. The field is dynamic, with new breakthroughs and applications emerging constantly. A passive approach, relying solely on past knowledge, will quickly leave you behind. Active, continuous learning is the key to remaining competitive and capitalizing on the opportunities presented by this transformative technology.

One of the most effective ways to stay informed is through targeted research and engagement with leading publications and research institutions. Numerous reputable journals and online platforms dedicate themselves to covering AI developments. Publications like *Nature* , *Science* , *MIT Technology Review* , and *IEEE Spectrum* regularly feature articles on cutting-edge research, practical applications, and ethical considerations surrounding AI. Beyond these general-interest sources, consider subscribing to specialized publications that focus on specific AI subfields, such as machine learning, deep learning, natural language processing, or computer vision, depending on your area of expertise or professional interest. This focused approach ensures you're receiving the most relevant and impactful information.

Beyond academic journals, industry-specific publications and blogs provide valuable insights into the practical applications of AI across various sectors. These resources often offer case studies, success stories, and analyses of emerging trends, providing a more applied perspective on the theoretical advancements. For example, if you're in the finance industry, following publications focused on fintech and AI's role in financial markets will keep you informed about relevant developments. Similarly, marketing professionals should focus on publications covering AI's applications in marketing automation, personalization, and predictive analytics. Actively seeking out these specialized resources allows you to understand how AI is transforming your specific industry and tailor your skills and knowledge accordingly.

Conferences and workshops offer an invaluable opportunity to network with leading experts and gain firsthand knowledge of the latest advancements. Attending conferences such as NeurIPS, ICML, AAAI, and CVPR provides access to cutting-edge research presented by top researchers and practitioners. These events are often complemented by workshops that delve deeper into specific topics, offering intensive training and opportunities for hands-on learning.

Beyond large-scale academic conferences, industry-specific conferences and workshops are equally valuable, often focusing on practical applications and real-world case studies. Actively participating in these events, attending presentations, engaging in discussions, and networking with peers and experts, significantly contributes to staying at the forefront of AI development.

Online learning platforms offer a flexible and accessible method for continuous professional development in AI. Platforms like Coursera, edX, Udacity, and fast.ai provide a vast array of courses, from introductory-level overviews to advanced specializations in specific AI areas. These courses often feature videos, assignments, and interactive exercises, facilitating a deep understanding of AI concepts and techniques. Many platforms also offer certifications that can enhance your professional profile and demonstrate your commitment to lifelong learning in this rapidly evolving field.

Selecting courses that align with your specific career goals and industry needs is paramount to maximizing their impact.

Engaging with online communities and forums is another effective way to stay updated on AI advancements. Platforms like Reddit, Stack Overflow, and specialized AI forums provide a space to discuss current issues, share knowledge, and learn from others' experiences. Participating in these communities provides access to a wealth of information, diverse perspectives, and real-time insights into the latest developments. The collaborative nature of these forums fosters a sense of community and shared learning, contributing to a deeper understanding of the field. Actively participating in discussions, asking questions, and sharing your own insights can significantly enhance your understanding and broaden your network within the AI community.

Podcasts and webinars offer another convenient method of staying informed. Numerous podcasts and webinars focus on AI, featuring interviews with leading experts, discussions of current trends, and analysis of new technologies. These formats provide a convenient way to consume information while commuting or during breaks, making them ideal for those with busy schedules. Subscribing to relevant podcasts and registering for webinars can ensure a consistent stream of updated information directly to your device. Seeking out podcasts and webinars from reputable sources, with established experts as speakers, helps ensure the quality and accuracy of the information received.

Beyond formal learning avenues, maintaining a habit of consistently reading news articles, blogs, and technical papers is indispensable. Setting aside dedicated time each week to explore the latest developments, either through curated newsletters or self-directed browsing, keeps you informed about the field's current state. Many reputable news outlets, such as the New York Times, Wired, and The Verge, regularly publish articles on AI. Combining these with specialized AI news sites and blogs, you can build a personalized, consistent information stream. Using RSS feeds or other news aggregation tools can further streamline this process, presenting the latest updates efficiently.

Finally, it is crucial to understand that staying updated on AI advancements isn't a passive activity. It's an active, ongoing engagement with the field. This requires a commitment to lifelong learning, a willingness to embrace new information, and a proactive approach to seeking out relevant resources. By actively pursuing these strategies, professionals can effectively navigate the evolving landscape of AI and maintain their competitive edge in the modern workplace. The constant influx of new information requires an adaptable mindset, a willingness to unlearn outdated approaches, and a commitment to embracing continuous learning. This isn't merely about staying informed; it's about actively shaping your career trajectory in a field that's rapidly redefining the future of work. Embracing this continuous learning process positions you not just as a survivor but as a thriving leader in the age of AI. The ability to adapt, learn, and innovate will be the defining skills in the years to come, and continuous engagement with AI advancements is the key to unlocking that potential.

Chapter 3: Cultivating Uniquely Human Skills

Emotional Intelligence Navigating Human Interaction

As artificial intelligence increasingly automates tasks across various industries, the uniquely human skills that were once considered secondary are now catapulting individuals to the forefront of their professions. Among these vital skills, emotional intelligence stands out as a critical differentiator, a capacity that AI currently lacks and is unlikely to replicate in the foreseeable future. Emotional intelligence is not merely a soft skill; it's a hard-wired advantage in a world increasingly shaped by technology.

Emotional intelligence encompasses four key components: self-awareness, self-regulation, empathy, and social skills. Self-awareness involves understanding one's own emotions, strengths, weaknesses, and values. It's the ability to accurately assess your emotional state in any given moment and recognize how your feelings influence your thoughts and behaviors. A self-aware individual is not ruled by their emotions; they understand them and use this understanding to make informed decisions. For instance, a self-aware project manager might recognize their frustration mounting during a particularly challenging project phase. Instead of lashing out at the team, they pause, acknowledge their feelings, and then consciously choose a more productive response, perhaps seeking clarification on a particular issue or delegating certain tasks to alleviate the pressure.

Self-regulation, the second pillar of emotional intelligence, is the ability to manage one's emotional responses. This doesn't mean suppressing emotions entirely; it's about channeling them constructively. It involves controlling impulses, thinking before acting, and adapting to changing circumstances with composure.

Imagine a sales professional facing a demanding client who is escalating their complaints. A self-regulated individual would remain calm, actively listen to the client's concerns, and respond with empathy and professionalism, finding solutions instead of getting drawn into a conflict. This ability to maintain emotional control under pressure is invaluable in any high-stakes environment.

Empathy, the capacity to understand and share the feelings of others, is another crucial component of emotional intelligence. It's about stepping into someone else's shoes, perceiving their emotions, and responding with compassion and understanding. In the context of leadership, empathy allows managers to foster strong relationships with their teams, build trust, and effectively motivate their employees. For instance, an empathetic leader would recognize signs of stress or burnout in their team members and take proactive steps to address these issues, perhaps by offering support, adjusting workloads, or promoting a healthier work-life balance.

This proactive approach can significantly improve team morale, productivity, and retention rates.

Social skills, the final component of emotional intelligence, encompass the ability to build rapport, communicate effectively, manage conflict, and work collaboratively with others. It's about navigating complex social dynamics, understanding nonverbal cues, and adapting communication styles to different individuals and situations. In a collaborative work environment, strong social skills are essential for effective teamwork. Individuals with high social skills can easily build consensus, resolve disagreements, and foster a positive and productive team dynamic. For example, a team member with strong social skills might recognize that a colleague is hesitant to share their ideas during a brainstorming session. They would proactively create a safe space for their colleague, encouraging their participation and ensuring their contributions are valued.

Developing emotional intelligence is not a passive process; it requires conscious effort and consistent practice. One effective strategy is self-reflection, regularly taking time to analyze your own emotional responses to different situations. Journaling can be a valuable tool for this purpose, allowing you to track your emotional patterns and identify areas for improvement. For example, by documenting your responses to challenging situations, you might notice recurring patterns of reactivity that you can then address through mindful practices or coaching.

Seeking feedback from trusted colleagues, mentors, or supervisors is another crucial element in developing emotional intelligence.

Constructive criticism, though often uncomfortable, provides invaluable insights into how your actions and emotional responses affect others. By actively soliciting and engaging with this feedback, you gain a more objective perspective on your strengths and weaknesses, enabling you to target specific areas for development.

Participating in training programs specifically designed to enhance emotional intelligence can significantly accelerate your growth in this area. Numerous workshops and courses focus on developing self-awareness, self-regulation, empathy, and social skills, using a range of interactive exercises and practical techniques. These programs often incorporate simulations of real-world scenarios, allowing participants to practice their emotional intelligence skills in a safe and controlled environment, preparing them for the complexities of the workplace.

Mindfulness practices, such as meditation or yoga, can also contribute significantly to improving emotional intelligence. By cultivating a greater awareness of your thoughts and feelings in the present moment, mindfulness enables you to respond to situations more thoughtfully and less reactively. This increased self-awareness allows you to better manage your emotions, fostering calm and clarity in even stressful situations. The practice of mindfulness is not simply about relaxation; it's about cultivating a heightened awareness of oneself and the environment, fostering more adaptive and compassionate responses.

Furthermore, actively seeking out opportunities to interact with diverse groups of people can significantly strengthen your social skills and empathy. Exposure to different perspectives and cultural norms fosters a deeper understanding of human behavior and broadens your emotional intelligence. Whether through volunteering, joining clubs, or participating in community events, seeking such experiences promotes understanding and respect for others, cultivating a capacity for empathetic communication and collaboration.

In conclusion, emotional intelligence is not merely a supplementary skill in the age of AI; it's a fundamental competitive advantage. By cultivating self-awareness, self-regulation, empathy, and social skills, individuals can not only navigate the complexities of the modern workplace but also flourish in the face of rapid technological advancements. The ability to build rapport, understand and manage emotions, and collaborate effectively—qualities currently beyond the scope of artificial intelligence—are becoming increasingly indispensable, placing those who master them firmly at the forefront of their careers. The conscious development and refinement of these uniquely human skills represents a powerful strategy for future-proofing one's career and capitalizing on the ever-evolving demands of the modern workplace. This investment in oneself is not simply about navigating the present; it's about building resilience and adaptability for the unpredictable future of work. The human touch remains invaluable, a crucial component in leadership, team collaboration, and client relationships, a factor that makes emotional intelligence a skill as critical as technical proficiency.

Complex Problem Solving: Thinking Critically and Creatively

While emotional intelligence provides a crucial human advantage in the age of AI, it's not the only skill set that will define success. The ability to tackle complex problems, think critically and creatively, and develop strategic solutions are equally, if not more, vital. These uniquely human skills are not easily replicated by algorithms, and their importance will only grow as AI increasingly automates routine tasks. This isn't about replacing human intelligence with artificial intelligence; it's about augmenting human capabilities to tackle problems of ever-increasing complexity.

AI excels at processing vast amounts of data and identifying patterns, but it often struggles with nuanced situations demanding intuitive leaps, creative solutions, and ethical considerations. These higher-order cognitive functions are what truly differentiate human problem-solving. The ability to synthesize information from diverse sources, identify underlying assumptions, consider multiple perspectives, and develop innovative solutions remains a uniquely human strength.

Critical thinking, a cornerstone of complex problem-solving, involves actively and skillfully conceptualizing, applying, analyzing, synthesizing, and/or evaluating information gathered from, or generated by, observation, experience, reflection, reasoning, or communication, as a guide to belief and action. It's more than simply absorbing information; it's about questioning assumptions, identifying biases, and evaluating evidence objectively. Consider a financial analyst faced with predicting market trends. AI can process historical data, but a critical thinker will consider geopolitical events, consumer sentiment, and regulatory changes –factors that are difficult for AI to fully contextualize. They can identify patterns, but a human can understand the *why* behind those patterns, adding a layer of understanding and foresight that AI lacks.

This skill is honed through practice. One effective method is to actively seek out diverse perspectives when examining a problem. Engage in debates and discussions with colleagues who hold different viewpoints. This challenges your assumptions and forces you to consider alternative explanations and solutions. Another technique is to meticulously examine the evidence, looking for flaws or inconsistencies. Are there any biases in the data? Are there alternative interpretations of the evidence? Developing a healthy skepticism and meticulously examining evidence are crucial in ensuring that your analysis is as objective and comprehensive as possible.

Creative problem-solving goes beyond critical thinking; it's about generating novel and effective solutions to complex challenges. This involves lateral thinking, brainstorming, and experimenting with different approaches. AI can suggest solutions based on existing data, but it lacks the ability to truly innovate. Humans, on the other hand, can combine seemingly unrelated ideas to develop groundbreaking solutions. Imagine a marketing team tasked with launching a new product in a saturated market. AI might analyze competitor campaigns, but a creatively minded team might devise a viral marketing strategy using unexpected collaborations or unique media formats. They can think "outside the box," drawing inspiration from unrelated fields or industries to create unique solutions that AI might not even consider.

Numerous techniques can enhance creative problem-solving skills.

Mind mapping, for example, helps visualize complex ideas and identify connections between seemingly disparate concepts.

Brainstorming sessions, conducted effectively, can generate a wide range of ideas, even those initially deemed impractical. The key is to create a safe and supportive environment where participants feel comfortable expressing even unconventional ideas. These ideas can then be refined, combined, and adapted through further discussion and analysis, leading to innovative solutions that might not have emerged through more traditional approaches.

Strategic thinking, a higher-level cognitive skill, combines critical thinking and creative problem-solving to develop long-term plans and strategies. It involves anticipating future trends, assessing potential risks, and adapting to changing circumstances. While AI can predict certain outcomes based on historical data, it can't easily account for unexpected events or evolving market dynamics. A strategically minded leader, on the other hand, anticipates these changes, preparing contingency plans and adjusting their strategies accordingly. This foresight is crucial in navigating complex and uncertain environments.

The development of strategic thinking often involves simulation and scenario planning. By creating hypothetical scenarios, individuals can anticipate potential challenges and develop effective responses. This practice improves decision-making under pressure and builds resilience in the face of unexpected events. In a rapidly changing environment, strategic thinkers are invaluable. They are the ones capable of anticipating shifts in the market, adjusting business strategies accordingly, and positioning their organizations for success in the long term. This adaptive thinking is a distinctly human trait.

Case studies illustrate the power of these combined skills. Consider a company facing declining market share. An AI might analyze the data and identify specific weaknesses. However, a team employing critical thinking might uncover deeper issues, such as a lack of innovation or a failure to adapt to changing consumer preferences.

Creative problem-solving could then lead to the development of new product lines, improved marketing strategies, or innovative business models. Finally, strategic thinking would involve developing a long-term plan to regain market share, accounting for potential risks and opportunities.

Further enhancing these skills requires active learning and consistent practice. Engage in complex problem-solving activities, such as puzzles or strategic games, to stimulate your critical and creative thinking. Participate in workshops and training programs that focus on developing these skills. Seek out feedback from colleagues and mentors, and learn from your mistakes. Continuous learning is essential in staying ahead of the curve in an environment where the demand for complex problem-solving skills is ever-increasing. Read widely, stay informed about current events, and explore different perspectives to broaden your understanding and enhance your ability to analyze complex situations.

In conclusion, while AI is revolutionizing the workplace, the uniquely human skills of complex problem-solving, critical thinking, creative problem-solving, and strategic thinking remain invaluable.

These are the skills that will differentiate individuals and organizations in the age of AI, enabling them to not only adapt but thrive in a rapidly changing world. Investing in the development of these skills is an investment in future success – a future where humans and AI collaborate to solve increasingly complex problems and create a more innovative and efficient world. The future belongs not to those who simply adapt to AI, but to those who learn to leverage its capabilities to enhance their uniquely human strengths, especially the complex and critical thinking abilities that shape strategic responses and innovative solutions.

Adaptability and Resilience Embracing Change

Adaptability and resilience are no longer optional traits; they're essential survival skills in today's rapidly evolving workplace, particularly in the face of accelerating AI-driven transformation.

The ability to navigate change, manage stress effectively, and embrace new opportunities will be paramount in securing career success and maintaining a sense of purpose in an increasingly automated world. This isn't about passively accepting change, but actively shaping one's response to it, proactively seeking new challenges, and viewing disruption as a catalyst for growth.

Developing a growth mindset is foundational to adaptability. This mindset shifts the perspective from viewing abilities as fixed and unchangeable to seeing them as malleable and improvable through dedication and effort. Instead of fearing failure, individuals with a growth mindset see it as an opportunity for learning and improvement. They embrace challenges, persist in the face of setbacks, learn from criticism, and find inspiration in the success of others. This perspective is crucial in navigating the uncertainties inherent in a technologically disrupted workplace. When AI introduces new tools and workflows, those with a growth mindset see it not as a threat, but as a chance to learn new skills and enhance their existing capabilities.

Managing stress effectively is another critical component of resilience. The fear of job displacement, the pressure to constantly upskill, and the rapid pace of technological change can lead to significant stress. Developing effective stress management strategies is therefore essential. These strategies might include mindfulness practices like meditation or yoga, which help to quiet the mind and reduce anxiety. Regular physical exercise is also crucial, not just for physical health but also for its stress-relieving effects. Maintaining a healthy work-life balance, prioritizing sleep, and engaging in activities that promote relaxation and enjoyment are also important components of a robust stress management plan. Creating a supportive network of colleagues, friends, and family can provide emotional support and encouragement during challenging times.

Upskilling and reskilling are not merely buzzwords; they are practical necessities in the age of AI. The skills valued in today's workplace may not be relevant tomorrow. Therefore, proactive engagement in continuous learning is crucial. This involves identifying future-proof skills – those less susceptible to automation– and acquiring them through online courses, workshops, professional development programs, and on-the-job training. The focus should be on developing skills that complement AI, rather than competing with it. For example, while AI might excel at data analysis, the ability to interpret that data, draw insightful conclusions, and communicate those findings effectively to non-technical audiences remains a highly valuable human skill.

Similarly, skills related to critical thinking, complex problem-solving, creativity, and emotional intelligence are difficult to replicate with current AI technology.

Re-skilling involves acquiring entirely new skill sets to transition to different roles or industries. This might involve a complete career change, moving from a field heavily impacted by automation to one that is less affected. For example, a data entry clerk might re-skill to become a data analyst, leveraging their existing knowledge of data handling while developing advanced analytical skills. A factory worker whose job is being automated might re-skill in areas like robotics maintenance or programming, gaining expertise in the very technology that is reshaping their industry. Such transitions require careful planning and execution. Identifying transferable skills –those relevant across different roles – is a key first step. Then, identifying training opportunities, developing a compelling resume and cover letter showcasing acquired skills, and actively networking to uncover new opportunities are all crucial parts of a successful reskilling journey.

Numerous resources are available to support upskilling and reskilling efforts. Online learning platforms like Coursera, edX, and Udacity offer a wide range of courses in various subjects, catering to different learning styles and schedules. Professional organizations often provide training and certification programs tailored to specific industries.

Community colleges and universities offer more structured learning pathways leading to formal qualifications.

Government programs and initiatives may also offer funding or support for upskilling and reskilling efforts. The key is to be proactive, identify relevant resources, and commit to consistent learning.

The successful navigation of career changes exemplifies the power of adaptability and resilience. Consider the case of a journalist whose role was significantly impacted by the rise of AI-powered content generation. Rather than succumbing to job losses, this journalist leveraged their writing skills and combined them with their newfound expertise in data analysis and visualization, transitioning to a role as a data storyteller, creating compelling narratives based on complex data sets. This individual's success was built upon their ability to identify transferable skills, embrace new technologies, and acquire additional knowledge, demonstrating the transformative potential of adaptability.

Another example is a manufacturing worker displaced by factory automation. Instead of accepting unemployment, this individual utilized government-sponsored training programs to acquire skills in robotics programming and maintenance. This allowed them to transition into a higher-skilled, higher-paying role within the same industry, showcasing the power of reskilling in mitigating the negative impacts of automation. These examples highlight that change, while daunting, can also be an opportunity for growth and career advancement.

The development of adaptability and resilience isn't a one-time event; it's a continuous process requiring ongoing self-reflection, learning, and adaptation. Regularly evaluating one's skills, identifying potential skill gaps, and proactively addressing them is critical. This includes seeking feedback from colleagues, mentors, and managers to gain insights into one's strengths and weaknesses.

It's also about embracing continuous learning as a way of life, consistently seeking out new challenges, and viewing setbacks as valuable learning opportunities.

Building a strong professional network is also essential. Networking provides access to information about emerging trends, new opportunities, and potential career paths. It also provides support and encouragement during challenging times. Attending industry events, joining professional organizations, and actively engaging with colleagues on social media are all effective ways to expand one's network.

Mentorship can provide invaluable guidance and support, particularly during career transitions or when navigating uncertain times. Finding a mentor who has successfully navigated similar challenges can offer practical advice and encouragement. This process of continuous learning, networking, and self-reflection builds a foundation of resilience that allows professionals to not just survive but thrive in the face of rapid technological change.

In conclusion, adaptability and resilience are not simply desirable traits; they are essential for success in the AI-driven workplace. By developing a growth mindset, managing stress effectively, and proactively engaging in upskilling and reskilling, individuals can equip themselves to navigate the uncertainties of a rapidly changing work environment. The examples of professionals who have successfully navigated career transitions showcase the transformative power of adaptability and resilience. Embracing change as an opportunity for growth, rather than a threat, is crucial to securing a prosperous and fulfilling career in the age of AI. The future belongs to those who are not only technologically savvy but also possess the human skills of adaptability, resilience, and a commitment to lifelong learning, allowing them to thrive in a world increasingly shaped by automation and technological advancement.

This proactive approach ensures not just survival but sustained professional growth and success in a world where change is the only constant.

Communication and Collaboration: Working Effectively with AI and Humans

The previous section focused on cultivating uniquely human skills like adaptability and resilience, essential for navigating the AI-driven transformation of the workplace. Now, we shift our attention to another critical area: communication and collaboration. Effective communication and collaboration, both with AI systems and human colleagues, are paramount for success in this new era. The ability to articulate needs clearly to AI, interpret its responses accurately, and work seamlessly with diverse human teams will determine your ability to leverage AI's potential while maintaining a strong human-centric approach to problem-solving and innovation.

The nature of communication itself is evolving. We are no longer solely reliant on traditional methods like email and in-person meetings. The integration of AI into our workflows introduces new communication channels and necessitates new approaches to ensure clarity and efficiency. AI-powered tools, such as chatbots and virtual assistants, demand precise instructions and clear expectations. Ambiguity is the enemy of effective AI interaction. Unlike human colleagues who can often infer meaning from context or incomplete instructions, AI operates based on the data provided. Therefore, mastering the art of precise and concise communication is crucial when interacting with AI systems.

This necessitates a shift in communication style. Instead of relying on informal language or implied meanings, we need to adopt a more structured and analytical approach. Clearly defined goals, explicit instructions, and well-defined parameters are essential for effective communication with AI. Consider the example of using an AI-powered writing assistant. Simply requesting "write a report" is insufficient. You need to specify the topic, target audience, desired length, and tone. The more detailed your instructions, the more accurate and effective the AI's output will be.

Furthermore, understanding the limitations of AI is crucial. While AI can process and analyze vast amounts of data, it lacks human judgment and intuition. Its responses should not be blindly accepted but critically evaluated for accuracy, relevance, and completeness. The human-in-the-loop approach remains vital. AI should be viewed as a tool to augment human capabilities, not replace them.

Therefore, the communication process with AI is iterative: input, evaluation, feedback, refinement – a continuous cycle of interaction to ensure the desired outcome.

This iterative process also applies to collaborating with human colleagues. In an increasingly diverse and globally distributed workforce, effective communication across geographical boundaries and cultural differences becomes crucial. The ability to communicate effectively in both written and verbal forms, to actively listen, and to understand differing perspectives are essential for fostering collaboration and achieving shared goals. This is particularly important when working in teams that include both human and AI components. We must develop strategies to ensure that humans and AI effectively complement each other's strengths.

The rise of AI necessitates the development of new collaboration frameworks. For example, agile methodologies, which emphasize iterative development and frequent feedback, are particularly well-suited for projects involving AI. These methodologies encourage close collaboration between team members, allowing for quick adaptation to emerging challenges and opportunities. Regular check-ins, clear communication channels, and collaborative workspaces are essential elements of this process.

Beyond the technical aspects of communication, the human element remains crucial. Empathy, emotional intelligence, and the ability to build strong interpersonal relationships are still highly valued in the workplace, even with the integration of AI. These uniquely human skills are essential for fostering trust, managing conflict, and motivating team members to achieve shared goals. They help bridge cultural differences, build consensus, and ensure effective communication within diverse teams.

Consider the challenge of managing a team where some members interact directly with AI systems, while others focus on more traditionally human tasks. Effective communication becomes crucial to ensure seamless integration and collaboration. This requires careful planning, clear communication channels, and training to ensure everyone understands their role and how they contribute to the overall success of the project. Regular team meetings, both in person and remotely, are essential for maintaining alignment and addressing potential challenges. Establishing clear expectations, defining roles and responsibilities, and establishing clear communication protocols are all essential for successful collaboration.

Moreover, the successful implementation of AI often requires overcoming resistance to change within organizations. Effective communication and leadership are crucial in navigating these challenges. Transparency about the goals of AI implementation, the benefits it offers, and how it will impact employees' roles and responsibilities are essential for building trust and encouraging buy-in. This requires proactive communication strategies, open forums for discussion, and ongoing training to ensure employees feel comfortable with the changes taking place.

Furthermore, the effective communication of AI's capabilities and limitations is crucial to prevent unrealistic expectations. AI is a powerful tool, but it's not a magic bullet. Overselling its potential or underestimating its limitations can lead to disappointment and mistrust.

Therefore, a balanced and realistic communication strategy is crucial. This approach involves clearly communicating the capabilities and limitations of AI to both internal stakeholders and external clients. This ensures a realistic and sustainable approach to integrating AI into the workplace.

The ability to clearly articulate complex technical information to non-technical audiences is another crucial communication skill.

Many AI projects require explaining complex algorithms, data analysis, or technological solutions to individuals without a deep understanding of these fields. This requires the ability to simplify complex concepts, use clear and concise language, and employ effective visual aids to explain technical information in an accessible and understandable way. This skill is crucial for building consensus, ensuring effective collaboration across departments, and communicating the value of AI projects to senior leadership.

In the context of collaboration, the importance of active listening cannot be overstated. In a world saturated with information, the ability to truly listen and understand the perspectives of others is essential for effective teamwork. Active listening involves paying attention not just to the words spoken but also to the non-verbal cues, understanding the underlying emotions, and asking clarifying questions to ensure accurate comprehension. This is especially critical when collaborating with colleagues from diverse backgrounds and cultures who might have different communication styles.

Finally, the art of constructive feedback is paramount. The rapid pace of change in the AI-driven workplace necessitates continuous learning and adaptation. The ability to provide and receive constructive feedback is essential for improving individual and team performance. This involves delivering feedback in a respectful and supportive manner, focusing on specific behaviors rather than personal attributes, and framing feedback in a way that helps individuals improve their performance.

In conclusion, effective communication and collaboration are not merely desirable traits in the AI-driven workplace; they are essential for success. By mastering the art of precise communication with AI systems, fostering effective collaboration among diverse human teams, and developing strong interpersonal skills, individuals can position themselves to thrive in this rapidly evolving landscape. The integration of AI into the workplace presents new challenges and opportunities, but the uniquely human skills of effective communication and collaboration will remain crucial in navigating this new world and achieving collective success. The future of work hinges not just on technological proficiency but on the ability to build strong human connections and foster productive interactions, leveraging the power of both AI and human ingenuity.

Creativity and Innovation: Generating New Ideas and Solutions

The previous section emphasized the crucial role of communication and collaboration in the AI-driven workplace. Now, we turn our attention to another uniquely human skill set that will become increasingly valuable: creativity and innovation. While AI can process vast quantities of data and identify patterns, it currently lacks the capacity for truly original, imaginative thought – the kind of thinking that generates groundbreaking ideas and solutions to complex, multifaceted problems. This is where humans hold a distinct advantage. The ability to think outside the box, to connect seemingly disparate concepts, and to envision novel approaches is not only valuable but essential for thriving in an AI-augmented world.

The integration of AI into the workplace doesn't diminish the need for creativity; it amplifies it. AI can automate repetitive tasks and analyze data at an unprecedented scale, freeing up human workers to focus on higher-level cognitive functions, including creative problem-solving and innovative design. Instead of replacing human creativity, AI acts as a powerful tool to augment and enhance it.

Imagine an architect using AI to analyze structural data and optimize building designs, but relying on their own creative vision to shape the aesthetic appeal and overall functionality of the building. The AI handles the technical specifications; the architect handles the artistic and conceptual vision. This synergy is at the heart of the future workplace.

So how do we cultivate and enhance creativity in a world increasingly shaped by AI? Several key strategies can be adopted. First, it's vital to foster a culture of curiosity and experimentation.

This involves encouraging risk-taking, embracing failure as a learning opportunity, and creating a safe space where individuals feel comfortable sharing unconventional ideas without fear of judgment.

Many successful companies already understand this. Organizations like Google, known for their innovative culture, actively promote brainstorming sessions, hackathons, and "20% time" initiatives, which encourage employees to dedicate a portion of their work time to pursuing their own creative projects. These seemingly frivolous pursuits can often yield surprising and valuable results.

Secondly, active learning plays a vital role in enhancing creativity.

Continuously seeking new knowledge, exploring different fields, and engaging in diverse experiences broadens our perspectives and expands our mental toolbox. This is particularly relevant in the AI age, where rapid technological advancements necessitate continuous learning and adaptation. Individuals who actively seek out new information, engage with different perspectives, and embrace lifelong learning will be better equipped to adapt to the evolving demands of the workplace and generate innovative solutions to unforeseen challenges. Consider the example of a marketing professional who combines their expertise in digital marketing with a newfound knowledge of AI-powered marketing tools. This blend of traditional skills and AI proficiency unlocks new levels of creativity and efficiency.

Techniques like brainstorming, mind mapping, and lateral thinking can be powerful tools for unlocking creative potential.

Brainstorming encourages the free flow of ideas, regardless of their initial feasibility. Mind mapping helps visualize connections between different concepts and ideas. Lateral thinking encourages unconventional approaches to problem-solving by challenging assumptions and exploring alternative perspectives. These techniques are not just theoretical; they are practical tools that can be applied in various contexts. Imagine a team tasked with designing a new AI-powered customer service platform. Using brainstorming, they might generate a wide range of ideas, some seemingly outlandish, which would then be refined and prioritized through mind mapping and lateral thinking, resulting in a creative and effective platform.

Furthermore, embracing collaboration significantly enhances creative output. Diversity in thought and experience leads to richer brainstorming sessions, enabling more innovative solutions to emerge. The exchange of ideas between individuals with different backgrounds and skill sets sparks unexpected connections and inspires unconventional thinking. The power of collaborative creativity has long been recognized. Many famous inventions and works of art emerged from the collaborative efforts of multiple individuals, highlighting the synergistic effect of teamwork on creativity. In the context of AI, this collaboration extends beyond human-to-human interaction. It involves learning to effectively collaborate with AI tools, viewing them not as replacements but as collaborators that enhance our creative capabilities. Another vital aspect of creativity in the AI era is the ability to effectively interpret and utilize AI-generated insights. While AI can process vast amounts of data and identify patterns, it's the human element that determines how those insights are translated into creative solutions. This necessitates a deep understanding of AI's capabilities and limitations, enabling humans to effectively guide and refine AI-generated outputs, ensuring that they align with broader strategic goals and creative visions. This process, in essence, is a collaborative endeavor. AI acts as a facilitator, providing data and insights, while human creativity shapes those insights into practical, innovative applications.

Finally, perseverance and resilience are crucial aspects of cultivating creativity. The process of developing creative solutions is rarely linear. It often involves setbacks, unexpected challenges, and moments of frustration. Individuals who demonstrate perseverance and resilience, who can learn from their mistakes and continue to explore new avenues, are more likely to achieve significant breakthroughs. History is replete with examples of inventors, artists, and entrepreneurs who encountered numerous obstacles on their path to success, yet their persistence ultimately led to groundbreaking innovations. This tenacity is no less essential in the AI age. The rapid pace of technological change demands a willingness to adapt, to learn from failures, and to persist in the face of unexpected challenges. These qualities are not just beneficial; they are vital for maintaining a competitive edge in the AI-driven workplace.

In conclusion, while AI will undoubtedly transform the workplace, it will not diminish the importance of human creativity and innovation. Indeed, it might very well amplify it. By cultivating a culture of curiosity, embracing active learning, utilizing creative thinking techniques, fostering collaboration, mastering the interpretation of AI-generated insights, and demonstrating resilience, individuals can not only adapt but thrive in this rapidly evolving landscape, generating innovative solutions that shape the future. The combination of human ingenuity and AI capabilities will lead to a more efficient, creative, and productive workplace for all.

Chapter 4: Positioning Yourself as an AI-Literate Leader

Understanding the Leadership Landscape in the Age of AI

The previous section highlighted the crucial role of human creativity and innovation in the age of AI. Now, we shift our focus to the individuals who guide and shape this new era: leaders. The leadership landscape is undergoing a dramatic transformation, and success in this evolving environment demands a new set of skills and attributes—those of the AI-literate leader. This isn't simply about adopting AI tools; it's about fundamentally rethinking leadership strategies and fostering an organizational culture capable of embracing and leveraging the transformative potential of AI.

The first and most fundamental aspect of AI-literate leadership is a deep understanding of AI itself. This doesn't require a computer science degree, but it does necessitate a grasp of AI's capabilities, limitations, and ethical considerations. Leaders need to understand how AI systems function, the types of problems they are best suited to solve, and the potential biases that can be embedded within them. This knowledge allows leaders to make informed decisions about AI implementation, to identify opportunities for optimization, and to mitigate potential risks. For example, a leader in the healthcare industry might understand how AI can be used to analyze medical images for early disease detection, but they would also need to understand the potential for algorithmic bias to lead to misdiagnosis or inequitable treatment. They would need to implement strategies to mitigate such risks.

Beyond technical understanding, AI-literate leaders must possess strong analytical and problem-solving skills. While AI can process data at an unprecedented scale, it's the human leader who frames the problems, interprets the results, and ultimately decides how to act. This involves critical thinking—the ability to assess information objectively, identify underlying assumptions, and consider alternative perspectives. Leaders need to be able to discern the significant insights from the noise, to extract actionable intelligence from the vast amounts of data that AI can generate. A leader in the financial sector, for example, might use AI to analyze market trends, but they would also need to use their own critical thinking to assess the validity of the predictions and to determine the appropriate investment strategy.

Equally crucial is the ability to effectively manage and motivate teams in a rapidly changing environment. The introduction of AI often generates anxiety among employees, who may fear job displacement or feel overwhelmed by the new technologies. AI-literate leaders must address these concerns openly and honestly, providing clear communication, ongoing training, and support to help their teams adapt. They need to cultivate a culture of trust and collaboration, emphasizing the human-centric aspects of the workplace and the opportunities AI creates for enhancing individual skills and contributing to collective success. A study by McKinsey & Company highlighted the critical role of leadership in successful AI adoption, emphasizing the need for clear communication strategies to alleviate employee anxieties and foster a sense of shared purpose.

Furthermore, AI-literate leaders must be adept at fostering a culture of innovation and continuous learning. This necessitates a willingness to experiment, to embrace failure as a learning opportunity, and to cultivate a climate where new ideas are welcomed and encouraged. This includes investing in employee development programs, providing access to relevant training and resources, and creating opportunities for employees to develop their AI-related skills. Leading companies are already implementing such initiatives. Many invest in internal training programs on AI and data science, offering employees the chance to upskill and gain expertise in these areas. This not only prepares them for the future but also enhances their overall value within the organization.

Effective change management is another vital skill for AI-literate leaders. Implementing AI systems often requires significant organizational restructuring, process re-engineering, and adjustments to established workflows. Leaders must be able to navigate these changes effectively, managing employee expectations, resolving conflicts, and ensuring a smooth transition to the new AI-augmented work environment. This requires strategic planning, clear communication, and strong leadership qualities to guide the organization through this significant period of transformation.

Ethical considerations are paramount in the age of AI. AI-literate leaders must be acutely aware of the ethical implications of AI technologies and ensure that their implementation aligns with ethical guidelines and organizational values. This includes addressing issues of bias, privacy, and accountability, and promoting responsible AI practices. This often involves developing clear policies and guidelines, providing ethics training to employees, and establishing mechanisms for oversight and accountability. Leaders in the field of social media, for example, face critical ethical decisions regarding the use of AI in content moderation and algorithmic bias, demanding constant vigilance and proactive measures to safeguard against harmful consequences.

Furthermore, successful AI-literate leaders excel at collaboration, both within their organizations and across external partnerships. They must be able to build and maintain strong relationships with stakeholders, including employees, customers, and other external partners. This involves effective communication, conflict resolution, and an ability to create a shared understanding of AI's potential and its impact on various aspects of the organization. Effective leadership in the AI age increasingly hinges on the ability to forge collaborative networks, bringing together expertise from diverse fields to tackle complex challenges. Consider the collaborative efforts between technology companies, research institutions, and government agencies in developing and implementing ethical guidelines for AI, highlighting the vital role of collaborative leadership.

Beyond technical expertise and management skills, AI-literate leaders need strong emotional intelligence. This involves the ability to understand and manage their own emotions, and the emotions of others. This is especially critical during times of organizational change, as employees may experience anxiety, uncertainty, or even resistance to the adoption of new technologies. Leaders with high emotional intelligence can create a supportive and inclusive environment, where employees feel heard, understood, and valued, facilitating smoother transitions and fostering greater resilience to change. The emotional support and empathy provided by AI-literate leaders will be increasingly important in navigating the anxieties associated with technological disruption.

Finally, AI-literate leaders are lifelong learners. The rapid pace of technological advancement necessitates continuous learning and adaptation. Leaders must remain abreast of the latest AI developments, industry best practices, and ethical considerations.

This involves seeking out new knowledge, participating in professional development programs, and staying engaged with the broader AI community. This continuous learning not only benefits the leader themselves but also ensures that their organizations remain competitive and at the forefront of innovation. Following industry trends, participating in conferences, and actively seeking out mentorship opportunities are all essential components of continuous learning for AI-literate leaders. In essence, the AI-literate leader is a continuous learner, constantly adapting and evolving to meet the ever-changing demands of the digital age.

In conclusion, the leadership landscape is being reshaped by AI, demanding a new type of leader—one who is not only technically proficient but also adept at managing change, fostering innovation, and promoting ethical AI practices. The AI-literate leader is a strategic thinker, an effective communicator, a strong collaborator, and a lifelong learner. These attributes are not simply desirable; they are essential for navigating the complexities of the AI-driven workplace and leading organizations towards a future where human ingenuity and AI capabilities converge to create unprecedented opportunities. The journey to becoming an AI-literate leader is ongoing, demanding constant learning, adaptation, and a commitment to fostering a thriving and ethical AI-powered future.

Leading Teams Through AI-Driven Transformations

Leading teams through AI-driven transformations requires a multifaceted approach that goes beyond simply introducing new technologies. It demands a profound understanding of the human element, acknowledging the anxieties, uncertainties, and potential resistance that often accompany technological change. Effective leadership in this context involves proactive communication, robust training programs, and a commitment to fostering a culture of continuous learning and adaptation.

One of the most significant challenges leaders face is managing employee anxieties surrounding AI. The fear of job displacement is a common and understandable concern. To address this, transparency is paramount. Leaders must openly communicate the organization's AI strategy, explaining how AI will be implemented, the potential impact on roles and responsibilities, and the opportunities for reskilling and upskilling. Instead of presenting AI as a threat, it should be framed as a tool to enhance productivity, improve efficiency, and create new opportunities for growth and innovation. This proactive approach builds trust and reduces uncertainty, mitigating anxieties before they escalate.

Furthermore, leaders should invest heavily in training and development programs tailored to the specific needs of their teams. These programs should not only focus on technical skills related to AI but also on developing uniquely human skills, such as critical thinking, problem-solving, creativity, and emotional intelligence –skills that are less susceptible to automation. By equipping employees with the skills needed to thrive in an AI-augmented workplace, leaders can empower them to embrace the change and see it as an opportunity for personal and professional growth.

Effective training programs should be interactive, engaging, and tailored to different learning styles, ensuring that all employees have the opportunity to enhance their skills and adapt to the evolving work environment. The use of simulations and real-world case studies can make the learning experience more practical and relevant.

Fostering a culture of continuous learning is essential for navigating the rapidly evolving landscape of AI. Leaders must create an environment where learning is not a one-time event but an ongoing process. This requires providing employees with access to the latest information and resources, encouraging experimentation, and embracing failure as a learning opportunity. Leaders should also promote knowledge sharing among team members, fostering a collaborative learning environment where individuals can learn from each other's experiences and expertise. Implementing regular knowledge-sharing sessions, internal mentorship programs, and access to online learning platforms can help cultivate this culture of continuous learning. It is crucial to create a safe space where employees feel comfortable experimenting and asking questions without fear of judgment.

The effective utilization of AI tools to enhance team performance is another key aspect of AI-literate leadership. Leaders should not simply implement AI for the sake of it, but strategically identify areas where AI can add the most value. This requires a clear understanding of the capabilities and limitations of AI, coupled with a deep understanding of the team's workflows and challenges.

Leaders should prioritize tasks that are repetitive, data-heavy, or require significant processing power, leaving more complex and creative tasks to human employees. This approach leverages the strengths of both AI and human intelligence, resulting in improved efficiency and productivity.

Effective change management is critical for successfully integrating AI into the workplace. This involves more than just introducing new technologies; it requires a systematic approach to managing the transition, addressing employee concerns, and ensuring a smooth and seamless integration of AI into existing workflows. Leaders should develop a comprehensive change management plan that addresses all aspects of the transition, including communication, training, and support. This plan should be clearly communicated to the team, keeping them informed of the progress and addressing any concerns promptly. Regular feedback sessions and open dialogues are essential to ensure that the change management process is responsive to the needs of the team.

Furthermore, change management in the context of AI implementation necessitates a clear understanding of the potential impact on various roles within the team. This necessitates careful consideration of how tasks will be redistributed, what new skills will be required, and how individuals will adapt to the evolving work environment. Leaders should proactively work with employees to identify opportunities for reskilling and upskilling, ensuring that they are equipped with the necessary competencies to thrive in the new AI-augmented workplace.

Beyond technical aspects, emotional intelligence plays a pivotal role in leading teams through AI-driven transformations. Leaders need to understand and empathize with the emotions and concerns of their team members, fostering an environment of trust and collaboration. This involves actively listening to employees' anxieties, addressing their concerns openly and honestly, and creating a safe space for them to express their feelings without fear of judgment. By demonstrating empathy and understanding, leaders can build strong relationships with their team members, facilitating smoother transitions and fostering greater resilience to change.

Regular one-on-one meetings and team-building activities can strengthen these relationships.

Crucially, the success of AI integration depends on effective collaboration. Leaders must foster a collaborative environment, both within their teams and with external partners. This requires building strong relationships, sharing information openly, and working together to overcome challenges. Effective communication is paramount, ensuring that everyone is informed, engaged, and working towards a common goal. Regular meetings, collaborative projects, and cross-functional teams can all contribute to fostering a collaborative environment. Open communication channels should be established to ensure that feedback is actively solicited and addressed, fostering a sense of ownership and commitment among team members.

Finally, continuous monitoring and evaluation are essential to ensure the successful implementation and ongoing effectiveness of AI within the team. Leaders should regularly assess the impact of AI on team performance, identify areas for improvement, and adapt their strategies accordingly. This might involve collecting data on key performance indicators (KPIs), conducting regular feedback sessions, and analyzing the results of AI-driven projects. This iterative approach ensures that AI tools are optimized for maximum efficiency and that the overall impact on team productivity is continuously positive.

In essence, leading teams through AI-driven transformations requires a proactive, human-centered approach. It's about more than just implementing technology; it's about managing change effectively, fostering a culture of continuous learning, and empowering employees to thrive in an evolving work environment. By embracing a holistic approach that prioritizes communication, training, collaboration, and emotional intelligence, leaders can guide their teams through this technological transformation, unlocking the full potential of AI while maintaining a human-centric workplace. The ongoing success of this transformation depends not just on technological proficiency but on leadership that fosters adaptation, resilience, and ongoing growth for the entire team.

Building an AI-Ready Workforce

Building a workforce capable of thriving in the age of AI requires a proactive and multifaceted approach that extends beyond simply acquiring new technologies. It necessitates a fundamental shift in organizational culture, training methodologies, and recruitment strategies. This transformation demands a leader's commitment to fostering a learning environment that embraces change, encourages continuous development, and values adaptability above all else.

One crucial aspect is the design and implementation of robust training and development initiatives. These programs must go beyond superficial introductions to AI terminology and delve into practical applications relevant to the specific roles within the organization. Rather than generic courses, tailor training to individual roles and skill gaps. A marketing team, for instance, might benefit from training on AI-powered marketing automation tools, while a finance team would need instruction in algorithmic trading or fraud detection systems. These specialized programs maximize the impact of training investment, ensuring employees gain immediately applicable skills.

Effective training requires a blended learning approach, incorporating various methods to cater to diverse learning styles. Online modules, interactive workshops, simulations, and mentoring programs should all be considered. Online learning platforms offer flexibility, while workshops provide opportunities for hands-on experience and peer-to-peer learning. Simulations allow employees to experiment with AI tools in a safe environment without risking real-world consequences. Mentorship programs, pairing experienced employees with those new to AI, facilitate knowledge transfer and provide personalized guidance. The integration of gamification techniques can also significantly improve engagement and retention of learning materials.

The content of the training itself should move beyond simple technical skills. Critical thinking, problem-solving, and creative thinking remain vital, even in an AI-driven environment. Employees need to learn how to interpret AI-generated insights, identify biases in algorithms, and utilize AI to enhance their creative processes rather than replace them entirely. For example, an AI might generate hundreds of marketing campaign options, but the human team member still needs the critical thinking skills to select the most effective and ethically sound choices. The training should equip employees with the ability to work *with* AI, not just be replaced *by* it.

Furthermore, the development of emotional intelligence is paramount. As AI handles more routine tasks, human employees will increasingly focus on tasks requiring empathy, interpersonal skills, and complex communication. Training should incorporate elements focused on active listening, conflict resolution, and effective teamwork—skills crucial for navigating the collaborative human-AI work environment. Workshops on emotional intelligence may cover areas like recognizing and managing emotional responses to technological change, fostering positive working relationships in a restructured workforce, and practicing empathetic communication with clients or colleagues.

Recruiting AI-literate talent is another critical aspect of building an AI-ready workforce. This requires a shift in recruitment strategies, moving beyond traditional skills-based assessments to incorporate assessments of adaptability, problem-solving skills, and a willingness to learn new technologies. Job descriptions need to be updated to reflect the changing nature of work, highlighting the opportunities for growth and development in an AI-enhanced environment. Attracting top talent may require organizations to offer competitive compensation packages, opportunities for professional development, and a work environment that encourages innovation and collaboration.

Beyond specific technical skills and soft skills, the ability to understand and effectively utilize data is becoming increasingly essential. Data literacy training is crucial across all organizational levels. Employees need to be equipped to not only interpret data generated by AI but also to critically analyze it, recognizing potential biases and limitations. This includes understanding data visualization techniques, statistical analysis, and the ethical implications of data usage. Effective data literacy empowers employees to confidently work with AI-generated insights and make informed decisions based on the information provided.

The recruitment process should also consider candidates with diverse backgrounds and experiences. Teams that reflect the diversity of their customer base and the broader society are more likely to produce innovative solutions and avoid biases inherent in AI systems. This diverse talent pool brings different perspectives, skills, and problem-solving approaches to the table, crucial for navigating the complexities of the AI-driven workplace.

Organizations should also review their existing recruitment processes to ensure they aren't inadvertently excluding qualified candidates based on outdated biases or traditional criteria.

Fostering a culture of continuous learning and adaptation is essential for long-term success. Organizations must create an environment where employees feel encouraged to learn new skills, experiment with new technologies, and embrace change as an opportunity rather than a threat. This can involve initiatives like establishing internal knowledge-sharing platforms, funding professional development opportunities, and creating dedicated time for employees to explore new technologies.

Several successful companies demonstrate effective strategies for building AI-ready workforces. For instance, companies like Google and Microsoft invest heavily in internal training programs, providing employees with access to cutting-edge AI technologies and expert instruction. Their approach extends beyond technical training; they emphasize the importance of human skills such as critical thinking, creativity, and collaboration. These organizations prioritize a culture of continuous learning, providing ongoing support and resources for their employees to stay ahead of the curve. Similarly, many financial institutions are actively reskilling their workforce to adapt to the rise of algorithmic trading and AI-powered risk management.

Another noteworthy strategy is to establish cross-functional teams dedicated to AI implementation. These teams, comprising experts from various departments, can collaborate on projects, sharing knowledge and experience to ensure seamless integration of AI across different functions. They provide a platform for learning and knowledge sharing, fostering a collaborative environment where employees learn from each other.

It's vital to acknowledge that building an AI-ready workforce is not a one-time event but an ongoing process. Organizations must continuously adapt their strategies, training programs, and recruitment practices to keep pace with the rapid advancements in AI. Leaders must prioritize not only the acquisition of technical skills but also the development of human skills that will remain essential in the age of AI – creativity, critical thinking, emotional intelligence, collaboration, and adaptability. By investing in their people and fostering a culture of continuous learning, organizations can position themselves to thrive in the age of AI. The future of work is not about humans versus AI, but about humans and AI working together to achieve remarkable results. Building an AI-ready workforce is about empowering individuals to embrace this collaborative future.

Leveraging AI for Strategic Decision Making

The transition to an AI-driven workplace isn't merely about replacing human workers with machines; it's about augmenting human capabilities and transforming how we make decisions.

Strategic decision-making, once the exclusive domain of experienced executives, is now being significantly enhanced by the power of artificial intelligence. AI's ability to process vast datasets, identify patterns invisible to the human eye, and generate predictive models offers a transformative potential for businesses across all sectors. Leveraging AI for strategic decisions isn't about relinquishing control; it's about empowering leaders with data-driven insights to make more informed, effective, and timely choices.

One of the most significant applications of AI in strategic decision-making lies in data analysis. Traditional methods often struggle to cope with the sheer volume and complexity of data generated in today's business environment. AI algorithms, however, can efficiently sift through massive datasets, identifying trends, correlations, and anomalies that would otherwise remain hidden.

This enhanced analytical capability empowers businesses to understand their customers better, optimize operational processes, and identify emerging market opportunities with greater accuracy.

For example, an e-commerce company can use AI to analyze customer purchase history, browsing behavior, and demographic data to personalize marketing campaigns and recommendations, increasing sales conversion rates. Similarly, a manufacturing firm can leverage AI to analyze sensor data from its production line, predicting equipment failures and optimizing maintenance schedules, thereby minimizing downtime and maximizing efficiency. The key here is the ability to translate raw data into actionable insights, a task AI excels at.

Beyond data analysis, AI's predictive capabilities are proving invaluable in strategic forecasting. By analyzing historical data and incorporating various external factors, AI algorithms can generate accurate forecasts for sales, demand, market trends, and other key business metrics. This enhanced predictive power allows businesses to anticipate challenges, mitigate risks, and capitalize on emerging opportunities. Consider a financial institution using AI to forecast market volatility. By analyzing vast amounts of financial data, news articles, and social media sentiment, the AI can predict potential market downturns, allowing the institution to adjust its investment strategies accordingly and minimize potential losses. In the energy sector, AI-powered forecasting can help predict energy demand fluctuations, enabling utilities to optimize energy generation and distribution, ensuring a stable and reliable power supply.

Scenario planning, a crucial aspect of strategic decision-making, also benefits significantly from AI's capabilities. Traditional scenario planning often relies on expert judgment and limited data sets. AI, however, can simulate a wide range of potential scenarios, factoring in multiple variables and uncertainties, providing a more comprehensive understanding of potential future outcomes. A logistics company, for instance, might use AI to simulate various scenarios related to supply chain disruptions, such as natural disasters or geopolitical instability. The AI can assess the impact of each scenario on its operations, enabling the company to develop contingency plans and strengthen its resilience. Similarly, a healthcare provider could use AI to simulate different treatment protocols for a specific disease, assessing their effectiveness and potential side effects, leading to more informed and personalized treatment plans.

The ethical considerations surrounding the use of AI in decision-making are paramount. AI algorithms are trained on data, and if that data reflects existing biases, the AI's decisions will inevitably inherit and potentially amplify those biases. Therefore, it's crucial to ensure that the data used to train AI systems is representative, unbiased, and free from discriminatory patterns. Furthermore, the transparency and explainability of AI algorithms are essential. Leaders need to understand how an AI arrives at its conclusions to ensure the decisions made are ethically sound and justifiable. The "black box" nature of some AI algorithms raises concerns about accountability and the potential for unforeseen consequences. Therefore, a balanced approach is necessary, combining the power of AI with the ethical judgment and oversight of human decision-makers. This involves rigorous testing, validation, and ongoing monitoring of AI systems to detect and mitigate potential biases.

The successful implementation of AI for strategic decision-making requires a combination of technological prowess, data management expertise, and human oversight. Organizations need to invest in robust data infrastructure, develop AI-literate teams, and establish clear guidelines for the ethical use of AI. This includes providing training to employees on data analysis, AI interpretation, and ethical decision-making in the context of AI. Furthermore, it's crucial to foster a culture of experimentation and continuous improvement, allowing teams to learn from successes and failures, adapting their strategies as AI technology evolves.

Several successful case studies demonstrate the transformative impact of AI on strategic decision-making. For instance, many large retailers leverage AI-powered recommendation systems to personalize customer experiences and drive sales. These systems analyze vast amounts of data to predict which products customers are most likely to purchase, leading to increased sales and improved customer satisfaction. Financial institutions use AI to detect fraudulent transactions and manage risk, protecting their assets and maintaining customer trust. Healthcare providers utilize AI to improve diagnostic accuracy, personalize treatment plans, and accelerate drug discovery. These examples highlight the versatility and potential of AI across diverse industries.

It's important to emphasize that AI is not a replacement for human judgment; rather, it's a powerful tool that augments human capabilities. The most effective approach involves a collaborative partnership between humans and AI, where humans provide the strategic direction, ethical considerations, and critical thinking skills, while AI handles the data analysis, predictive modeling, and scenario planning. This synergy allows leaders to make more informed, efficient, and ethical decisions, positioning their organizations for success in the ever-evolving landscape of the modern business world. The future of strategic decision-making is not about choosing between human intuition and AI-driven analysis; it's about harnessing the power of both to achieve truly impactful and sustainable results. This collaborative approach requires a cultural shift within organizations, one that embraces data-driven decision making while retaining the crucial role of human intuition, ethical considerations and creative problem-solving. The leaders who successfully navigate this transition will be those who empower their teams with the knowledge and tools to effectively utilize AI, fostering a collaborative environment where technology and human expertise work in perfect harmony.

Communicating the Value of AI to Stakeholders

Communicating the value of AI to stakeholders is paramount for successful AI integration within any organization. This requires a multifaceted approach that tailors messaging to specific audiences, addressing their unique concerns and expectations. Ignoring this crucial aspect can lead to resistance, mistrust, and ultimately, the failure of AI initiatives.

For employees, the initial reaction to AI implementation can range from excitement to apprehension, often fueled by fears of job displacement. Open and honest communication is vital in addressing these anxieties. Instead of framing AI as a job-replacement tool, it should be presented as a technology designed to augment human capabilities, freeing employees from repetitive tasks and allowing them to focus on more strategic and creative work. This requires demonstrating how AI can streamline workflows, improve efficiency, and enhance job satisfaction.

Concrete examples are essential. For instance, in a customer service setting, demonstrate how AI-powered chatbots can handle routine inquiries, freeing human agents to address complex issues requiring empathy and problem-solving skills. In a marketing department, show how AI-driven tools can automate repetitive tasks like social media posting or email marketing, allowing marketers to focus on more strategic initiatives like developing creative campaigns or refining marketing strategies.

Transparency is critical in gaining employee trust. Explain how AI systems work, what data they utilize, and the decision-making processes involved. Addressing concerns about data privacy and security head-on is vital. Establishing clear guidelines on data usage and ensuring compliance with relevant regulations builds confidence and trust. Furthermore, providing ample opportunities for employees to ask questions and express concerns in a safe and supportive environment is crucial for creating a culture of open dialogue. This could involve town hall meetings, Q&A sessions with AI specialists, or even internal communication platforms dedicated to AI-related discussions. Investing in training programs that equip employees with the skills to effectively use and interact with AI technologies also demonstrates a commitment to their development and reduces the fear of obsolescence.

Communicating the value of AI to customers requires a different approach. Focus should be on the improved products or services AI enables. Highlight the benefits customers will directly experience, such as faster response times, personalized recommendations, or more efficient problem resolution. For example, a bank could showcase how AI-powered fraud detection systems enhance security and protect customer accounts. An e-commerce platform could demonstrate how AI-driven personalization improves the shopping experience and delivers relevant product suggestions. Transparency in data usage, particularly regarding customer data privacy, is crucial to build customer trust. Customers need to understand how their data is collected, used, and protected. Clear and concise privacy policies, readily accessible to customers, are essential.

Furthermore, actively soliciting customer feedback on AI-related features and improvements demonstrates a commitment to customer-centricity and continuous improvement. This feedback loop not only helps improve the AI system but also fosters a sense of partnership and collaboration with customers.

Investors, on the other hand, are primarily interested in the financial implications of AI integration. They need to see a clear return on investment (ROI), including enhanced efficiency, increased revenue, reduced costs, and improved risk management. Presenting compelling financial projections supported by data and case studies is essential to gain investor confidence. Demonstrate how AI can help achieve specific business goals, such as optimizing supply chains, improving customer retention, or entering new markets. Highlighting successful implementations of AI in similar companies can further strengthen the argument for investment. Transparency regarding the costs involved in AI implementation, including infrastructure, software, and personnel, is equally important. Investors need a complete and accurate picture of the financial implications to make informed decisions. Addressing any potential risks associated with AI implementation, such as data security breaches or algorithmic biases, is also critical for investor confidence.

Ethical considerations permeate all aspects of AI communication. Transparency regarding the algorithms used, their limitations, and potential biases is vital to build trust with all stakeholders. Explain how steps are being taken to mitigate bias and ensure fairness in AI systems. Clearly articulating the company's commitment to ethical AI development and deployment is crucial. This could involve adhering to ethical guidelines established by industry organizations or creating internal ethical review boards to oversee AI initiatives.

Proactive communication about any unforeseen consequences or unintended biases identified in AI systems demonstrates accountability and responsibility. This open and honest approach builds credibility and trust, mitigating potential negative consequences.

Effective communication strategies go beyond simply disseminating information. It's about building a narrative that resonates with each stakeholder group. This includes using various communication channels tailored to each audience, from formal reports and presentations for investors to informal workshops and Q&A sessions for employees. Leveraging storytelling to illustrate the benefits of AI can make abstract concepts more relatable and engaging. Case studies, testimonials, and interactive demonstrations can all enhance the effectiveness of communication efforts. Regularly monitoring and assessing the effectiveness of communication initiatives is essential for continuous improvement. Gathering feedback from stakeholders through surveys, focus groups, or social media can provide invaluable insights into how to refine communication strategies and address emerging concerns.

Finally, building a culture of AI literacy within the organization is crucial for successful communication and implementation.

Providing training and education to employees at all levels helps equip them with the knowledge and understanding needed to effectively use and interact with AI technologies. This training should not only focus on technical aspects but also on ethical considerations, societal implications, and the potential impact of AI on the workforce. By fostering a culture of continuous learning and adaptation, organizations can better manage the transition to an AI-driven workplace and maximize the benefits of AI while minimizing the risks. The goal is not merely to inform stakeholders about AI, but to build a shared understanding and a collective commitment to its ethical and responsible application. Only through such a comprehensive and proactive communication strategy can organizations truly unlock the transformative potential of AI.

Chapter 5: Securing Promotions and High-Paying Opportunities

Identifying High Demand AI-Related Roles

The rapid advancement of artificial intelligence is not simply reshaping industries; it's fundamentally redrawing the career landscape. While anxieties about AI-driven job displacement are valid, they often overshadow a crucial reality: AI is also creating a plethora of new, high-demand roles, many offering lucrative salaries and significant career growth potential. Understanding these emerging opportunities is key to navigating the changing job market and securing a prosperous future.

One of the most prominent high-demand roles is that of the **AI specialist**. These professionals are the architects and engineers of AI systems. Their expertise spans a broad range of disciplines, including machine learning, deep learning, natural language processing (NLP), and computer vision. AI specialists are responsible for designing, developing, and implementing AI algorithms, training models on large datasets, and deploying these models into production environments. They need a strong foundation in mathematics, statistics, and computer science, along with practical experience in programming languages like Python or R and familiarity with various AI frameworks such as TensorFlow or PyTorch. The required skillset extends beyond technical proficiency; strong problem-solving abilities, critical thinking, and a keen eye for detail are essential for identifying and resolving issues within complex AI systems. Salary ranges for AI specialists vary significantly based on experience and location, but can easily reach six-figure incomes, particularly for those with advanced degrees and specialized expertise.

Closely related to the AI specialist is the **data scientist**. While AI specialists focus on the algorithms and models themselves, data scientists play a critical role in preparing and analyzing the data that fuels these systems. They are responsible for collecting, cleaning, transforming, and visualizing large datasets, identifying patterns and insights, and using statistical methods to draw meaningful conclusions. Data scientists need a strong background in statistics, data mining, and database management, along with programming skills and experience with data visualization tools.

They must also possess excellent communication skills to effectively present their findings to both technical and non-technical audiences. The demand for data scientists remains exceptionally high across various sectors, from finance and healthcare to technology and marketing, leading to competitive salaries that often surpass those of many other technical roles. The ability to leverage AI tools to automate data analysis tasks further enhances a data scientist's value.

The ethical implications of AI are increasingly gaining recognition, leading to the emergence of the **AI ethicist** as a crucial role. AI ethicists are responsible for ensuring that AI systems are developed and deployed responsibly, ethically, and without bias. They assess the potential societal impacts of AI, identify and mitigate risks, and develop guidelines and policies to promote fairness and accountability. This role demands a strong understanding of AI technology, ethical principles, and societal values. Excellent communication and collaboration skills are vital for engaging with diverse stakeholders, including developers, policymakers, and the public. The field of AI ethics is relatively nascent, but the demand for qualified professionals is growing rapidly, as organizations recognize the importance of ethical considerations in their AI initiatives. Salaries for AI ethicists are competitive, reflecting the critical nature of their work and the increasing awareness of responsible AI development.

Another high-demand role is that of the **AI project manager**. These individuals are responsible for overseeing the entire lifecycle of AI projects, from conception to deployment and maintenance.

They manage project timelines, budgets, and resources, ensuring projects stay on track and deliver on their objectives. AI project managers need a strong understanding of AI technologies, project management methodologies, and business needs. They must possess excellent organizational, communication, and leadership skills to effectively lead cross-functional teams and manage complex projects. The ability to communicate technical concepts to non-technical stakeholders is crucial for successful project execution. Given the complexities and large-scale nature of many AI projects, experienced and skilled AI project managers are highly sought after, commanding substantial salaries.

Beyond these core roles, other high-demand positions are emerging within the AI ecosystem. **AI trainers** are responsible for fine-tuning and improving the performance of AI models, using techniques like reinforcement learning or transfer learning. **AI cybersecurity specialists** focus on protecting AI systems from attacks and vulnerabilities, a critical area given the increasing reliance on AI in critical infrastructure. **AI explainability engineers** aim to make the decision-making processes of AI models more transparent and understandable, addressing concerns about "black box" AI systems.

Even traditional roles are being redefined by AI. For instance, **marketing managers** who can effectively leverage AI-driven tools for marketing automation, personalization, and campaign optimization are in high demand. Similarly, **financial analysts** proficient in using AI-powered tools for risk assessment, algorithmic trading, and fraud detection have significant career advantages.

The career paths within these AI-related fields are diverse and promising. Many entry-level positions require a bachelor's degree in a relevant field, such as computer science, data science, or engineering. However, advanced degrees, such as master's or doctoral degrees, are increasingly becoming essential for higher-level positions and specialized roles. Continuous learning and upskilling are paramount in this rapidly evolving field. Staying abreast of the latest advancements in AI, acquiring new skills through online courses, workshops, and certifications, and actively participating in the AI community are crucial for career progression.

The potential salary ranges for these roles are highly variable, dependent on factors like experience, location, company size, and specific skills. However, it's safe to say that many AI-related roles offer significantly higher earning potential than many traditional professions. Entry-level positions may start at competitive salaries, but with experience and expertise, professionals in these fields can quickly command six-figure incomes, and sometimes much more.

The high demand and relatively short supply of qualified professionals in many AI specializations drive up salaries, creating attractive career opportunities for those willing to invest the time and effort to acquire the necessary skills.

Securing these high-paying opportunities requires a proactive and strategic approach. Building a strong foundation in relevant technical skills is essential. This includes proficiency in programming languages, statistical modeling, machine learning techniques, and relevant AI frameworks. Equally important is developing strong soft skills, including communication, teamwork, problem-solving, and critical thinking. Networking within the AI community is crucial for uncovering hidden job opportunities and building relationships with potential employers. Attending industry conferences, joining professional organizations, and participating in online forums are excellent ways to expand your professional network. Tailoring your resume and cover letter to highlight your relevant skills and experience for each specific job application demonstrates your understanding of the role's requirements.

Practice your interviewing skills, preparing answers to common interview questions and showcasing your passion for AI. A portfolio of personal projects, demonstrating your practical skills and abilities, can significantly enhance your job application. Finally, a commitment to continuous learning and professional development, staying updated on the latest trends and technologies within the rapidly evolving AI landscape, will solidify your position as a highly competitive candidate for high-demand roles in the field. The future of work is intertwined with AI, and those who embrace this technology and develop the relevant skills will be well-positioned to secure not just employment, but rewarding and high-paying careers.

Crafting a Compelling Resume and LinkedIn Profile

The previous section outlined the burgeoning job market within the AI sector and the high-demand roles it encompasses. Now, let's shift our focus to a crucial element in securing those lucrative positions: presenting yourself effectively to potential employers. Your resume and LinkedIn profile are your first impression, acting as gatekeepers to interviews and job offers. In the age of AI, simply listing your skills is insufficient; you need to strategically showcase your capabilities in a way that resonates with recruiters and hiring managers – often aided by AI-driven applicant tracking systems (ATS).

Crafting a compelling resume requires a strategic approach that moves beyond a chronological listing of your work history. Think of your resume as a marketing document, highlighting your unique value proposition and demonstrating why you are the ideal candidate for the specific role. Instead of merely stating your responsibilities, quantify your achievements. For example, instead of writing "Managed social media accounts," try "Increased social media engagement by 30% within six months through targeted advertising campaigns and engaging content creation, resulting in a 15% increase in lead generation." This approach showcases tangible results and demonstrates your impact.

When tailoring your resume for AI-related positions, incorporate relevant keywords strategically throughout the document. Utilize job descriptions as your guide, identifying keywords frequently used by recruiters and incorporating them organically into your resume's narrative. AI-powered ATS scan resumes for specific terms, and failing to include them can prevent your application from even reaching human eyes. Keywords may include "machine learning," "deep learning," "natural language processing," "computer vision," "Python," "TensorFlow," "PyTorch," "data mining," "data visualization," "big data," and other relevant technologies and tools. However, avoid keyword stuffing – unnatural and excessive use of keywords will be easily flagged by more sophisticated ATS algorithms and harm your application rather than help it. Aim for a natural integration of keywords that accurately reflects your skills and experience.

Beyond simply listing technical skills, emphasize your problem-solving abilities and critical thinking. Describe situations where you encountered challenges, how you approached them, and the successful outcomes you achieved. These narrative examples provide concrete evidence of your analytical prowess, a highly valued trait in AI-related roles. For instance, if you developed a machine learning model, don't merely state that you did so. Detail the specific problem you addressed, the datasets used, the algorithms employed, the challenges overcome (e.g., handling imbalanced datasets, mitigating bias), and the final performance metrics achieved. This narrative provides much more context and shows a deeper understanding of the process.

Similarly, highlighting projects undertaken outside of formal employment significantly enhances your resume. These projects demonstrate initiative, passion, and the ability to apply your skills independently. If you've developed any AI-related projects, include a concise description of the project, its goals, your contributions, and the results achieved. Include links to GitHub repositories or project websites whenever possible to allow recruiters to examine your work firsthand. Even personal projects, such as developing a chatbot or building a predictive model for a hobby, can significantly bolster your application, showcasing your self-motivation and commitment to the field.

Your LinkedIn profile serves as your professional online presence and should complement, not simply duplicate, your resume. Ensure your profile is complete and up-to-date, reflecting your current skills and experience accurately. Use a professional headshot, and write a compelling headline that succinctly summarizes your expertise and aspirations. Your summary section provides an opportunity to showcase your passion for AI and highlight your unique contributions to the field. Don't just list your accomplishments; tell a story that conveys your enthusiasm and career goals.

On LinkedIn, strategically utilize keywords similar to those used in your resume. Ensure your experience section details your achievements quantitatively, mirroring the approach adopted in your resume. Connect with individuals in your field, participating in relevant groups and engaging in discussions. This expands your network and provides opportunities for organic discovery by recruiters. LinkedIn also allows you to showcase your skills.

Endorse and recommend colleagues, and actively solicit endorsements for your own skills to establish credibility and expertise. By actively cultivating your LinkedIn profile, you transform it from a static online resume into a dynamic professional networking hub.

Remember that visual appeal matters. Your resume and LinkedIn profile should be visually clean, easy to navigate, and free of grammatical errors. Use a professional font, maintain consistent formatting, and ensure your content is concise and easy to read. Before submitting your resume or updating your LinkedIn profile, have a trusted colleague or mentor review your work for any potential improvements or omissions. A second pair of eyes can often identify subtle improvements that significantly elevate your presentation.

In the AI landscape, continuous learning is paramount. Showcase your commitment to professional development by listing relevant certifications, online courses, workshops, and conferences attended. Highlight any involvement in open-source projects or contributions to the broader AI community. This demonstrates your proactive approach to staying current with the latest advancements in the field, a highly desirable trait for employers.

Examples of successful resumes and LinkedIn profiles can be found online, but remember to tailor them to your specific circumstances and career goals. Generic templates rarely capture the unique essence of your capabilities and experience. Authenticity and a well-crafted narrative will always trump a generic template. Focus on highlighting your individual contributions, quantifying your accomplishments, and showcasing your passion for the field. Your resume and LinkedIn profile should reflect not just your technical skills, but also your personality, work ethic, and professional aspirations.

In summary, your resume and LinkedIn profile are more than just documents – they're your professional calling card in the competitive landscape of the AI industry. By strategically crafting these documents, leveraging keywords effectively, quantifying your achievements, and building a compelling online presence, you significantly increase your chances of landing interviews and ultimately securing high-paying opportunities within the exciting and rapidly evolving world of artificial intelligence. Remember, it's not just about having the skills; it's about effectively showcasing them to the right audience at the right time. With careful planning and attention to detail, you can make your application stand out from the crowd and secure the career you deserve. The effort invested in crafting a compelling narrative of your skills and accomplishments will yield significant returns in securing those coveted high-paying AI roles.

Acing the Interview: Showcasing Your AI Skills

Now that you've meticulously crafted your resume and LinkedIn profile to highlight your AI expertise, the next crucial step in securing a high-paying AI role is acing the interview. This isn't merely a formality; it's your opportunity to demonstrate your practical knowledge, problem-solving skills, and passion for the field—all in a dynamic, conversational setting. The interview process, much like the application itself, is increasingly influenced by AI, with some companies using AI-powered tools to analyze candidate responses and assess suitability. Therefore, preparation is key.

Preparation transcends simply reviewing common interview questions; it involves strategically anticipating the types of questions likely to be posed, given your specific background and the role you're pursuing. For example, a role in machine learning will necessitate a deeper understanding of algorithms and model evaluation than a position focused on data analysis. Tailor your preparation accordingly, ensuring you are well-versed in the specific technologies and methodologies relevant to the position.

Let's address some common interview questions and strategies for crafting compelling answers:

Technical Proficiency: Expect questions designed to gauge your technical proficiency. These might include inquiries about specific algorithms (e.g., explaining the differences between linear regression and logistic regression, or detailing the workings of a convolutional neural network), programming languages (Python, R, Java), or relevant frameworks (TensorFlow, PyTorch, scikit-learn).

Don't simply provide definitions; illustrate your understanding through examples. For instance, if asked about the bias-variance trade-off, explain it conceptually and then describe a situation where you had to navigate this trade-off in a real-world project, outlining the choices made and the resulting impact.

Project-Based Questions: Be ready to discuss your past projects in detail. This is where the narrative approach emphasized in resume preparation becomes crucial. Instead of simply listing project elements, weave a story that highlights the challenges you encountered, your problem-solving strategies, the technologies you employed, and the outcomes you achieved. Quantify your achievements wherever possible. Did you improve a model's accuracy by a certain percentage? Did you reduce processing time significantly? These tangible metrics provide concrete evidence of your impact. Prepare for follow-up questions that delve deeper into the technical aspects of your projects. For example, if you built a recommendation system, be prepared to explain the algorithm you used, the data preprocessing steps, and how you evaluated the system's performance.

Problem-Solving Scenarios: Many AI interviews include problem-solving scenarios. These scenarios are designed to assess your critical thinking and analytical abilities. For example, you might be presented with a hypothetical problem requiring the development of a machine learning model for a specific task. The interviewer isn't necessarily looking for a perfect solution; they're evaluating your approach to the problem. Clearly outline your steps: defining the problem, identifying the relevant data, selecting appropriate algorithms, considering potential biases, and outlining the evaluation metrics you would use. Showcase your ability to think critically and systematically, demonstrating a structured approach to problem-solving.

Ethical Considerations: AI is rife with ethical considerations. Be prepared to discuss ethical dilemmas in AI, such as bias in algorithms, privacy concerns, and the potential impact of AI on society. Demonstrate your awareness of these challenges and your ability to consider the ethical implications of your work. For example, you might discuss how you addressed bias in a dataset or how you ensured the privacy of user data in a project. This showcases your responsible approach to AI development.

Teamwork and Collaboration: Most AI projects involve teamwork. Highlight your collaborative experiences, emphasizing your communication skills, ability to work effectively within a team, and contributions to a shared goal. Provide specific examples of collaborative projects, describing your role, your contributions, and the overall outcome.

Continuous Learning: The AI field is rapidly evolving. Demonstrate your commitment to continuous learning by discussing the resources you use to stay up-to-date with the latest advancements, such as attending conferences, participating in online courses, or engaging with the AI community through open-source projects. Highlight specific technologies, techniques, or concepts you've recently learned, demonstrating your proactive approach to professional development.

Behavioral Questions: Beyond technical skills, expect behavioral questions designed to assess your personality and work style. These often begin with phrases like "Tell me about a time when..." or "Describe a situation where...". Use the STAR method (Situation, Task, Action, Result) to structure your answers, providing specific examples that illustrate your skills and experiences. For example, if asked about a time you failed, honestly describe the situation, the actions you took, the lessons you learned, and how you applied those lessons to future endeavors.

Asking Questions: The interview is a two-way street. Prepare insightful questions to ask the interviewer. This demonstrates your engagement and interest in the role and the company. Avoid questions easily answered through online research; instead, focus on questions that reveal your deeper understanding of the company's culture, the challenges faced by the team, and the opportunities for growth. Questions about specific projects, the company's AI strategy, or the team's approach to ethical considerations are excellent choices.

Practicing Your Delivery: Rehearse your answers to common interview questions. This helps you refine your responses, ensuring they are clear, concise, and impactful. Practice speaking confidently and articulately, conveying your enthusiasm and passion for the field. Consider practicing with a friend or mentor to receive constructive feedback. Record yourself to identify areas for improvement in your delivery.

Understanding the Company's AI Initiatives: Thoroughly research the company's AI-related activities. Understand their products, services, or research areas that involve AI. This allows you to tailor your responses to their specific needs and demonstrate your understanding of their business. Mention specific projects or initiatives that resonate with you, showing genuine interest and initiative.

In summary, acing the AI job interview requires a multi-faceted approach that blends technical expertise with strong communication and problem-solving skills. By meticulously preparing for common questions, showcasing your projects effectively, demonstrating your ethical awareness, and showcasing your passion for continuous learning, you'll significantly increase your chances of securing that high-paying AI role. Remember, it's not just about what you know; it's about how effectively you communicate that knowledge and enthusiasm to the interviewer. The interview is your opportunity to bring your resume and online presence to life, demonstrating why you are the ideal candidate for the position. With thorough preparation and a confident presentation, you can navigate the interview process successfully and embark on a rewarding career in the exciting field of artificial intelligence.

Negotiating Your Salary and Benefits

Having successfully navigated the interview process and secured a coveted AI role, the next critical step is negotiating your salary and benefits package. This is not merely a matter of accepting the initial offer; it's an opportunity to maximize your earning potential and secure a compensation package that reflects your value and expertise. A well-negotiated salary can significantly impact your financial well-being and long-term career trajectory. Remember, your skills in AI are in high demand, and you deserve to be compensated accordingly.

Before entering any salary negotiation, thorough research is paramount. Understanding the market rate for your specific skillset and experience level is crucial. Numerous online resources provide salary data based on location, job title, and years of experience.

Sites like Glassdoor, Payscale, and Salary.com offer valuable insights into salary ranges for similar roles in your geographic area. Don't limit yourself to general averages; try to find data specific to AI roles within your industry and company size. Consider factors such as the company's financial performance, its standing within the industry, and the complexity and responsibility of the role you are filling.

Beyond general salary surveys, leverage your network. Connect with colleagues, former classmates, and mentors who have experience in AI roles. Informal conversations can offer invaluable insights into salary expectations and benefit packages offered by similar companies. This informal research provides context beyond the numbers found on websites, giving you a more nuanced understanding of the prevailing market dynamics. Remember to respect confidentiality and avoid disclosing your own salary expectations during these informal discussions.

Once you've established a realistic salary range based on your research, it's time to define your value proposition. This involves clearly articulating the unique skills and experience you bring to the table. This isn't just about listing your technical proficiencies; it's about showcasing the tangible impact you expect to make on the organization. Quantify your achievements whenever possible.

For instance, if you developed a machine learning model that improved efficiency by 15%, or significantly reduced error rates, highlight these accomplishments prominently. Emphasize how your skills and experience directly address the company's needs and contribute to its overall goals. Preparing a concise and impactful statement summarizing your value proposition can be incredibly helpful during the negotiation process.

When presenting your salary expectations, be confident and assertive, but also maintain a professional and respectful demeanor.

Avoid presenting a rigid number; instead, frame your expectation as a range, allowing for flexibility and compromise. For example, you might state, "Based on my research and experience, I'm targeting a salary range of $X to $Y." Justify your expectations by citing your accomplishments and research findings. Remember, you are not simply asking for a higher salary; you are presenting a compelling case for your value and the return on investment the company will receive by employing you.

Negotiating benefits is just as crucial as negotiating salary. Explore options beyond the basic health insurance and paid time off.

Consider asking for professional development opportunities, such as attending conferences or taking specialized AI courses. This demonstrates your commitment to continuous learning and signals your long-term dedication to the company. Furthermore, inquire about flexible working arrangements, such as remote work options or flexible hours, which can significantly enhance your work-life balance. Stock options or other performance-based incentives could also be part of your negotiation, especially if you're joining a fast-growing tech company.

Consider the entire compensation package. Don't solely focus on the base salary; analyze the total compensation, which includes benefits like health insurance, retirement contributions, paid time off, and bonuses. A company might offer a lower base salary but compensate with a more comprehensive benefits package. Carefully evaluate the total value proposition before making a final decision. Often, a slightly lower salary with superior benefits might offer a better overall return in terms of long-term financial security and well-being.

During the negotiation, actively listen to the employer's perspective.

Understand their constraints and priorities. A collaborative approach, rather than an adversarial one, often yields the best results. Be prepared to make concessions, but ensure that those concessions do not significantly compromise your overall compensation package. Negotiation is a two-way street, and finding common ground requires mutual understanding and compromise.

Don't be afraid to walk away if the offered compensation is significantly below your expectations. This may seem drastic, but it's better to prioritize your own worth and find an opportunity that properly values your skills and experience. A strong job market, especially in the high-demand field of AI, provides you with leverage. Remember, you deserve to be compensated fairly for your expertise and contributions.

Prepare counter-arguments for potential objections. For instance, if the employer argues that the offered salary is at the high end of their budget, you might offer a phased-in salary increase contingent upon meeting performance goals or mastering specific new skills within a reasonable time frame. This shows your commitment to exceeding expectations while providing the employer with a financially responsible solution.

Successful salary negotiation is not about being aggressive or demanding; it's about being prepared, assertive, and confident. By thoroughly researching the market, clearly defining your value proposition, and approaching the negotiation with a collaborative mindset, you can secure a compensation package that reflects your worth and sets you up for long-term career success in the dynamic world of AI. Remember, your skills are in high demand, and you deserve to be rewarded fairly for your expertise.

Let's consider some specific examples of successful salary negotiation strategies.

Example 1: The Value-Added Approach: Imagine you're interviewing for a senior AI engineer role. During the negotiation, you could highlight a past project where you significantly improved a model's accuracy, leading to a substantial cost saving for the previous employer. Quantifying this success – for instance, "increased efficiency by 18%, saving the company $500,000 annually" – directly demonstrates your value. You can then frame your salary request by linking it to this tangible impact, suggesting a salary that reflects the return on investment the company will gain from your expertise.

Example 2: The Counter-Offer Strategy: Suppose the initial offer falls below your expectations. Instead of simply rejecting it, prepare a thoughtful counter-offer. This might involve proposing a slightly lower salary in exchange for improved benefits, such as a signing bonus or additional vacation days. This demonstrates flexibility while still ensuring you receive fair compensation in a different form. For example, you could say, "While I appreciate the offer, I'm hoping for a salary closer to $X. However, I am flexible. Perhaps we could discuss a slightly lower salary with the addition of a $Y signing bonus to compensate."

Example 3: Negotiating Beyond Salary: Beyond salary, consider other aspects of the compensation package. Perhaps the company offers a limited professional development budget. You could negotiate for a larger budget, allowing you to attend relevant conferences or pursue advanced certifications. This demonstrates your commitment to continued learning and aligns with the company's long-term interest in upskilling its workforce.

Example 4: The Phased Increase: If the company is hesitant to meet your desired salary upfront, you might propose a phased salary increase over a specific timeframe. This might involve a higher starting salary with periodic reviews and potential increases based on performance metrics. This strategy shows your commitment to meeting performance expectations while easing the financial burden on the company.

Example 5: The Leverage of Multiple Offers: In a highly competitive job market, having multiple job offers can significantly enhance your negotiating power. This isn't about being manipulative, but about honestly showcasing your attractiveness to other companies. You could state something like, "I have received another offer for a similar role at a different organization that is closer to my target salary range. While I'm genuinely interested in this opportunity, I need to consider all my options." This is not intended as a threat, but rather as factual information that can influence the negotiations.

By understanding the strategies behind successful salary negotiations, you can confidently enter the conversation and secure a compensation package that reflects your value as an AI professional. Remember, it's a discussion, not a battle. Preparation and clear communication are key to achieving a successful outcome. This is an investment in your future, and it's worth the effort to maximize your financial well-being and secure a career path that sets you up for success in the exciting field of artificial intelligence.

Building Your Personal Brand and Network

In the fiercely competitive landscape of artificial intelligence, securing high-paying opportunities and promotions isn't solely about possessing technical expertise; it's equally, if not more, about cultivating a strong personal brand and a robust professional network. Your technical skills are the foundation, but your brand and network are the scaffolding that elevates your career to new heights. This section delves into the strategic building of both, providing actionable steps to enhance your visibility, credibility, and ultimately, your earning potential.

Building a compelling personal brand within AI requires a multifaceted approach. It's about strategically showcasing your expertise, accomplishments, and unique value proposition to potential employers, collaborators, and industry leaders. Think of it as creating a consistent and memorable narrative around your professional identity. This isn't about self-promotion; it's about authentically conveying your capabilities and passions within the AI domain.

One of the most potent tools for personal branding is your online presence. This encompasses your LinkedIn profile, personal website (if you choose to have one), and any contributions you make to online communities and platforms related to AI. Your LinkedIn profile, in particular, should be more than just a resume; it should be a dynamic showcase of your expertise. Instead of simply listing your responsibilities, quantify your achievements. For example, instead of saying "Developed machine learning models," state"Developed machine learning models resulting in a 20% increase in customer engagement." Showcase your skills and endorsements.

Make sure your headline clearly reflects your current area of specialization within AI. Include a professional headshot and keep your profile up-to-date.

Consider creating a personal website. This offers a more comprehensive platform to display your work, publications, and thought leadership. It provides a space to express your unique perspectives and demonstrate a deeper understanding of the AI field beyond a simple resume or LinkedIn profile. A well-designed website can significantly enhance your credibility and demonstrate professionalism to recruiters and potential employers. Think of it as your digital portfolio.

Another crucial aspect of personal branding is engaging with the AI community online. This could involve participating in discussions on platforms like Reddit, participating in AI-focused forums, or contributing to relevant blog posts or articles. By actively contributing your expertise and insights, you are not only establishing yourself as a thought leader, but also demonstrating your commitment to the field. It allows you to engage with other professionals, learn from their experiences, and showcase your knowledge in a way that goes beyond a static profile. This is about showcasing active participation and demonstrating a commitment to the AI field that goes beyond just having a profile.

Beyond your online presence, attending industry events is paramount. Conferences, workshops, and meetups offer invaluable opportunities for networking, learning, and showcasing your expertise. This is where you can establish face-to-face connections with potential employers, collaborators, and mentors. Prepare a concise and impactful "elevator pitch" that summarizes your skills and experience. Actively listen to others, ask engaging questions, and be genuinely interested in learning from their experiences.

Networking isn't just about collecting business cards; it's about building genuine relationships. Focus on establishing authentic connections, understanding people's interests, and offering value in your interactions. Follow up after events with personalized messages, connecting on LinkedIn, or even sharing relevant articles. These follow-up interactions are crucial for solidifying relationships. You're not just building a network; you're building a community of professionals who can support and advance your career.

Leveraging your network for career advancement requires a strategic approach. Don't hesitate to reach out to your connections for advice, information, or introductions to potential opportunities. A simple message expressing your interest in their work or seeking their insights can open doors. Be prepared to offer value in return; perhaps by sharing your expertise or connecting them with other professionals in your network. Remember, networking is a two-way street.

Developing relationships with key individuals in the AI industry can provide significant career advantages. This could involve mentors, senior professionals, or researchers who can provide guidance, support, and insights. Seek out mentors who possess the skills and experience you admire and who can provide valuable feedback and support. These relationships can offer invaluable guidance, access to opportunities, and even sponsorship for promotions or new roles.

Successful personal branding extends beyond online platforms and networking events; it reflects your overall professional conduct and behavior. Maintain a consistent professional image, both online and offline. Always be respectful, courteous, and approachable in your interactions with colleagues, mentors, and potential employers. Your reputation within the industry is a significant factor in your career trajectory. A positive reputation, based on integrity and professionalism, will open many doors.

Consider the power of storytelling in personal branding. Develop compelling narratives that highlight your accomplishments and experiences. These stories can showcase your abilities, resilience, and unique contributions to the AI field. When networking or interviewing, use these stories to illustrate your skills and experience, making your profile more memorable and engaging.

Let's examine a few examples of effective personal branding strategies in action:

Example 1: The Thought Leader: A data scientist regularly contributes insightful articles to AI-focused blogs and participates actively in online forums. Their consistent contributions establish them as a thought leader, attracting attention from recruiters and fostering valuable connections with other professionals. Their online presence doesn't just showcase skills, it showcases intellectual curiosity and engagement.

Example 2: The Community Builder: An AI engineer organizes and leads monthly meetups for AI enthusiasts in their city. This active involvement in the community builds their reputation as a leader and connector, attracting opportunities and recognition. Their community building demonstrates passion and leadership.

Example 3: The Strategic Networker: A machine learning specialist strategically targets conferences and workshops relevant to their specialized area of expertise. They meticulously plan their networking interactions, following up with personalized messages to cultivate meaningful relationships. They understand that networking is a long-term investment.

Example 4: The Portfolio Showcase: A software engineer creates a comprehensive online portfolio showcasing their AI projects, complete with detailed descriptions, code samples, and performance metrics. This digital portfolio clearly demonstrates their skills and abilities, acting as a powerful visual resume.

Example 5: The Mentor-Mentee Relationship: A seasoned AI researcher actively mentors junior professionals, providing guidance, support, and valuable networking opportunities. This not only helps others, but solidifies the researcher's position as a respected leader within the field, potentially generating future opportunities.

By implementing these strategies – cultivating a strong online presence, actively networking, attending industry events, and building genuine relationships – you will significantly enhance your personal brand and solidify your position within the AI industry. Remember, building a personal brand and network is a continuous process, requiring dedication, consistency, and a genuine commitment to building relationships and contributing to the broader AI community. The payoff, however, is substantial – increased visibility, greater opportunities, and ultimately, a more fulfilling and successful career in the ever-evolving world of artificial intelligence.

Chapter 6: Case Studies: Real-World Examples of Success

Case Study Marketing Professional Adapting to AI

Sarah Chen, a seasoned marketing professional with over a decade of experience, found herself at a crossroads in 2018. The buzz around artificial intelligence was no longer a distant hum; it was a roaring engine rapidly transforming her industry. She had witnessed firsthand the incremental automation of tasks – email marketing campaigns optimized by algorithms, social media ad targeting refined by machine learning, and even rudimentary content generation powered by natural language processing. While initially apprehensive, Sarah recognized that resisting the tide of AI was futile; adapting and mastering its tools was the only path to not just survival, but continued success and upward mobility.

Sarah's initial response was proactive education. She enrolled in online courses focusing on AI's applications in marketing. These weren't coding boot camps; instead, she focused on understanding the strategic implications of AI-driven tools and how they could enhance, not replace, human creativity and strategy. She learned about predictive analytics, customer segmentation using AI, and how to interpret the vast amounts of data generated by AI-powered marketing platforms. This wasn't about becoming a data scientist; it was about becoming AI-literate. This foundational knowledge formed the bedrock of her adaptation strategy.

Her next step was strategic implementation within her existing role at a mid-sized consumer goods company. Sarah began by identifying areas where AI could augment her team's efficiency. She spearheaded the adoption of an AI-powered marketing automation platform, significantly streamlining their email campaigns and improving open and click-through rates. This demonstrably improved efficiency freed up her team's time to focus on more strategic initiatives, like brand development and creative content generation. She meticulously tracked and quantified the impact of this change, documenting the improved ROI and presenting this data to her superiors. This wasn't just about applying AI; it was about demonstrating its value through concrete results.

Beyond operational efficiency, Sarah explored AI's role in enhancing marketing strategy. She began utilizing predictive analytics to better understand customer behavior and preferences. By analyzing vast datasets using AI-powered tools, she was able to identify previously unseen patterns and segment her audience with unparalleled precision. This led to more effective targeting of advertising campaigns, resulting in a measurable increase in conversion rates and a significant reduction in wasted ad spend. She presented these findings to senior management, positioning herself as a key innovator within the organization, someone who wasn't just reacting to AI, but actively shaping its application to drive business growth.

Sarah's success wasn't solely about technical prowess; it was equally about leadership and communication. She proactively educated her team about the benefits and potential of AI, dispelling anxieties and fostering a culture of adaptation. She organized workshops and training sessions, ensuring that her colleagues felt comfortable navigating the new technological landscape. She understood that a successful AI integration demanded buy-in from the entire team, not just technical proficiency. By building this internal consensus and promoting a culture of continuous learning, she mitigated potential resistance and fostered collaboration.

As her expertise grew, Sarah began seeking out opportunities to expand her network within the AI-driven marketing community.

She attended industry conferences, joined relevant professional organizations, and actively participated in online forums dedicated to AI in marketing. These interactions allowed her to stay abreast of the latest innovations, learn from other professionals, and establish valuable connections within the industry. This proactive networking didn't just broaden her knowledge base; it also enhanced her professional visibility and opened doors to new opportunities.

In 2020, Sarah transitioned to a new role as Head of Digital Marketing at a rapidly growing tech startup. This move was a direct result of her demonstrable success in integrating AI into marketing strategies. Her reputation as an AI-savvy marketing leader had preceded her. The new role demanded a more strategic, long-term approach to AI implementation, extending beyond immediate operational efficiency to encompass overall brand building and product development.

In her new position, Sarah oversaw the development of a completely new AI-powered customer relationship management (CRM) system. This wasn't simply selecting an off-the-shelf solution; she led the design and implementation of a bespoke system that leveraged AI to personalize customer interactions, predict future behavior, and provide invaluable insights into customer preferences. This involved close collaboration with data scientists, engineers, and other stakeholders, showcasing her ability to navigate complex projects and collaborate effectively across different teams. The successful implementation of this CRM system further solidified her reputation as a visionary leader.

Moreover, Sarah leveraged AI to enhance the company's content marketing strategy. Instead of relying solely on human writers, she implemented AI-assisted content creation tools that helped automate the creation of routine content, like social media posts and product descriptions. This allowed the human writers on her team to focus on more strategic and creative content, like blog posts and thought leadership pieces that would resonate deeply with their target audience. It wasn't about replacing human creativity; it was about intelligently augmenting it.

By 2023, Sarah's career had reached new heights. Her strategic integration of AI not only propelled her career forward but demonstrated its transformative potential within marketing. She became a sought-after speaker at industry conferences, sharing her insights and experience with others. Her work has been featured in leading industry publications, further cementing her position as a recognized authority in the field. Her success showcases a compelling narrative: successful adaptation to AI is not about fear or resistance; it's about proactive learning, strategic implementation, and a genuine understanding of how AI can empower human potential.

Sarah's journey highlights a crucial aspect: the importance of continuously learning and adapting. The AI landscape is constantly evolving; new technologies and applications emerge rapidly.

Therefore, continuous learning isn't simply a nice-to-have; it's a necessity for long-term success. Sarah's ongoing commitment to professional development reflects her understanding of the dynamic nature of the industry and her dedication to remaining at the forefront of innovation.

Furthermore, Sarah's experience underscores the importance of embracing lifelong learning. She didn't merely acquire technical skills; she developed a holistic understanding of AI's impact on her field. She understood the strategic implications of AI, how it could impact organizational culture, and how to communicate its value effectively to diverse stakeholders. This broader perspective is essential for those seeking leadership roles in the age of AI.

In conclusion, Sarah Chen's story is a testament to the potential for personal and professional growth in the age of artificial intelligence.

Her proactive approach, strategic implementation, and consistent dedication to learning enabled her to not only survive the AI revolution but thrive within it, achieving remarkable career success and recognition as a leader in the field. Her experience serves as a powerful case study for those seeking to navigate the transformative impact of AI on their own careers. The key takeaway isn't simply about learning specific AI tools, but about embracing a mindset of continuous learning, adaptability, and strategic integration of technology to enhance, not replace, human capabilities. The future of work is not about humans versus AI; it's about humans *with* AI.

Case Study Financial Analyst Leveraging AI Tools

David Lee, a financial analyst at a major investment bank, found himself facing a deluge of data in 2019. His typical day involved sifting through mountains of financial reports, market analyses, and economic indicators, a process that was not only time-consuming but also prone to human error. The sheer volume of information often made it difficult to identify crucial trends and patterns quickly enough to make timely and informed investment decisions. The pressure to perform, coupled with the ever-increasing pace of the financial markets, left him feeling overwhelmed. David recognized that his current workflow was unsustainable and that he needed to find a way to leverage technology to enhance his efficiency and accuracy.

His initial exploration of AI tools within the finance industry was a steep learning curve. He began by researching various AI-powered platforms and tools relevant to his field. He discovered that several sophisticated programs offered automated data analysis, predictive modeling, and real-time market trend identification capabilities.

These tools promised to significantly reduce the time spent on manual data processing, allowing him to focus on higher-level tasks requiring strategic thinking and decision-making. However, implementing these tools wasn't a simple plug-and-play process. He needed to understand their functionalities, limitations, and the potential biases inherent in their algorithms.

He started with smaller, manageable projects, focusing on specific tasks that were highly repetitive and data-intensive. For example, he began using AI-powered tools to automate the process of compiling and analyzing financial statements. These tools could extract key data points from various reports, perform complex calculations, and identify any inconsistencies or anomalies far quicker than manual analysis. This freed up significant amounts of his time, allowing him to focus on identifying investment opportunities that required human intuition and strategic thinking.

One of the initial challenges David encountered was the integration of these AI tools into his existing workflow. The bank's systems were not initially designed to seamlessly interact with these new technologies, creating compatibility issues and requiring significant technical adjustments. He had to work closely with the IT department to ensure smooth data transfer and efficient integration.

This collaborative effort showcased his ability to work across departments, demonstrating a critical skill in today's interconnected work environment.

Beyond basic data processing, David delved into more advanced AI applications, like predictive modeling. He used machine learning algorithms to analyze historical market data, economic indicators, and company financials to forecast future stock prices and identify potentially lucrative investment opportunities. This involved experimenting with various models, adjusting parameters, and evaluating the accuracy of the predictions. The process was iterative, requiring continuous refinement and optimization. He learned that understanding the underlying algorithms and the potential for bias was critical for accurate and reliable predictions.

However, David discovered that relying solely on AI predictions could be risky. The tools offered valuable insights, but they didn't replace the need for human judgment and critical thinking. He found that the best results came from a synergistic approach, combining the speed and efficiency of AI with his own expertise in financial analysis and market understanding.

He treated the AI tools as powerful assistants, augmenting his abilities rather than replacing them.

To effectively utilize these tools, David invested significant time in upskilling himself. He completed online courses in machine learning, data analytics, and AI in finance. He also attended workshops and conferences to network with other professionals in the field and stay abreast of the latest developments in AI technology. This continuous learning was essential for his success, as the AI landscape is constantly evolving, requiring professionals to stay updated to remain competitive.

The improvement in David's efficiency was substantial. He could now analyze vast datasets in a fraction of the time previously required, allowing him to identify patterns and make investment recommendations much faster. The accuracy of his predictions also increased due to the reduced risk of human error and the ability of AI tools to identify subtle correlations that might otherwise have gone unnoticed.

The impact on his career was equally significant. His ability to leverage AI tools to improve his productivity and accuracy caught the attention of his superiors. He was recognized for his innovative use of technology and the positive impact it had on the firm's investment performance. He received promotions and was entrusted with more complex and high-stakes projects. His success demonstrates that embracing AI in the workplace is not just about staying relevant; it's about achieving remarkable career advancement.

But David's journey wasn't without challenges. He encountered resistance from some colleagues who were apprehensive about the introduction of AI into their workflows. He addressed these concerns by actively educating his colleagues on the benefits of AI, showcasing how it could enhance their work rather than replace it. He organized training sessions and workshops to help them become more comfortable with the new tools. He emphasized that AI was not a threat, but a powerful ally that could help them become more efficient and effective in their work. This proactive approach to change management was critical to the successful implementation of AI within his team.

Furthermore, David faced the challenge of interpreting AI-generated insights critically. He learned that AI algorithms, while powerful, can be prone to bias or produce inaccurate results if not properly trained or interpreted. He developed a rigorous process for validating the output of the AI tools, cross-referencing the findings with other sources of information and applying his own judgment before making any investment decisions. This careful approach ensured that he was not blindly following the AI's recommendations but using them as a valuable source of information within a broader analytical framework.

David's success story highlights the critical importance of data literacy and critical thinking in the age of AI. While AI tools can process and analyze data at an unprecedented scale, the ability to interpret the results effectively and make informed judgments remains a uniquely human skill. His ability to blend technical proficiency with critical thinking and strategic decision-making allowed him to leverage AI to its full potential and achieve remarkable career success. He wasn't replaced by AI; he became a master of its application, transforming himself into a highly sought-after financial analyst. His experience serves as a powerful case study, showcasing how professionals can not only survive but thrive in the age of artificial intelligence. The future of finance, like many other fields, is not about humans versus AI, it's about humans *with* AI, working synergistically to achieve unprecedented levels of efficiency, accuracy, and insight.

Case Study Sales Representative Embracing AI-Powered CRM

Sarah Chen, a sales representative for a mid-sized technology company, found herself facing a familiar challenge in 2022: managing an ever-growing pipeline of leads while battling limited time and resources. Her days were a whirlwind of emails, phone calls, and spreadsheets, leaving little time for strategic planning and building meaningful relationships with potential clients. She felt the pressure mounting, knowing that her performance was directly tied to the company's revenue growth. The existing CRM system, while functional, was cumbersome and lacked the intelligence to prioritize leads effectively or provide actionable insights. She knew there had to be a better way.

Sarah's initial foray into AI-powered CRM solutions was driven by a desire to streamline her workflow and improve her efficiency. She researched various platforms, comparing their features, functionalities, and integration capabilities with her company's existing systems. She quickly realized that AI could significantly improve several aspects of her sales process, from lead qualification and prioritization to personalized communication and sales forecasting.

The chosen CRM solution offered several key AI-driven features that proved invaluable. Firstly, its lead scoring algorithm analyzed various data points – website activity, email engagement, social media interactions, and even demographic information – to assign a numerical score to each lead, indicating their potential to convert into paying customers. This sophisticated algorithm, powered by machine learning, learned and adapted over time, becoming increasingly accurate in predicting which leads were most likely to close. This eliminated the need for Sarah to manually sift through hundreds of leads, prioritizing her time and effort on those most likely to yield positive results.

Secondly, the AI-powered CRM incorporated a powerful predictive analytics engine. By analyzing historical sales data, market trends, and customer behavior, the system could predict future sales outcomes with remarkable accuracy. This allowed Sarah to forecast her pipeline more effectively, identifying potential shortfalls or areas of strength, enabling her to adjust her strategies proactively. This predictive capability allowed her to better allocate her time and resources, ensuring she focused her energy on the most promising opportunities.

Beyond lead scoring and forecasting, the AI-powered CRM also personalized Sarah's communications. The system automatically generated customized email templates and messaging based on individual lead profiles. This level of personalization improved engagement rates significantly, making her communications more relevant and persuasive. It also freed her from the repetitive task of composing individual emails, allowing her to spend more time engaging with potential clients on a deeper level.

The impact on Sarah's sales performance was immediate and dramatic. Her conversion rates increased by 30% within the first six months of using the AI-powered CRM. This significant improvement was attributable to several factors. Firstly, the AI-driven lead scoring system ensured she focused her time on the most promising leads. Secondly, the personalized communications increased engagement and improved her ability to connect with potential clients on a personal level. Finally, the predictive analytics engine allowed her to anticipate market trends and adjust her strategies accordingly.

Furthermore, the AI-powered CRM provided Sarah with valuable insights into her sales process. The system tracked key metrics such as conversion rates, deal sizes, and sales cycles, providing granular data that helped her identify areas for improvement. She was able to analyze her performance across different segments, products, and channels, allowing her to refine her sales strategies and optimize her efforts.

The AI-powered CRM not only improved Sarah's sales performance but also had a profound impact on her career progression. Her demonstrable improvement in sales figures and her ability to leverage technology to enhance her productivity and efficiency caught the attention of her superiors. She was recognized for her innovative use of AI, her proactive approach to problem-solving, and her ability to adapt to the ever-evolving technology landscape.

Her success, however, wasn't without its challenges. Initially, there was a learning curve associated with mastering the AI-powered CRM's various features and functionalities. She dedicated time to understanding the system's capabilities, exploring its various options, and refining her processes to optimize its usage. This required ongoing learning and adaptation, highlighting the importance of continuous professional development in the age of rapid technological advancements.

Moreover, Sarah encountered some initial resistance from colleagues who were hesitant about embracing new technology. She addressed these concerns by actively educating and mentoring her colleagues, demonstrating the benefits of the AI-powered CRM and helping them integrate it into their workflows. This collaborative approach fostered a more receptive environment, proving that effective change management is critical for successful AI adoption.

She also realized the importance of critical thinking and human judgment. While the AI-powered CRM provided valuable insights and automation, it didn't eliminate the need for human interaction and strategic decision-making. She learned to view the AI as a powerful tool that augmented her abilities, not replaced them. She used the insights provided by the AI to inform her decisions, but she retained control and ultimate responsibility for her sales activities.

Sarah's story exemplifies the transformative power of AI in the workplace. Her success is not solely a testament to the capabilities of the

AI-powered CRM; it's also a demonstration of her adaptability, her willingness to learn and embrace new technologies, and her ability to combine technological advancements with her own unique skills and experience. She didn't simply adopt AI; she mastered it, transforming her career in the process. Her journey serves as a powerful case study, illustrating how professionals can harness the power of AI to enhance their productivity, elevate their performance, and propel their careers to new heights. The future of sales, much like other professions, isn't about humans versus AI; it's about humans working synergistically with AI to achieve remarkable results, a partnership that fosters growth, innovation, and ultimately, success. The ability to adapt, learn, and effectively integrate AI into existing workflows will increasingly determine career trajectory in the coming decades. Sarah's experience highlights the necessity of continuous learning, proactive adoption, and a critical, human-centered approach to AI integration for maximizing its positive impacts. The potential for AI-driven tools to reshape individual careers, and indeed entire industries, is profound and transformative, promising a future where human ingenuity and artificial intelligence work in perfect harmony.

Case Study Leadership Team Integrating AI into Organizational Strategy

The leadership team at Global Dynamics Corporation, a multinational manufacturing firm, faced a significant challenge in 2023: maintaining their competitive edge in a rapidly evolving global market. Their traditional reliance on manual processes and outdated data analysis methods was hindering their ability to respond quickly to shifting market demands, optimize production, and improve overall efficiency. Recognizing the transformative potential of artificial intelligence, the leadership team embarked on an ambitious initiative to integrate AI across all aspects of their operations, from supply chain management to customer service.

Their approach was methodical and multifaceted, recognizing that successful AI integration requires more than just acquiring the latest technology. It demanded a comprehensive strategy addressing change management, employee training, and careful implementation. The first step involved a thorough assessment of their current operational processes and data infrastructure. This involved identifying areas where AI could have the greatest impact, prioritizing those with the highest potential for return on investment. This assessment wasn't a top-down dictate; instead, cross-functional teams comprising employees from various departments were assembled. This ensured buy-in from the ground up and allowed for the identification of nuanced challenges and opportunities specific to each department. The result was a prioritized roadmap outlining the phased integration of AI technologies.

The next crucial step was addressing the potential anxieties of the workforce. Many employees feared that AI would lead to job displacement, mirroring anxieties common across many industries adopting similar technologies. The leadership team tackled these concerns head-on through a comprehensive communication strategy and a robust employee training program. Instead of portraying AI as a replacement for human workers, they emphasized its role as a tool to augment human capabilities, enabling employees to focus on higher-value tasks. They emphasized that AI wouldn't eliminate jobs but would transform them, requiring employees to adapt and acquire new skills. This messaging was crucial in fostering a culture of acceptance and collaboration around AI adoption.

The training program wasn't a one-off event; rather, it was an ongoing process designed to equip employees with the knowledge and skills necessary to work effectively with AI tools. The program covered various aspects, including AI fundamentals, ethical considerations, data analysis using AI-powered tools, and practical application within their respective roles. The training was tailored to different skill levels and departments, ensuring that all employees felt supported and adequately prepared for the transition. The leadership actively participated in these training sessions, demonstrating their commitment and fostering a sense of shared purpose within the company. This visible commitment from leadership served as a potent signal, dissipating skepticism and encouraging active participation among employees.

The implementation of AI technologies was phased, starting with pilot projects in specific departments to test the effectiveness and identify potential challenges before scaling up. This approach allowed the leadership team to refine their strategy based on real-world experience, minimizing disruptions and maximizing the benefits. Each pilot project was closely monitored, with data collected and analyzed to assess its impact on productivity, efficiency, and employee satisfaction. The feedback gathered during these pilot phases was invaluable in informing subsequent implementation stages and making necessary adjustments to the overall strategy. This iterative approach minimized the risks associated with large-scale AI adoption and ensured a smoother transition for employees.

One particularly successful pilot project involved the integration of AI-powered predictive maintenance in their manufacturing facilities. By analyzing sensor data from their machinery, the AI system could predict potential equipment failures with remarkable accuracy, allowing for proactive maintenance and minimizing downtime. This resulted in a significant reduction in maintenance costs and an increase in overall production efficiency. The data generated by the system was further analyzed to reveal patterns and areas for improvement in the manufacturing process itself, leading to further optimization and cost savings.

In the customer service department, the implementation of AI-powered chatbots significantly improved response times and customer satisfaction. The chatbots handled routine inquiries, freeing up human agents to focus on more complex issues requiring human judgment and empathy. This also allowed the company to offer 24/7 customer support, expanding their reach and enhancing customer experience. Analyzing the chatbot interactions further provided valuable insights into customer preferences, pain points, and unmet needs, informing product development and marketing strategies.

The success of Global Dynamics' AI integration can be attributed to several key factors. Firstly, their proactive and comprehensive approach to change management mitigated employee concerns and fostered a culture of acceptance. Secondly, their well-designed and ongoing employee training program ensured that employees were adequately prepared to work effectively with AI tools. Thirdly, their phased implementation approach allowed them to learn from experience, refine their strategy, and minimize disruptions.

Furthermore, the leadership team's commitment to data-driven decision-making played a crucial role. They continuously monitored the impact of AI implementation, analyzing data to assess its effectiveness and make necessary adjustments. This iterative approach ensures continuous improvement and optimization of their AI strategies. By embracing a culture of continuous learning and adaptation, Global Dynamics positioned itself for sustained success in the age of AI. However, the journey wasn't without its challenges. Integrating AI required significant investment in both technology and employee training. The company also had to address data security concerns, ensuring that sensitive data was protected from unauthorized access. The leadership team also faced the challenge of managing the ethical implications of AI, particularly in areas such as data privacy and algorithmic bias. They tackled these challenges by establishing robust data governance policies, incorporating ethical considerations into their AI development processes, and engaging in ongoing discussions with stakeholders on responsible AI use.

The success of Global Dynamics Corporation serves as a compelling case study, demonstrating that successful AI integration requires a holistic and well-planned approach. It's not simply about acquiring the latest technology; it's about creating a supportive organizational culture, investing in employee training, and adopting a data-driven, iterative approach. The lessons learned from Global Dynamics'experience are applicable across industries, providing a blueprint for organizations seeking to leverage the power of AI to enhance their competitiveness and achieve sustainable growth. The company's journey underscores the importance of proactive planning, transparent communication, and continuous learning in navigating the transformative potential of artificial intelligence.

Their success emphasizes the necessity of viewing AI not as a replacement for human workers, but as a powerful tool that enhances human capabilities, fosters innovation, and paves the way for a future where human ingenuity and artificial intelligence work in seamless harmony to achieve remarkable results. Their proactive approach showcases how integrating AI isn't merely about technological advancement but also about fostering a culture of collaboration, continuous improvement, and ethical considerations that are crucial for maximizing the benefits of this transformative technology. The long-term implications of their successful integration, from improved efficiency and customer satisfaction to enhanced decision-making and innovation, highlight the transformative power of strategically implemented AI. Their case study serves as a valuable template for other businesses seeking to successfully integrate AI into their operations, underscoring the importance of a carefully considered, human-centric approach to realize the full potential of this disruptive technology.

Case Study An Entrepreneur Building an AI-Powered Startup

The narrative of successful AI integration extends beyond established corporations; it also thrives in the dynamic ecosystem of startups. Consider the journey of Anya Sharma, founder and CEO of "Predictive Insights," a company specializing in AI-powered predictive analytics for the retail sector. Anya, a data scientist with a PhD from MIT, identified a significant gap in the market: the lack of accessible and affordable predictive analytics tools specifically tailored to small and medium-sized retail businesses. These businesses often lacked the resources and expertise to leverage the power of big data and AI, leaving them at a competitive disadvantage compared to their larger counterparts.

Anya's vision was to democratize access to advanced analytics. She envisioned a user-friendly platform that could process vast amounts of retail data – sales figures, customer demographics, inventory levels, social media trends – and provide actionable insights to improve forecasting, inventory management, and personalized marketing. This vision formed the cornerstone of Predictive Insights' business model: a Software-as-a-Service (SaaS) platform offered on a subscription basis, making it financially accessible to a wide range of retail businesses.

However, translating this vision into reality presented a formidable set of challenges. Securing seed funding was the first hurdle. Anya spent months pitching her business plan to venture capitalists and angel investors, navigating the often-daunting process of securing funding in the competitive world of AI startups. Her pitch wasn't just about the technical prowess of her AI algorithms; it emphasized the market need, the scalability of her SaaS model, and the potential for significant returns on investment. She meticulously crafted her pitch deck, highlighting the market opportunity, her team's expertise, the competitive landscape, and a detailed financial projection. She emphasized the ease of use of the platform, emphasizing that it required minimal technical expertise to operate, thus minimizing training costs for her clients. This understanding of the client's needs was crucial in securing funding.

A key differentiator in Anya's pitch was her focus on ethical AI. She proactively addressed concerns about data privacy and algorithmic bias, highlighting the robust security measures implemented in her platform and the rigorous testing procedures employed to ensure fairness and accuracy. This emphasis on ethical AI resonated strongly with investors who are increasingly aware of the societal implications of AI technology. She outlined processes for data anonymization and de-identification and committed to transparent algorithm development and deployment. This commitment to ethical AI proved to be a significant asset, not just in attracting investors but also in establishing trust with her clients.

Once funding was secured, the next challenge was building the platform. Anya assembled a talented team of data scientists, software engineers, and marketing professionals, carefully selecting individuals with not only technical expertise but also a shared passion for her vision. The team worked tirelessly to develop a user-friendly platform capable of handling large datasets and providing accurate and actionable insights. Agile development methodologies were employed, allowing for iterative development, regular feedback, and rapid adaptation based on user testing. This iterative process also allowed Anya to adjust her platform based on client feedback, resulting in a much more useful product.

The launch of Predictive Insights' platform was met with positive reception. The platform's intuitive interface and accurate predictions quickly gained traction among small and medium-sized retail businesses. Word-of-mouth referrals further fueled the company's growth. Anya recognized the importance of marketing and branding; she crafted a brand identity that communicated trust, expertise, and user-friendliness. She invested in targeted marketing campaigns through online channels and industry events, focusing her marketing efforts on the specific needs and challenges of her target audience.

Predictive Insights' success wasn't solely attributable to technological innovation. Anya cultivated a strong company culture characterized by collaboration, innovation, and a commitment to excellence. She prioritized employee well-being and professional development, fostering a supportive environment that attracted and retained top talent. Regular team-building activities and open communication channels helped to foster a strong sense of team cohesion and shared purpose. This investment in human capital was a significant driver of the company's success.

However, the path to success wasn't without its setbacks. Anya faced unexpected technical challenges during the platform's development, requiring her to adapt her plans and allocate resources effectively. She also had to navigate the complexities of scaling her business, ensuring that the platform could handle the increasing demand from a growing customer base. Moreover, she faced competition from larger, established companies offering similar services. To counter this, Anya focused on her niche market, emphasizing the personalized support and accessibility of her platform. She built strong relationships with her clients, providing personalized onboarding and ongoing support, fostering loyalty and positive word-of-mouth marketing.

Anya's entrepreneurial journey provides valuable insights for aspiring AI entrepreneurs. Her success stemmed from a combination of factors: a clear vision, a well-defined business model, a strong emphasis on ethical AI, a talented team, effective marketing, and a persistent commitment to innovation and adaptation. Her story demonstrates that building a successful AI-powered startup requires more than just technical expertise; it requires a holistic approach encompassing market understanding, business acumen, strong leadership, and a unwavering commitment to delivering value to clients. Anya's emphasis on building a strong company culture, valuing her employees, and fostering a supportive and innovative environment stands as a testament to the human element in the successful deployment of AI. Her story highlights the importance of balancing technological advancement with a human-centric approach to business, making her a compelling example of entrepreneurship in the age of AI. The ability to adapt and pivot in response to unexpected challenges, along with a commitment to continuous learning and improvement, were crucial to her success, ultimately demonstrating that the ability to navigate the complexities of the market and manage the human aspects of a business are just as important as the technological innovations themselves. This multifaceted approach cemented Anya's success and made Predictive Insights a beacon of innovation and a model for ethical AI entrepreneurship.

Chapter 7: The Ethics of AI in the Workplace

Bias in AI Systems and Mitigation Strategies

The preceding examples showcase the transformative potential of AI in various business sectors, yet the ethical dimensions of this technology cannot be overlooked. A crucial aspect of responsible AI implementation is the mitigation of bias, a pervasive issue that can significantly impact fairness and equity in the workplace. AI systems, unlike humans, do not inherently possess prejudices; however, they are trained on data, and this data often reflects existing societal biases. This means that if the data used to train an AI algorithm contains biases related to gender, race, age, or other protected characteristics, the resulting AI system will likely perpetuate and even amplify those biases in its decision-making processes.

Consider, for instance, the use of AI in recruitment. Many companies utilize AI-powered tools to screen resumes and select candidates for interviews. If the training data for this AI system primarily reflects historical hiring practices that favored certain demographic groups, the AI might unintentionally discriminate against candidates from underrepresented groups, even if the stated goal is to achieve a more diverse workforce. Similarly, AI systems used for loan applications or risk assessment can perpetuate existing biases if the training data reflects historical lending practices that discriminated against specific communities. This can lead to discriminatory outcomes, denying individuals access to crucial financial services.

The sources of bias in AI systems are multifaceted and complex. One primary source is the data itself. Data used to train AI algorithms is often incomplete, inaccurate, or simply reflective of existing societal inequalities. For example, if a facial recognition system is trained primarily on images of individuals from a specific demographic group, it may perform poorly when identifying individuals from other groups, leading to misidentification and potentially harmful consequences. This is particularly concerning in law enforcement, where facial recognition technology is increasingly being used. Another source of bias stems from the algorithms themselves. The design and implementation of algorithms can inadvertently introduce biases, even if the training data is unbiased. For instance, a poorly designed algorithm might inadvertently weigh certain factors more heavily than others, leading to skewed outcomes. Furthermore, the selection and interpretation of data can introduce biases. Even with seemingly neutral data, the choices made during the data collection, preprocessing, and feature selection stages can significantly influence the AI system's performance and potentially lead to biased outcomes.

The ethical implications of bias in AI systems are profound and far-reaching. Biased AI systems can perpetuate and exacerbate existing societal inequalities, leading to unfair and discriminatory outcomes in various aspects of life, including employment, lending, healthcare, and even the criminal justice system. These biases can undermine trust in AI systems, leading to public skepticism and resistance to their adoption. Moreover, the use of biased AI systems can have significant legal and reputational consequences for organizations, leading to lawsuits, fines, and damage to their brand image. Organizations must therefore prioritize the development and deployment of fair and unbiased AI systems to ensure ethical and responsible use of this transformative technology.

Mitigating bias in AI systems requires a multifaceted approach encompassing various strategies throughout the entire AI lifecycle. The first crucial step is to ensure the quality and representativeness of the training data. This involves collecting data from diverse sources and employing various techniques to identify and address biases in the data. For example, techniques such as data augmentation can help increase the diversity of the training data, while resampling techniques can address class imbalances. Data cleaning and preprocessing steps are also crucial to eliminate inconsistencies and irrelevant information that might bias the AI model. Careful data annotation is crucial to avoid introducing human biases during the labelling process. Using multiple independent datasets for training and testing can also provide valuable insights into the robustness and fairness of the AI model, highlighting potential biases that might otherwise be overlooked.

Beyond data, algorithm design plays a crucial role in mitigating bias. Researchers are actively developing algorithms that are inherently more robust to bias and less prone to amplifying existing societal inequalities. These techniques often involve incorporating fairness constraints into the algorithm's design, which can lead to more equitable outcomes. Moreover, employing explainable AI (XAI) techniques allows for greater transparency in the decision-making process of AI systems. XAI aims to make the reasoning behind AI decisions more understandable and interpretable, enabling the identification and rectification of biases. By providing insights into how an AI system arrives at its conclusions, XAI can help uncover and correct any biases present in the algorithm or the data. This increased transparency strengthens trust and accountability in AI systems.

Regular audits and monitoring of AI systems are essential for identifying and addressing emerging biases. These audits should involve analyzing the system's performance across different demographic groups to identify any disparities in outcomes. This ongoing monitoring helps catch and rectify biases that may emerge over time as the AI system learns and adapts to new data.

Employing diverse teams involved in the development and deployment of AI systems is crucial. A team composed of individuals with diverse backgrounds, perspectives, and expertise can help identify and address potential biases more effectively. This ensures that different viewpoints are considered throughout the AI lifecycle, from data collection to model deployment, leading to more robust and ethical outcomes.

Furthermore, establishing clear ethical guidelines and standards for the development and deployment of AI systems is imperative. These guidelines should address issues of fairness, accountability, transparency, and privacy. Organizations should integrate these guidelines into their internal policies and procedures to ensure responsible AI development and use. Regular training for employees on ethical AI considerations helps raise awareness and promote responsible practices. This includes training on how to identify and report biases in AI systems and best practices for working with AI tools ethically. Establishing effective grievance mechanisms for individuals who believe they have been subjected to unfair treatment by an AI system is crucial. These mechanisms should provide clear pathways for redress and ensure that complaints are investigated thoroughly and impartially.

Finally, ongoing research and development in the field of fair and unbiased AI are critical to the advancement of responsible AI. This involves exploring novel algorithms and techniques to mitigate bias, as well as developing new methods for evaluating the fairness and equity of

AI systems. Collaboration between researchers, developers, policymakers, and stakeholders is crucial to fostering innovation and ensuring that AI is developed and deployed in an ethical and responsible manner.

The journey towards fair and unbiased AI is continuous and requires a commitment to ongoing learning and improvement. The strategies outlined here represent a starting point, and their effectiveness depends on consistent application and refinement. Addressing bias in AI systems is not merely a technical challenge but a fundamental ethical imperative, crucial for ensuring fairness, equity, and trust in this transformative technology within the workplace and beyond. The responsible implementation of AI demands a vigilant and proactive approach to identifying and mitigating biases, fostering a workplace that values both technological advancement and human dignity.

Data Privacy and Security in the Age of AI

The ethical considerations surrounding AI extend far beyond bias mitigation; they encompass the crucial realm of data privacy and security. The proliferation of AI in the workplace necessitates a robust framework to protect the sensitive data that fuels these intelligent systems. This data, ranging from employee records and customer information to proprietary business strategies, represents a valuable asset but also a significant vulnerability. The careless handling of such information can lead to serious legal repercussions, financial losses, and reputational damage, undermining the very foundation of trust upon which successful business operations rely.

The sheer volume of data collected and processed by AI systems is staggering. Machine learning algorithms thrive on vast datasets, often encompassing personal information, health records, financial details, and other sensitive data. This necessitates a careful examination of the ethical implications of data collection, usage, and storage. The question arises: What data is necessary for AI functionality, and what constitutes an unnecessary invasion of privacy? The line between legitimate business needs and unwarranted data collection is often blurred, requiring a careful ethical compass to navigate this complex terrain. The temptation to collect "just in case" data must be resisted in favor of a more focused and privacy-respecting approach.

Existing regulations, such as the General Data Protection Regulation (GDPR) in Europe and the California Consumer Privacy Act (CCPA) in the United States, provide a legal framework for protecting personal data. These regulations outline specific requirements for data collection, processing, and storage, emphasizing transparency and individual rights. Businesses must adhere to these regulations diligently, implementing robust data governance practices to ensure compliance. This includes obtaining informed consent for data collection, providing clear explanations of how data will be used, and offering individuals the right to access, correct, or delete their personal information. Beyond legal compliance, businesses should strive to exceed the minimum standards set by regulations, demonstrating a commitment to proactive data protection.

The implementation of strong security measures is paramount in safeguarding data from unauthorized access, use, or disclosure. This requires a multi-layered approach, incorporating physical, technical, and administrative controls. Physical security involves protecting data centers and other physical locations where data is stored. Technical security measures include employing robust encryption techniques, implementing access control systems, and regularly updating software and systems to patch security vulnerabilities. Administrative controls involve establishing clear data governance policies, conducting regular security audits, and providing employee training on data security best practices.

The ethical use of data in AI systems requires more than simply adhering to regulations and implementing security measures; it demands a proactive and transparent approach to data handling.

This includes clearly articulating the purpose of data collection, ensuring that data usage remains aligned with stated objectives, and minimizing the retention period for data. Regular audits of data practices are essential to identify potential vulnerabilities and ensure that data is being handled responsibly. The principle of data minimization, which advocates for collecting only the necessary data, should be embraced to limit the potential for misuse.

Furthermore, the ethical implications extend beyond the initial collection and usage of data. The ongoing maintenance and disposal of data require careful consideration. Data should be securely disposed of when no longer needed, employing methods that ensure the complete destruction of sensitive information. The potential for data breaches remains a significant concern, requiring continuous vigilance and a proactive approach to incident response.

Organizations must have robust plans in place to respond to data breaches swiftly and effectively, minimizing the potential impact on individuals and the business. Transparency is key in the event of a breach; informing affected individuals promptly and openly is crucial for maintaining trust.

The development and deployment of AI systems should incorporate privacy by design principles, embedding data protection considerations throughout the entire lifecycle of the system. This involves carefully evaluating the potential privacy implications of each stage of development, from data collection to model deployment. Privacy-enhancing technologies, such as differential privacy and federated learning, can be employed to reduce the risk of privacy violations. Differential privacy adds noise to the data, making it more difficult to identify individual data points, while federated learning allows for training models on decentralized data without directly accessing the sensitive data.

The responsible use of AI in the workplace requires a collaborative effort between developers, policymakers, and users. Developers should prioritize the development of AI systems that respect privacy and security, while policymakers should create robust regulatory frameworks to protect individuals' rights. Users should be empowered to understand and control how their data is being used, fostering a culture of data literacy and awareness. Open communication and transparency between all stakeholders are crucial for establishing a robust ethical framework for AI in the workplace. This includes providing individuals with clear and accessible information about how their data is being collected, processed, and used.

The ethical challenges surrounding data privacy and security in the age of AI are multifaceted and constantly evolving. Technological advancements continually reshape the landscape, requiring a proactive and adaptive approach to ethical considerations. The pursuit of responsible AI development necessitates a continuous learning process, encompassing ongoing research, education, and collaboration among stakeholders. Regular evaluation of existing practices and policies is crucial for ensuring that they remain relevant and effective in addressing emerging challenges. The ethical use of AI is not a destination but a journey, requiring sustained commitment and vigilance. The long-term success of AI in the workplace hinges on the ability to balance technological innovation with a robust commitment to data privacy and security, fostering a workplace culture that values both technological advancement and human dignity. Failure to do so risks undermining trust, stifling innovation, and ultimately jeopardizing the potential benefits of AI. The ethical implications must be front and center in every stage of development and implementation. Only by prioritizing ethics can we harness the full potential of AI while safeguarding individual rights and societal well-being.

Algorithmic Transparency and Accountability

The ethical considerations surrounding AI in the workplace extend beyond data privacy and security to encompass the critical need for algorithmic transparency and accountability. While the previous section focused on the responsible handling of data, this section delves into the equally important issue of understanding and controlling the decision-making processes of AI systems themselves.

Many contemporary AI algorithms, particularly deep learning models, operate as "black boxes," their internal workings opaque and their decision-making processes inscrutable. This lack of transparency raises significant ethical concerns, particularly in employment contexts where AI systems increasingly influence hiring, performance evaluation, promotion decisions, and even termination processes.

Consider a scenario where an AI system is used to screen job applications. The system, trained on historical data, might inadvertently perpetuate existing biases present in that data. For example, if the historical data reflects a bias against female applicants in a specific field, the AI might unfairly penalize qualified female candidates, even if this bias is unintentional and unrecognized by the human developers. The opacity of the algorithm makes it difficult, if not impossible, to identify and correct this bias, leading to potentially discriminatory outcomes.

Without understanding *how* the AI arrived at its decision, it's impossible to ensure fairness and equity. This lack of transparency undermines trust and accountability, creating a system that is both unjust and difficult to challenge.

This issue is not limited to hiring. In performance management, AI-driven systems might evaluate employee performance based on metrics that fail to capture the full complexity of an individual's contributions. A system focused solely on quantifiable outputs, for instance, might unfairly penalize employees who dedicate time to mentoring junior colleagues or engage in crucial but less easily measurable collaborative activities. The lack of transparency in the algorithm's weighting of different performance indicators makes it difficult to assess whether the evaluation is accurate and fair.

Furthermore, the use of AI in decision-making processes raises concerns about accountability. If an AI system makes a flawed decision, who is responsible? Is it the developers who created the algorithm, the company that implemented it, or the individuals who used the system's output? The absence of clear lines of responsibility creates a vacuum where errors can go unaddressed and individuals can be unfairly impacted without recourse. This lack of accountability can have devastating consequences, particularly in situations involving layoffs or other significant employment decisions.

Promoting algorithmic transparency and accountability requires a multifaceted approach. One crucial step involves developing more interpretable AI models. While deep learning models often excel in accuracy, their complexity often comes at the cost of interpretability. Researchers are actively exploring techniques to enhance the explainability of AI systems, making it easier to understand the factors that drive their decisions. These methods include rule-based systems, decision trees, and techniques like LIME (Local Interpretable Model-agnostic Explanations) and SHAP (SHapley Additive exPlanations), which provide insights into the contributions of individual features in the AI's decision-making process.

Beyond developing more interpretable models, companies should implement robust auditing mechanisms to regularly assess the fairness and accuracy of AI systems used in the workplace. These audits should involve both technical experts and domain specialists who can evaluate the system's performance and identify potential biases or inaccuracies. The results of these audits should be transparently communicated to employees, fostering trust and allowing for timely corrections.

Furthermore, companies should invest in employee training programs to educate employees about how AI systems are used in the workplace and how they can challenge or appeal AI-driven decisions. This empowers employees to understand their rights and advocate for fair treatment. Transparency about the limitations and potential biases of AI systems is critical to managing expectations and fostering trust.

Legal frameworks also play a vital role in promoting algorithmic transparency and accountability. Regulations that require companies to explain the decision-making processes of AI systems used in employment contexts can ensure that individuals are not unfairly treated. These regulations might mandate impact assessments, where the potential risks and benefits of AI systems are carefully evaluated before deployment.

The development of industry best practices and ethical guidelines is another essential element in fostering accountability. Industry bodies can play a key role in establishing standards for algorithmic transparency and accountability, providing guidance for companies on how to responsibly implement AI systems in the workplace.

These guidelines should cover the entire lifecycle of AI systems, from development and testing to deployment and monitoring.

Finally, fostering a culture of ethical AI within organizations is critical. This involves embedding ethical considerations into the organizational culture and decision-making processes, from the boardroom to the development team. Organizations should establish clear ethical principles for the use of AI, incorporating principles of fairness, transparency, and accountability into all stages of the development and deployment process. This may involve creating ethics review boards or committees to oversee AI initiatives and ensure alignment with organizational values.

The ethical use of AI in the workplace is not a one-time task but an ongoing process that requires vigilance, adaptation, and continuous improvement. Algorithmic transparency and accountability are not merely desirable goals but essential prerequisites for ensuring fairness, trust, and the ethical implementation of AI systems. A failure to address these critical aspects risks not only undermining the potential benefits of AI but also eroding trust in organizations and causing significant harm to individuals. Only through a proactive and multi-faceted approach that encompasses technological advancements, regulatory frameworks, and a strong ethical commitment can we harness the transformative power of

AI while simultaneously safeguarding the rights and dignity of workers. This requires ongoing dialogue, collaboration, and a commitment to continuous learning and improvement, constantly adapting to the rapidly evolving landscape of AI technology and its societal impact. The future of work in the age of AI hinges on our ability to develop and implement AI systems that are not only efficient and effective but also just, transparent, and accountable.

The Impact of AI on Workplace Diversity and Inclusion

The ethical considerations surrounding AI in the workplace extend far beyond data privacy and algorithmic transparency; they encompass the crucial and often overlooked area of diversity and inclusion. While the previous discussion highlighted the importance of understanding and controlling AI decision-making processes, this section delves into how AI systems, if not carefully designed and implemented, can exacerbate existing biases and inequalities in the workplace, potentially undermining efforts to foster a diverse and inclusive environment. The very power of AI to analyze vast datasets and identify patterns also means it can inadvertently amplify pre-existing societal prejudices, leading to unfair and discriminatory outcomes.

One of the primary concerns is the potential for AI systems to perpetuate and even amplify existing biases present in the data they are trained on. This is particularly relevant in areas like recruitment and hiring. If, for example, an AI system is trained on historical hiring data that reflects gender or racial bias—a common occurrence in many industries—the system may learn to replicate these biases, resulting in a disproportionate rejection of qualified candidates from underrepresented groups. The algorithm, without human intervention or oversight, might identify seemingly innocuous correlations between certain demographic characteristics and less successful outcomes, thereby reinforcing harmful stereotypes. This is not a matter of malicious intent; rather, it's a consequence of the inherent limitations and potential biases embedded within the data itself.

The problem extends beyond simply replicating historical biases. AI systems can also create new forms of bias through their design and application. For instance, if the criteria used to evaluate job applicants focus heavily on quantifiable metrics—such as years of experience or specific skill sets—it might inadvertently disadvantage individuals from diverse backgrounds who may possess valuable, albeit less easily measurable, qualities like adaptability, creativity, or emotional intelligence. Similarly, AI systems used for performance evaluation might inadvertently favor certain communication styles or work habits that are more common among individuals from specific demographic groups, leading to unfair assessments and potential discrimination.

Furthermore, the lack of transparency in many AI algorithms—the "black box" problem—compounds the issue. It makes it exceptionally difficult to identify and rectify biases once they've been embedded within the system. Without understanding the specific factors that influence an AI's decisions, it becomes almost impossible to determine whether a particular outcome is the result of bias or a legitimate assessment of qualifications. This opacity not only hinders efforts to achieve fairness and equity but also undermines trust in the AI system itself, potentially eroding employee morale and creating a sense of injustice among those who feel unfairly treated.

Addressing these challenges requires a multi-pronged approach. First, it is crucial to ensure that the data used to train AI systems is representative of the desired demographic diversity. This involves actively collecting and utilizing data from a broad range of sources and taking steps to mitigate any existing biases in the data. This might involve techniques like data augmentation, where synthetic data is generated to balance underrepresented groups, or re-weighting algorithms to account for skewed datasets. Careful data curation and pre-processing are critical steps in preventing the perpetuation of biases.

Second, the design and implementation of AI systems themselves must prioritize fairness and equity. This necessitates careful consideration of the metrics and criteria used to evaluate individuals, ensuring that they are inclusive and do not inadvertently disadvantage certain groups. It also requires rigorous testing and validation to identify and mitigate any potential biases in the system's output. This testing should not only focus on technical accuracy but also involve human review and assessment of the ethical implications of the AI's decisions. Blind testing, where evaluators are unaware of the demographic characteristics of the candidates, can help uncover and address underlying biases.

Third, transparency and explainability are vital. Developing AI systems that are more interpretable — that is, systems whose decision-making processes are transparent and understandable—is crucial for identifying and addressing biases. This involves utilizing techniques like decision trees, rule-based systems, and explainable AI (XAI) methods that offer insights into the factors driving the system's decisions. These methods allow for a better understanding of how the AI arrived at a particular outcome, enabling the identification and correction of biases. This transparency also fosters trust among employees, allowing them to understand the rationale behind AI-driven decisions and potentially appeal or challenge unfair outcomes.

Fourth, companies need to establish robust auditing mechanisms to regularly assess the fairness and accuracy of their AI systems. These audits should involve both technical experts and individuals from diverse backgrounds who can provide valuable perspectives and help identify potential biases or inaccuracies. The results of these audits must be transparently communicated to employees, fostering trust and enabling timely corrections. Moreover, organizations must invest in ongoing training programs to educate employees about how AI systems are used in the workplace and how to challenge or appeal AI-driven decisions. This empowers employees to understand their rights and advocate for fair treatment.

Finally, legal frameworks and industry best practices are crucial. Regulations that require companies to explain the decision-making processes of AI systems used in employment contexts can help prevent discrimination and ensure fairness. Similarly, industry bodies can play a significant role in establishing ethical guidelines and standards for the development and deployment of AI systems, promoting responsible innovation and ensuring that these technologies are used to foster a more inclusive and equitable workplace.

The pursuit of diversity and inclusion in the age of AI is an ongoing and evolving process. It demands a proactive and multi-faceted approach encompassing technological advancements, regulatory frameworks, and a strong ethical commitment from organizations.

Addressing the potential biases embedded in AI systems is not merely a matter of ethical responsibility; it's also critical for ensuring the successful and equitable implementation of AI in the workplace. By embracing transparency, accountability, and a commitment to ongoing improvement, organizations can leverage the power of AI while safeguarding the rights and dignity of all employees, creating a truly diverse and inclusive workplace for the future. The failure to do so risks perpetuating existing inequalities and undermining the potential benefits of this transformative technology. The future of work depends on our collective ability to address these challenges proactively and responsibly.

Responsible AI Development and Deployment

Building upon the previous discussion of bias and fairness in AI systems, responsible AI development and deployment requires a comprehensive and proactive approach, extending far beyond simply mitigating biases in data. It necessitates a fundamental shift in how we conceive of and implement AI within the workplace, placing ethical considerations at the forefront of every stage, from initial design to ongoing monitoring and evaluation. This involves a careful consideration of not only the technical aspects but also the broader societal implications of these powerful technologies.

A cornerstone of responsible AI development is the establishment of clear ethical principles and guidelines. These should be integrated into the organizational culture and serve as the bedrock for all AI-related initiatives. These principles should go beyond mere compliance with existing regulations; they should reflect a genuine commitment to fairness, transparency, and accountability in the use of AI. Key elements of such a framework might include: a commitment to privacy and data security, ensuring the responsible collection, use, and storage of employee data; a focus on fairness and non-discrimination, actively seeking to eliminate bias in AI systems and ensure equitable treatment of all employees; a commitment to transparency and explainability, striving to create AI systems whose decision-making processes are understandable and auditable; and a focus on accountability, establishing clear lines of responsibility for the development, deployment, and ongoing monitoring of AI systems. These ethical principles should be regularly reviewed and updated to reflect evolving technological advancements and societal values.

The importance of human oversight cannot be overstated. While AI systems can automate various tasks and processes, they should never operate entirely autonomously, particularly in decision-making that affects employees' lives and careers. Human oversight is crucial to ensure that AI systems are used in accordance with ethical principles and legal regulations, and to provide a crucial check against unintended consequences or biases. This oversight should not be limited to a single point in the AI lifecycle; rather, it should be an integral part of the entire process, from initial design and data selection to deployment, monitoring, and evaluation. Human-in-the-loop systems, where human intervention is integrated at critical decision points, are essential for maintaining ethical standards and accountability.

The design phase of AI systems should explicitly incorporate ethical considerations. This involves carefully considering the potential impacts of the system on individuals and groups, ensuring that the system is designed to be fair, transparent, and accountable. The selection of data for training AI systems is particularly critical. Bias embedded in training data will inevitably manifest in the AI's output. Therefore, rigorous data cleaning, pre-processing, and validation are essential to minimize bias and ensure that the data is representative of the diverse population it will affect. Moreover, the choice of algorithms and models should be carefully evaluated for their potential biases and limitations, and alternative approaches should be explored if necessary. The development process should also incorporate mechanisms for identifying and mitigating potential biases throughout the system's lifecycle. Regular audits and reviews of the system's performance are crucial to ensure that it continues to operate ethically and fairly.

Beyond the design phase, the deployment of AI systems necessitates careful consideration of their potential impact on the workforce. This includes a thorough assessment of the potential displacement of workers, the need for retraining and upskilling initiatives, and the potential for new job creation. Transparent communication with employees about the introduction of AI systems is paramount. This should include clear explanations of how the AI system will be used, its limitations, and its potential impact on their jobs. This open communication helps to foster trust and address employee concerns. Companies should also invest in retraining programs to equip employees with the skills they need to adapt to the changing workplace, ensuring a just transition for workers impacted by automation.

Ongoing monitoring and evaluation are essential for maintaining the ethical integrity of AI systems. Regular audits should be conducted to assess the system's fairness, transparency, and accountability. These audits should involve both technical experts and individuals from diverse backgrounds to ensure that the system's performance is assessed from multiple perspectives. The findings of these audits should be made publicly available to ensure transparency and accountability. Furthermore, feedback mechanisms should be implemented to allow employees to report any concerns or issues related to the AI system's operation. This continuous feedback loop is crucial for identifying and addressing any ethical lapses or biases that may arise over time.

The responsibility for responsible AI development and deployment extends beyond the individual organization. Collaboration across industries, academic institutions, and government bodies is crucial for establishing shared standards and best practices. Industry-wide guidelines and regulatory frameworks can help to set clear expectations for the ethical development and use of AI. Open-source tools and resources can facilitate the adoption of best practices and promote the development of more ethical and responsible AI systems. Government regulations can also play a crucial role in enforcing ethical standards and protecting employees from discrimination and unfair treatment.

The development and implementation of explainable AI (XAI) techniques are vital for enhancing transparency and accountability. XAI aims to create AI systems whose decision-making processes are understandable and interpretable by humans. This allows for the identification and mitigation of biases, fostering trust and accountability. XAI techniques can help to clarify the reasoning behind AI-driven decisions, providing valuable insights for both employees and managers. These insights can be critical for identifying and addressing instances of bias or unfairness. The development and adoption of XAI are thus a critical step in promoting responsible AI development and deployment in the workplace.

Finally, fostering a culture of ethical AI within organizations is crucial. This necessitates a shift in organizational mindset, prioritizing ethical considerations alongside technical advancements. Training programs for employees should emphasize ethical AI principles, promoting responsible use and raising awareness of potential ethical pitfalls. Companies should also create mechanisms for reporting and addressing ethical concerns, ensuring that there are avenues for raising concerns and seeking redress. Leadership commitment to ethical AI is essential, setting the tone and demonstrating a genuine commitment to using AI responsibly and ethically.

In conclusion, the responsible development and deployment of AI in the workplace are not merely technological challenges; they are fundamentally ethical imperatives. By prioritizing ethical considerations throughout the AI lifecycle, through a combination of robust ethical frameworks, human oversight, transparent design, ongoing monitoring, and industry-wide collaboration, organizations can harness the power of AI while safeguarding the rights and dignity of their employees, fostering a truly equitable and inclusive future of work. The failure to do so risks perpetuating existing inequalities and undermining the potential benefits of this transformative technology. The future of work depends on our collective ability to address these challenges proactively and responsibly, ensuring that AI serves as a force for good in the workplace.

Chapter 8: The Future of Work: Predictions and Possibilities

Emerging Trends in AI and Their Impact on the Workplace

The rapid advancement of artificial intelligence (AI) is not just reshaping existing industries; it's forging entirely new landscapes of opportunity and disruption. Understanding these emerging trends is crucial for navigating the future of work, preparing for both the challenges and the unprecedented possibilities that lie ahead. One of the most significant developments is the rise of generative AI, a category of AI that focuses on creating new content rather than simply analyzing or processing existing data. Generative AI models, trained on massive datasets, can produce text, images, audio, and even video, opening up a world of creative potential across diverse fields.

In marketing and advertising, generative AI is already transforming how campaigns are conceived and executed. Instead of relying solely on human creativity, marketers can leverage AI to generate multiple variations of ad copy, images, and video content, testing different approaches and optimizing campaigns for maximum impact. This not only speeds up the creative process but also enables more personalized and targeted advertising, catering to individual customer preferences and behaviors. This increase in efficiency and personalization may lead to a reduction in the need for large teams dedicated to purely creative tasks, but simultaneously creates demand for professionals who can manage, refine, and interpret the outputs of generative AI, ensuring brand consistency and ethical considerations.

The impact extends beyond marketing. In software development, generative AI can assist in code generation, debugging, and testing, significantly accelerating the software development lifecycle. This allows developers to focus on higher-level design and problem-solving, rather than getting bogged down in repetitive coding tasks.

The rise of "no-code" and "low-code" platforms, powered by AI, further democratizes software development, enabling individuals with limited programming expertise to build and deploy applications. However, this also raises questions about the future skillsets required for software engineers – the focus will shift from rote coding to architecting complex systems and managing AI-powered tools.

In the realm of finance, generative AI is finding applications in fraud detection, risk assessment, and algorithmic trading. AI models can analyze vast amounts of financial data to identify patterns and anomalies that might indicate fraudulent activities. They can also assist in developing more sophisticated risk management strategies and automating trading decisions. However, the implementation of such systems requires careful oversight and ethical considerations, as algorithmic bias could lead to unfair or discriminatory outcomes. The need for human expertise in financial analysis and regulation remains critical, even in an AI-driven environment. Instead of replacing human analysts, AI will augment their capabilities, allowing them to handle larger datasets and make more informed decisions.

The creative industries, traditionally seen as immune to automation, are also undergoing significant transformations thanks to generative AI. Artists and designers can now use AI tools to generate novel ideas, explore different design options, and refine their work more efficiently. AI can assist with tasks such as image generation, music composition, and even the creation of virtual environments. This opens up exciting possibilities for collaboration between humans and AI, creating new forms of art and design that blend human creativity with AI's computational power. The artistic role, however, may shift. Instead of being purely execution-focused, artists may need to be adept at prompting and guiding the AI, while retaining their unique artistic vision and style.

The impact of generative AI extends beyond specific industries to the very nature of work itself. The potential for new job roles focused on AI development, maintenance, and management is substantial. Professionals specializing in prompt engineering, AI ethics, and AI training will become increasingly sought after. Furthermore, the increasing sophistication of AI tools will require a workforce with strong analytical and problem-solving skills, a capacity for critical thinking, and a high level of adaptability. The ability to understand and effectively use AI tools will be a critical skill across all sectors, transforming the workforce into one where human-AI collaboration is the norm.

Beyond generative AI, other emerging trends are equally transformative. The convergence of AI with other technologies like the Internet of Things (IoT) and blockchain is creating powerful new capabilities. AI-powered IoT devices can collect and analyze vast amounts of data from the physical world, leading to improved efficiency and decision-making in various sectors, from manufacturing and logistics to healthcare and agriculture. Blockchain technology, with its decentralized and secure nature, can enhance the transparency and security of AI systems, addressing concerns related to data privacy and bias.

The increasing availability of open-source AI tools is further democratizing access to AI technology. This allows smaller companies and individuals to leverage the power of AI without the need for significant investment in proprietary technologies. This democratization can lead to a wave of innovation and entrepreneurship, fostering the creation of new businesses and services powered by AI. However, it also presents challenges related to the ethical considerations and quality control of AI tools widely available for use.

Another notable trend is the rise of explainable AI (XAI). As AI systems become more complex, the need for transparency and understanding of their decision-making processes is increasingly crucial. XAI aims to make AI systems more interpretable, enabling users to understand how AI arrives at its conclusions. This is especially important in industries where decisions have significant ethical or legal implications, such as healthcare and finance.

Developing and implementing XAI techniques remains a major technological challenge, but one that is essential for fostering trust and accountability in AI systems.

The future of work will be characterized by a continuous cycle of automation, job displacement, and the emergence of new roles. Industries will evolve, and business models will be redefined by AI-powered innovations. Understanding these evolving trends is essential not just for individual career planning but also for shaping public policy and workforce development strategies. Addressing the potential for job displacement through proactive investment in education and reskilling initiatives will be critical to ensuring a just transition to an AI-driven economy.

The potential benefits of AI are immense, but realizing these benefits requires a careful and considered approach. Addressing concerns related to bias, fairness, privacy, and security is paramount. Establishing clear ethical guidelines and regulatory frameworks is crucial for ensuring the responsible development and deployment of AI technologies. Collaboration among governments, industry leaders, and researchers is essential for navigating the ethical and societal implications of AI and shaping a future where AI serves humanity. The future of work is not simply about surviving the AI revolution; it's about actively shaping it, ensuring that the transformative power of AI benefits all members of society. This requires a proactive approach to education, reskilling, and the development of ethical guidelines to navigate the complexities of this rapidly evolving technological landscape. The journey into the future of work is not a passive one; it demands active participation, adaptation, and a commitment to building a future where human ingenuity and artificial intelligence work in harmony.

The Human-AI Collaboration Model A Synergistic Approach

The previous sections have outlined the transformative power of AI across various industries, highlighting both the opportunities and challenges it presents. However, the narrative shouldn't be framed as a simple human versus AI competition; rather, the future of work will be defined by a powerful synergy between human ingenuity and artificial intelligence. This section explores the human-AI collaboration model, a synergistic approach that leverages the unique strengths of both to achieve unprecedented levels of productivity and innovation.

The fundamental principle underpinning this model is the understanding that humans and AI possess complementary capabilities. Humans excel at tasks requiring creativity, critical thinking, emotional intelligence, complex problem-solving, and nuanced judgment. These are areas where AI currently lags, despite its rapid advancements. Conversely, AI possesses strengths in processing vast amounts of data at incredible speeds, identifying patterns humans might miss, performing repetitive tasks with unwavering precision, and providing data-driven insights that enhance human decision-making.

A truly effective human-AI collaboration model, therefore, requires a thoughtful division of labor. This isn't about replacing humans; it's about augmenting human capabilities and freeing them from tedious or repetitive tasks. Consider, for example, a financial analyst. Instead of spending hours sifting through financial reports and spreadsheets, the analyst could leverage AI tools to automate data analysis, identify potential risks and investment opportunities, and generate predictive models. The analyst then focuses their time and expertise on interpreting these insights, making strategic decisions, and communicating their findings to clients or stakeholders. The AI becomes a powerful assistant, enhancing the analyst's ability to perform their job more effectively and efficiently.

This principle extends across numerous professions. In healthcare, AI can assist doctors in diagnosing diseases, analyzing medical images, and personalizing treatment plans based on patient-specific data. The physician, however, remains central to the process, providing crucial clinical judgment, interacting with patients, and making critical decisions based on the AI's recommendations. In manufacturing, AI-powered robots can automate assembly lines and perform repetitive tasks with greater precision and speed than humans. However, human workers are still needed to oversee the process, troubleshoot problems, and ensure the quality of the final product. Even in creative fields, such as writing or music composition, AI tools can assist with brainstorming, generating drafts, and refining ideas. The human artist, however, remains responsible for the overall vision, ensuring originality, and injecting their unique style and perspective into the work.

Best practices for effective human-AI collaboration involve several key components. Firstly, clear communication is paramount.

Humans need to be able to effectively communicate their needs and objectives to the AI system, and the AI must provide clear, understandable outputs that humans can easily interpret. This necessitates a focus on designing user-friendly interfaces and developing clear protocols for human-AI interaction. Furthermore, ongoing training and education are essential for both humans and AI systems. Humans need to develop the skills and knowledge required to effectively use and manage AI tools, while AI systems must be continually trained and updated to improve their performance and accuracy. This includes addressing potential biases within AI algorithms and ensuring fairness and transparency in their decision-making processes.

The development of strong ethical frameworks is crucial for ensuring the responsible implementation of human-AI collaboration. This includes establishing clear guidelines on data privacy, algorithmic accountability, and the equitable distribution of benefits and risks associated with AI technologies. It's also critical to consider the potential societal impacts of widespread AI adoption and develop strategies to mitigate any negative consequences, such as job displacement or increased inequality. This requires proactive investment in education and retraining programs to equip workers with the skills needed to thrive in an AI-driven economy.

Furthermore, ongoing monitoring and evaluation of human-AI systems are essential to identify and address any unintended consequences or ethical concerns.

Building a successful human-AI collaboration model also requires a significant shift in organizational culture. Companies need to foster an environment where humans and AI are seen as complementary assets, rather than competitors. This requires investing in training programs to equip employees with the skills needed to work effectively alongside AI, promoting collaboration between human teams and AI systems, and fostering a culture of continuous learning and adaptation. Leadership plays a critical role in this transition, guiding the organization through the changes and ensuring that the benefits of AI are shared broadly throughout the workforce.

The implementation of human-AI collaboration requires careful consideration of organizational structure and processes.

Organizations might need to restructure teams, redefine job roles, and develop new workflows to optimize the integration of AI systems. This might involve creating new roles dedicated to AI management, training, and ethical oversight. Investing in robust IT infrastructure and data management systems is also crucial for supporting the seamless operation of human-AI systems.

Beyond the immediate workplace, the human-AI collaboration model has significant implications for society as a whole. AI-powered tools can enhance human capabilities in various aspects of life, from education and healthcare to transportation and environmental sustainability. However, it's crucial to address the potential risks and challenges associated with widespread AI adoption. This includes the potential for job displacement, algorithmic bias, and the ethical implications of using AI in decision-making processes. Careful planning and policy development are essential to ensure that the benefits of AI are broadly shared, and potential harms are mitigated. This necessitates a collaborative effort between governments, industry, and civil society to establish clear ethical guidelines and regulations governing the development and deployment of AI technologies.

The human-AI collaboration model is not merely a technological advancement; it's a fundamental shift in the way we approach work, innovation, and even the very definition of human potential. By understanding the complementary strengths of humans and AI, and by implementing best practices for collaboration, we can unlock unprecedented levels of productivity, creativity, and problem-solving. The path forward requires a commitment to ethical considerations, robust education and training initiatives, and a cultural shift embracing human-AI synergy as the foundation for a prosperous and equitable future. The future of work isn't about humans versus AI; it's about humans *with* AI, a partnership that promises to redefine what's possible. The journey toward this future demands proactive engagement, adaptable strategies, and a shared vision for a world where technological advancement serves humanity's best interests.

The Gig Economy and AI Opportunities and Challenges

The previous sections examined the profound implications of AI on the traditional workplace, highlighting the potential for both synergistic collaboration and significant disruption. We now turn our attention to the gig economy, a landscape already characterized by fluidity and independent contracting, and analyze how AI is reshaping its contours. The gig economy, with its inherent flexibility and project-based work, presents a unique case study in understanding the evolving relationship between humans and AI in the workplace.

The most immediate impact of AI on the gig economy is the creation of entirely new gig opportunities. The rise of online platforms connecting businesses with freelance workers has already created a vast and dynamic market. AI is further expanding this market, generating demand for specialists in AI-related fields like data annotation, machine learning model training, and AI-assisted content creation. Individuals with expertise in these areas can find lucrative opportunities through freelance platforms, contributing to the development and refinement of AI technologies while maintaining the flexibility inherent in gig work. Moreover, the automation of routine tasks by AI frees up businesses to focus on more complex and creative endeavors, often outsourcing these specialized needs to gig workers. This creates a trickle-down effect, broadening the range of available gig work beyond simple data entry or transcription. For instance, AI-powered tools for graphic design are becoming increasingly sophisticated. While these tools can automate basic tasks, they still require human intervention for the nuanced aspects of visual communication, generating opportunities for gig workers who specialize in fine-tuning AI-generated designs and adding a human touch. Similarly, in the field of writing, AI can assist with generating initial drafts or conducting research, but the skill of crafting compelling narratives, persuasive arguments, or emotionally resonant copy remains distinctly human.

This necessitates a continued demand for freelance writers and editors to refine AI-generated content and ensure its quality and effectiveness.

However, the integration of AI into the gig economy also presents significant challenges. One major concern is the potential for AI to displace gig workers in certain sectors. Tasks traditionally performed by freelance writers, graphic designers, and even programmers are becoming increasingly automatable. AI-powered tools can now generate basic marketing materials, translate languages, and write simple code, potentially reducing the demand for gig workers in these areas. This displacement isn't necessarily a complete elimination of jobs, but a shift in the nature of the work required. The gig workers who thrive will be those who can adapt and leverage AI to augment their skills, focusing on tasks that require uniquely human capabilities such as critical thinking, creative problem-solving, and emotional intelligence— skills that remain beyond the current capabilities of AI. The competitive landscape is shifting, demanding a higher level of specialization and adaptability from gig workers. Success will hinge on acquiring skills that complement AI, not compete with it.

Another critical challenge stems from the inherent precariousness of the gig economy. While AI can generate new opportunities, it also has the potential to exacerbate existing inequalities. The lack of traditional employee benefits, such as health insurance and retirement plans, is a persistent issue for gig workers. As AI-driven automation displaces some gig workers, those displaced may find it even more difficult to secure stable, well-paying employment. This could lead to a widening income gap, with a growing disparity between those who can adapt to the changing demands of the AI-driven gig economy and those who are left behind. The algorithmic nature of many gig platforms raises further concerns. These algorithms, often designed to optimize efficiency and profitability, may unintentionally create biased outcomes, disproportionately impacting certain demographics or worker groups. For instance, an algorithm designed to prioritize speed and efficiency might inadvertently favor gig workers who are willing to work long hours for lower wages, potentially suppressing wages overall. These biases, while potentially unintentional, can have significant consequences for gig workers' earnings and overall economic well-being.

Addressing these challenges requires a multi-faceted approach.

Firstly, there needs to be a renewed focus on education and retraining programs designed to equip gig workers with the skills needed to thrive in an AI-driven world. This includes not only technical skills, such as AI literacy and programming, but also soft skills, such as communication, teamwork, and critical thinking. Governments and educational institutions need to work together to develop programs that are accessible and relevant to the needs of gig workers, focusing on bridging the skills gap created by AI-driven automation. Furthermore, policymakers must address the issue of income inequality within the gig economy. This might involve exploring alternative models of social safety nets that better protect gig workers, such as portable benefits or universal basic income schemes. These policies are crucial not only for protecting individual workers but also for fostering a more equitable and inclusive society.

The design of AI algorithms themselves needs careful scrutiny.

Promoting transparency in the development and application of these algorithms is essential to identify and mitigate any potential biases that might disadvantage certain groups of gig workers.

Regular audits and independent reviews of gig platforms' algorithms can help ensure fairness and accountability. Furthermore, fostering a culture of ethical AI development within the tech industry is crucial, ensuring that AI is developed and deployed in a way that benefits all stakeholders, including gig workers. This requires collaborative efforts between industry, policymakers, and civil society.

Beyond policy interventions, gig workers themselves need to take a proactive approach to future-proofing their careers. Continuous learning and upskilling are essential for staying ahead of the curve in an ever-evolving AI-driven landscape. Embracing new technologies and developing skills that complement AI, such as critical thinking, creativity, and emotional intelligence, will be crucial for securing high-paying opportunities. Developing a strong personal brand and networking effectively will also be key to finding work in the gig economy. The focus should be on becoming irreplaceable, offering skills and services that AI cannot yet replicate.

The future of the gig economy will be defined by the interplay between human ingenuity and artificial intelligence. While AI poses significant challenges, it also presents exciting opportunities for those who are willing to adapt and embrace change. By investing in education, promoting ethical AI development, and implementing policies that address inequality, we can harness the transformative power of AI to create a more inclusive and equitable gig economy that benefits both workers and businesses. This requires a collective effort, with governments, educational institutions, businesses, and gig workers themselves working collaboratively to navigate the complex landscape of an AI-driven future. The success of this transition depends on a shared understanding of the challenges and opportunities, and a concerted commitment to ensuring a fair and prosperous future for all. The ultimate goal is not to compete with AI, but to collaborate with it, leveraging its capabilities to enhance human potential and create a more dynamic and fulfilling work experience for all.

The Role of Governments and Policymakers

The previous sections have explored the multifaceted impact of artificial intelligence on the evolving landscape of work, focusing particularly on the gig economy and its inherent complexities. We've seen how AI simultaneously creates new opportunities and presents significant challenges, particularly concerning job displacement and income inequality. Now, we shift our focus to the crucial role governments and policymakers play in navigating this transformative period and shaping a future of work that is both prosperous and equitable.

The most immediate and pressing need is a comprehensive overhaul of education and retraining programs. The skills gap, already a significant concern, is being widened by the rapid advancements in AI. Traditional educational models, often slow to adapt to technological change, are ill-equipped to prepare workers for the jobs of tomorrow. Governments must invest heavily in creating agile, responsive programs that equip individuals with the skills needed to thrive in an AI-driven economy. This requires a move beyond simply teaching specific technical skills, although proficiency in AI-related technologies like machine learning and data analysis is undeniably crucial. The focus must also be on cultivating "future-proof" skills – critical thinking, complex problem-solving, creativity, adaptability, and emotional intelligence. These human-centric skills are less susceptible to automation and are increasingly valuable in a world where collaboration between humans and AI is the norm.

Retraining programs should not be viewed as a one-time fix but rather as an ongoing process, reflecting the dynamic nature of AI and its continued evolution. Lifelong learning must be promoted, with readily accessible resources and opportunities for upskilling and reskilling throughout an individual's career. This might involve partnerships between governments, educational institutions, and the private sector to offer subsidized training programs, online courses, and apprenticeships specifically focused on AI-related fields and complementary human skills. Furthermore, these programs should be tailored to meet the diverse needs of different demographics, ensuring that individuals from marginalized communities, often disproportionately affected by technological disruption, are not left behind. This involves addressing potential barriers to access, such as financial constraints, geographical limitations, and lack of digital literacy.

Beyond education and retraining, governments must confront the issue of income inequality exacerbated by AI-driven automation. The traditional social safety net, often designed for a more stable employment landscape, struggles to adequately protect gig workers and those displaced by automation. Exploring alternative models of social protection is crucial. Universal Basic Income (UBI) schemes, while controversial, warrant serious consideration as a potential solution to address income insecurity in a future where traditional employment models may become less relevant. UBI, by providing a guaranteed minimum income, could offer a safety net for those transitioning between jobs or facing displacement due to automation, allowing individuals the time and resources to acquire new skills and adapt to changing market demands.

Other strategies could include portable benefits, allowing individuals to maintain access to essential benefits like health insurance and retirement plans regardless of their employment status. This would lessen the precarity of gig work and incentivize workers to invest in their skills without fearing the loss of essential benefits. Expanding access to affordable healthcare and childcare is another crucial element, recognizing that these factors often pose significant barriers to individuals seeking to upskill or re-enter the workforce. These policies, while demanding substantial investment, are essential for fostering a more equitable society and mitigating the potential for social unrest stemming from technological unemployment.

The role of government also extends to regulating the development and deployment of AI. While fostering innovation is critical, ensuring ethical and responsible AI development is equally important. Regulations are needed to prevent algorithmic bias, which can disproportionately harm certain groups of workers. Transparency in AI algorithms is essential, allowing for scrutiny and identification of potential biases that might disadvantage certain demographics. Governments can mandate audits and independent reviews of AI systems used in hiring processes, performance evaluations, and other aspects of employment.

Furthermore, standards for data privacy and security must be strengthened to protect workers' data and prevent misuse.

Collaborations between governments, industry, and labor unions are vital to developing effective regulatory frameworks. This collaborative approach allows for the incorporation of diverse perspectives and ensures that regulations are practical and effective, promoting both innovation and ethical considerations. The ultimate goal is to create a regulatory landscape that encourages responsible AI development while safeguarding the rights and well-being of workers. This includes addressing issues like algorithmic transparency, data security, and worker protections within the gig economy.

Further, governments can play a significant role in fostering a culture of lifelong learning and adaptation. Public awareness campaigns can highlight the transformative impact of AI on the workplace and encourage individuals to embrace lifelong learning. Government-funded initiatives can support community colleges and vocational schools in providing relevant training programs and fostering partnerships with employers. This approach helps bridge the gap between education and the changing demands of the job market.

It is crucial to remember that the transition to an AI-driven economy is not solely a technological challenge but a profound societal one. Governments play a pivotal role in navigating this transition, ensuring that the benefits of AI are shared widely and that the negative consequences are mitigated. This requires a proactive and multifaceted approach, encompassing education reform, social safety net enhancements, and thoughtful regulations to govern AI's development and deployment. The success of this transition depends on a shared commitment to fostering a future of work that is both equitable and prosperous for all. The focus must be on harnessing the transformative potential of AI to enhance human capabilities, rather than allowing it to create deeper societal divides. By proactively addressing the challenges and opportunities presented by AI, governments can play a crucial role in shaping a future of work that benefits everyone. The ultimate goal is not just to manage the transition but to leverage the transformative power of AI to build a more just, equitable, and prosperous future for all.

Preparing for the Unexpected Adaptability in the Age of AI

The previous discussion focused on the crucial role of governments in navigating the societal shifts brought about by AI. However, the onus of adaptation doesn't solely rest on policymakers. Individuals must also actively prepare for the unpredictable nature of the future of work, embracing a mindset of continuous learning and proactive career development. The speed at which AI is evolving necessitates a flexible and adaptable approach, ready to meet unexpected technological advancements and unforeseen shifts in the job market. This requires more than just acquiring new skills; it involves cultivating a fundamentally adaptable mindset and a proactive approach to career navigation.

One of the most significant challenges lies in predicting the specific skills that will be in demand in the future. While current trends point towards a growing need for data scientists, AI ethicists, and AI trainers, the rapid evolution of AI itself makes long-term predictions unreliable. New roles and specializations will undoubtedly emerge, ones that we can't even conceive of today. Instead of focusing on mastering a specific, potentially obsolete skillset, individuals should concentrate on developing transferable skills that remain valuable regardless of technological advancements.

Critical thinking, problem-solving, and creative thinking are paramount. While AI can process vast amounts of data and identify patterns, it still struggles with nuanced judgment, original thought, and innovative solutions to complex problems. Cultivating these uniquely human capabilities positions individuals for success in an environment where collaboration between humans and AI is becoming the norm. This collaborative approach will require individuals to effectively interpret AI's outputs, understand its limitations, and leverage its capabilities to enhance human decision-making and problem-solving. The ability to articulate complex ideas clearly and concisely, both orally and in writing, is another critical transferable skill. In a collaborative setting, effectively communicating ideas is critical for success.

Emotional intelligence is another increasingly valuable asset. The ability to understand and manage one's own emotions, as well as empathize with and connect with others, is crucial for effective teamwork and leadership. As AI becomes increasingly integrated into the workplace, these human-centric skills will become even more essential in building trust, fostering collaboration, and navigating complex interpersonal dynamics. These are capabilities that currently remain firmly in the human domain. AI can analyze data to predict human behavior patterns, but it can't genuinely empathize or understand the nuances of human interaction.

Adaptability itself needs to be cultivated as a crucial skill. This involves embracing lifelong learning as a core principle. The workforce of tomorrow will need to continuously update their knowledge and skills to stay relevant in a rapidly changing environment. This continuous learning process should not be seen as a burden but as an opportunity for growth, exploration, and professional development. It requires a proactive approach, seeking out new learning opportunities, and embracing challenges as chances to develop new capabilities. This proactive mindset requires a willingness to experiment, to step outside one's comfort zone, and to embrace new technologies and methodologies.

The adoption of a growth mindset is critical. Individuals must view challenges not as setbacks but as opportunities for learning and growth.

This mindset fosters resilience and enables individuals to adapt to unexpected changes and setbacks with greater ease. The ability to bounce back from adversity is a crucial asset in a dynamic work environment constantly evolving due to technological advancements. This involves developing effective strategies for stress management, time management, and learning from mistakes.

It also means cultivating a willingness to seek feedback and incorporate it into their approach.

Networking and collaboration are also pivotal. Building strong professional networks allows individuals to access new information, learn from others, and identify new opportunities. Collaboration, particularly with individuals from diverse backgrounds, fosters creativity and innovation, allowing for a broader range of perspectives and approaches. These networks can serve as valuable resources during periods of uncertainty or transition, providing support and guidance as one navigates a changing professional landscape. Active participation in professional organizations and online communities will broaden your knowledge and enable you to stay abreast of current trends.

Proactive career planning, rather than reactive responses, is essential. This requires an ongoing assessment of one's skills and interests, a thorough analysis of current and future job market trends, and a strategic approach to career development. This could involve pursuing advanced education, certifications, or acquiring new skills through online courses or workshops. Regularly evaluating one's career trajectory and making adjustments as needed will prevent being caught off guard by sudden shifts in the job market. Continuous exploration of new fields and industries is needed, which may require a certain level of risk-taking. This could lead to unexpected yet beneficial opportunities.

Financial planning should also be integrated into this adaptive approach. The unpredictable nature of the future of work necessitates financial security to allow for periods of retraining or transition. This could involve diversifying income streams, creating an emergency fund, and prioritizing financial literacy. Having a financial safety net will provide a buffer during times of uncertainty and allow for more flexibility in making career changes. Having such a safety net allows for more calculated risks and investments in career development, without the immediate pressure of financial instability.

The development of a personal brand, relevant to the individual's field of expertise and highlighting the human skills that complement AI, will also be highly advantageous. This involves cultivating a strong online presence, highlighting your unique capabilities and experience, and showcasing your expertise through publications, presentations, and community involvement. This helps to stand out in a competitive job market and attract attention from employers. This personal brand needs to be dynamic and adaptable to showcase the evolving skills and expertise of the individual.

Ultimately, preparing for the unexpected in the age of AI requires a holistic approach encompassing continuous learning, adaptable skill development, proactive career planning, and robust financial security. It's not about predicting the future but about developing the capacity to adapt to whatever the future brings. By cultivating a flexible mindset, embracing lifelong learning, and strategically developing human-centric skills, individuals can not only survive but thrive in the ever-evolving world of work shaped by artificial intelligence. The key is to embrace the unknown, not fear it, and to see change as an opportunity for growth and innovation. This proactive approach, while demanding effort and a willingness to adapt, will ultimately prove to be the most effective strategy for navigating the unpredictable terrain of the future of work. The future is not predetermined; it is shaped by our individual responses to the challenges and opportunities presented by technological advancements.

Chapter 9: Building Your AI-Ready Toolkit

Essential Resources for AI Learning and Development

The journey towards becoming AI-ready is a continuous process of learning and adaptation. While the previous section highlighted the crucial human skills and proactive strategies needed to thrive in an AI-driven world, this section provides a practical guide to the essential resources available for acquiring the necessary knowledge and skills. The resources are categorized to help navigate the vast landscape of AI learning and development, tailoring your learning path to your specific needs and career aspirations.

For those new to the field of AI, understanding fundamental concepts is paramount. Many excellent introductory resources cater to this need. Coursera and edX, two leading massive open online course (MOOC) platforms, offer a wealth of introductory courses on AI. Look for courses focusing on the basics of machine learning, deep learning, and AI ethics. These courses often provide a solid foundation without requiring prior programming experience, making them accessible to individuals from diverse backgrounds.

Within these platforms, look for courses taught by renowned universities and institutions. Pay attention to student reviews and ratings to gauge the quality and effectiveness of the course materials.

Beyond MOOCs, several excellent books serve as foundational resources for AI comprehension. "Artificial Intelligence: A Modern Approach" by Stuart Russell and Peter Norvig is a widely regarded textbook, offering a comprehensive overview of AI concepts and techniques. While academically rigorous, its clarity makes it approachable even for those without a strong technical background. For a more practical, hands-on approach, consider books focusing on specific AI applications relevant to your career path. For example, professionals in marketing might benefit from books on AI-powered marketing automation, while those in finance might find resources on algorithmic trading and risk management valuable. When choosing a book, consider the author's credentials, the book's reviews, and its alignment with your learning objectives.

Once you have grasped the fundamental concepts, the next step is to delve deeper into specific AI techniques and applications. This requires a more focused approach, targeting resources tailored to your chosen field. Consider specializing in areas like natural language processing (NLP), computer vision, or reinforcement learning, depending on your career aspirations. Many specialized online courses and workshops cater to these areas, offered by platforms such as Udacity, DataCamp, and Fast.ai. These resources often combine theoretical knowledge with practical exercises, allowing for hands-on experience with AI tools and techniques. Prioritize courses that provide opportunities for real-world projects, allowing you to apply what you've learned in a practical setting and build a portfolio of your work.

Advanced learning involves engaging with research papers, participating in online communities, and attending conferences.

Staying up-to-date with the latest advancements in AI requires actively participating in the AI research community. Platforms like arXiv provide access to the latest research papers, allowing you to understand cutting-edge developments in the field. Regularly browsing through these publications and engaging in discussions on online forums can greatly enhance your understanding of the field.

Additionally, attending AI conferences and workshops provides opportunities to network with professionals and learn from leading experts. These events often feature workshops and tutorials offering a deeper dive into specific AI techniques and tools. Networking opportunities can help you connect with mentors, colleagues, and potential employers, fostering growth and career advancement.

The choice of resources depends significantly on your career path.

For data scientists, mastering programming languages such as Python and R is crucial. Many online resources focus on these languages within the context of AI and machine learning. For AI ethicists, an interdisciplinary approach is required, blending technical knowledge with ethical and philosophical perspectives.

Resources on ethics, law, and social science will be equally important. Professionals in management roles may benefit from resources focusing on AI strategy and implementation, understanding how AI can be integrated into business processes to enhance productivity and efficiency. Tailoring your learning path to your specific career goals ensures that your efforts are focused and effective.

Beyond formal courses and books, several communities and online forums provide invaluable support and resources for AI learning.

Online forums such as Reddit's r/artificialintelligence and Stack Overflow offer spaces for asking questions, sharing knowledge, and collaborating with other learners. These platforms are excellent for clarifying concepts, troubleshooting technical problems, and staying up-to-date with industry trends. Active participation in these communities can significantly enhance your understanding and build a strong network of fellow AI enthusiasts. Don't hesitate to seek help when facing challenges; many experienced professionals are willing to assist.

Practical application is key. The best way to solidify your AI knowledge is to work on real-world projects. This can involve contributing to open-source projects, participating in AI hackathons, or building personal projects to showcase your skills. Creating a portfolio of AI projects not only demonstrates your capabilities to potential employers but also solidifies your understanding of AI concepts and techniques. The experience gained through practical application is invaluable in bridging the gap between theoretical knowledge and real-world implementation.

It is also important to remember that the AI field is constantly evolving. Continuous learning is not just recommended but essential for staying relevant and competitive. Regularly updating your knowledge through online courses, workshops, and the latest research publications ensures that you remain at the forefront of AI advancements. Consider incorporating continuous learning into your routine, dedicating a specific amount of time each week to expanding your knowledge and skills.

Finally, don't underestimate the power of mentorship. Connecting with experienced professionals in the AI field can provide invaluable guidance and support. Mentors can offer insights into career paths, offer advice on navigating the field, and provide feedback on your projects. Many online and offline platforms facilitate mentor-mentee relationships. Actively seeking out mentors and participating in mentorship programs can significantly accelerate your progress and increase your chances of success.

This curated list of resources, while not exhaustive, offers a starting point for embarking on your AI learning journey. Remember, the key is to be proactive, persistent, and adaptable. Embrace the challenges, celebrate the successes, and enjoy the continuous process of growth and discovery that comes with navigating the ever-evolving landscape of artificial intelligence. The future of work is being shaped by AI, and by proactively engaging in learning and development, you can not only survive but significantly thrive in this exciting and transformative era. Your proactive approach will shape your destiny within the AI-powered future. The path to success is paved with continuous learning, practical application, and a willingness to embrace the unknown.

AI Tools and Software for Enhanced Productivity

Having established the foundational knowledge and learning pathways for navigating the AI revolution, we now turn to the practical application of AI tools and software. This section will explore a range of AI-powered applications designed to enhance productivity across various professions. The rapid advancement of AI has yielded a wealth of tools that can streamline workflows, automate repetitive tasks, and provide insightful data analysis, ultimately boosting individual and organizational efficiency. While a comprehensive list is impossible given the ever-evolving landscape, we will examine key categories and examples to illustrate the transformative potential of these resources.

One of the most significant impacts of AI is in the realm of automation. Repetitive tasks that once consumed considerable time and effort can now be efficiently handled by AI-powered tools. In administrative roles, for example, tools like Zapier and IFTTT (If This Then That) can automate routine tasks such as email management, scheduling appointments, and data entry. These platforms connect various applications and automate workflows based on predefined triggers, freeing up valuable time for more strategic and creative work. The power of these tools lies in their simplicity and versatility; they require minimal technical expertise to set up and manage. For businesses operating across multiple platforms, the ability to automate data transfer and synchronize information across different systems can significantly reduce errors and streamline operations.

Moving beyond simple automation, AI is revolutionizing data analysis. Tools like Tableau and Power BI leverage AI algorithms to visualize complex data sets, identify patterns, and generate actionable insights. These platforms go beyond simple data representation; they employ AI to discover hidden trends, predict future outcomes, and assist in decision-making. For marketers, understanding customer behavior and predicting trends is crucial.

AI-powered analytics platforms can analyze vast amounts of customer data to identify purchasing patterns, preferences, and demographic trends, providing invaluable insights for targeted marketing campaigns. Similarly, financial analysts can utilize these tools to assess investment risks, predict market fluctuations, and optimize investment portfolios. The ability to rapidly analyze large data sets and extract meaningful insights is a significant competitive advantage in any field.

Project management has also been significantly impacted by AI.

Platforms like Asana and Monday.com incorporate AI-powered features to improve task management, prioritize tasks based on urgency and dependency, and predict potential project delays. These features help teams better manage their workloads, identify potential bottlenecks, and ensure projects stay on schedule. These AI features offer predictive capabilities, analyzing historical data to forecast project timelines and resource allocation. This proactive approach minimizes disruptions and enables teams to allocate resources more effectively. For large-scale projects involving multiple teams and stakeholders, the ability to centralize information and track progress efficiently is paramount for success. The collaborative features of many AI-powered project management tools further enhance team communication and efficiency.

In the realm of customer service, AI-powered chatbots are increasingly prevalent. These chatbots can handle routine customer inquiries, provide instant support, and resolve common issues without human intervention. This automation frees up human agents to focus on more complex and demanding tasks, ensuring faster response times and improved customer satisfaction. Many sophisticated chatbot systems utilize natural language processing (NLP) to understand and respond to a wide range of inquiries, mimicking human conversation in a way that is often indistinguishable from a human agent. This technological leap provides a seamless customer experience, ensuring 24/7 availability and a consistent level of service. The implementation of such chatbots has demonstrably reduced customer service costs while simultaneously improving customer satisfaction.

Beyond these broad categories, numerous other AI-powered tools enhance productivity in specific professions. For writers, grammar and style checkers like Grammarly leverage AI to improve writing quality, identify errors, and suggest improvements. For designers, AI-powered tools can generate design options, optimize layouts, and automate repetitive design tasks. Even in the legal field, AI is being used to analyze legal documents, identify relevant precedents, and streamline the process of legal research. The breadth of applications is continually expanding, highlighting the pervasive impact of AI on various aspects of professional life.

The key to effectively leveraging these AI tools is understanding their capabilities and limitations. While these tools can significantly enhance productivity, they are not a replacement for human judgment and expertise. AI should be viewed as a tool to augment human capabilities, not replace them. Effective integration requires a strategic approach, identifying areas where AI can best assist human efforts, and ensuring that the tools are appropriately integrated into existing workflows. Moreover, ethical considerations are paramount. The use of AI should always align with ethical principles and respect user privacy and data security.

The selection of appropriate AI tools will vary depending on the specific needs and priorities of the individual or organization. It's crucial to evaluate available tools based on factors like cost, ease of use, integration with existing systems, and the level of AI-powered features offered. Regularly reviewing and updating the toolkit is also essential, as new AI-powered solutions are continually emerging. The dynamic nature of this field necessitates an ongoing assessment and adaptation process to ensure that the chosen tools remain effective and aligned with evolving needs.

In addition to individual tools, there are broader ecosystem considerations. Many companies are developing integrated AI suites that combine multiple tools and functionalities. These integrated platforms offer a cohesive approach to AI-powered productivity, streamlining workflows and minimizing the need for multiple disparate systems. The move towards integrated solutions reflects a trend towards greater interoperability and seamless integration within the professional landscape. The benefits of integrated systems include reduced complexity, enhanced data flow, and improved overall efficiency.

Finally, it's vital to develop the skills needed to effectively use these AI tools. While many tools are designed for ease of use, a basic understanding of AI concepts and techniques can significantly enhance their effective application. This understanding allows for better decision-making, improved problem-solving, and a more strategic approach to integrating AI into workflows. Investing in training and development in this area is not merely a worthwhile endeavor; it's a necessary step in leveraging the full potential of AI-powered tools. The ongoing development of skills ensures not only proficiency in using existing tools but also the adaptability necessary to embrace future innovations. The future of work depends on a proactive, continuous embrace of the transformative potential of AI.

Networking and Mentorship Opportunities in the AI Field

Building a successful career in the rapidly evolving field of AI requires more than just technical skills; it demands a strong network and access to insightful mentorship. The AI community, while technically driven, thrives on collaboration and shared knowledge. Leveraging the opportunities for networking and mentorship is crucial for staying abreast of the latest advancements, gaining valuable insights, and navigating the complexities of the industry. This section outlines various avenues for building your professional network and securing mentorship within the AI landscape, categorized for clarity and tailored to different career stages and interests.

For those early in their AI journey, perhaps still in academia or pursuing entry-level roles, focusing on building a foundational network is paramount. Student organizations focused on AI, machine learning, or data science offer invaluable opportunities to connect with peers and faculty. Many universities have dedicated AI clubs or societies that organize workshops, hackathons, and guest speaker events. These events provide a low-pressure environment to learn, network, and begin building professional relationships.

Actively participating in these activities not only enhances your technical skills but also exposes you to different perspectives and potential mentors within the academic community. Attending local meetups focused on specific AI technologies, like natural language processing or computer vision, can also broaden your horizons and introduce you to individuals working in those domains. These smaller, niche events often foster a more intimate and engaging atmosphere, facilitating more meaningful connections. Online forums and communities, such as Reddit's r/artificialintelligence or dedicated Slack channels for specific AI technologies, provide a virtual space for engagement, question-asking, and networking.

These platforms allow you to connect with people across geographical boundaries, learning from their experiences and contributing your own insights.

As you progress in your career and gain more experience, the networking opportunities expand significantly. Professional organizations such as the Association for the Advancement of Artificial Intelligence (AAAI), the Institute of Electrical and Electronics Engineers (IEEE) – Computer Society, and the Association for Computing Machinery (ACM) SIGAI offer numerous benefits, including conferences, publications, and networking events. These organizations often host regional chapters and local meetings, providing more accessible networking opportunities.

Membership provides access to a vast network of professionals, including researchers, developers, and industry leaders. Attending their conferences is not just about listening to presentations; it's about actively participating, engaging in discussions, and exchanging contact information with like-minded individuals.

Conferences frequently include dedicated networking events, providing structured opportunities to meet professionals and expand your network. Moreover, many professional organizations maintain online forums and communities, providing year-round opportunities for connection and knowledge-sharing.

The importance of mentorship cannot be overstated. Seeking out mentorship, particularly from seasoned professionals in the AI field, provides invaluable guidance and support throughout your career.

Mentors offer insights into navigating career paths, developing crucial skills, and making strategic decisions. Several platforms are specifically designed to connect mentees with mentors.

Organizations like MentorCruise and others specialize in matching individuals with experienced mentors in various fields, including AI. These platforms often provide structured mentorship programs, including regular check-ins, goal-setting, and feedback mechanisms. Mentorship relationships can significantly enhance your career trajectory by providing personalized guidance, support, and access to valuable industry contacts.

For those focusing on specific AI applications or industries, targeted networking is crucial. For example, individuals interested in AI in finance should seek out networks within the financial services industry, such as attending industry conferences, joining relevant professional organizations like the CFA Institute, and participating in online communities focused on fintech and AI. Similarly, those interested in AI in healthcare should focus their networking efforts on healthcare-specific conferences and professional organizations, engaging with communities and researchers in medical AI. Tailoring your networking efforts to your specific area of interest ensures you connect with individuals who share your passion and can offer relevant guidance and support.

Beyond formal organizations and platforms, informal networking opportunities are abundant. Participating in open-source AI projects allows you to collaborate with developers worldwide, contributing to real-world projects and building your portfolio while simultaneously building a network of fellow contributors. Attending workshops and training sessions focused on specific AI technologies provides opportunities to interact with instructors and fellow participants, broadening your network. Moreover, engaging in online discussions and contributing to AI-related blogs or articles can increase your visibility and connect you with other experts in the field. Presenting your work at conferences or publishing your research can also significantly elevate your profile within the AI community, attracting mentors and collaborators.

The effectiveness of networking hinges on active participation and engagement. It's not simply about collecting business cards; it's about building genuine relationships based on mutual respect and shared interests. Actively participate in discussions, share your knowledge and insights, and genuinely listen to others. Follow up with contacts after networking events, maintaining connections and building rapport over time. Networking is an ongoing process that requires sustained effort and genuine engagement. It's about cultivating relationships that can last a lifetime and provide ongoing support and opportunities.

Leveraging online platforms effectively can drastically enhance your networking reach. LinkedIn, for instance, is an indispensable tool for connecting with professionals in the AI field. Building a professional profile that showcases your skills, experience, and interests is crucial. Actively engaging with content, participating in relevant groups, and connecting with individuals in your field significantly expands your network. Twitter also plays a vital role; following key influencers and researchers in the AI field allows you to stay updated on the latest advancements and engage in discussions. Utilizing platforms like GitHub to showcase your code and contributions allows potential collaborators and mentors to assess your technical abilities. The strategic use of these online platforms can significantly amplify your networking efforts.

Finally, remember that networking is a two-way street. As you build your network, be mindful of offering value to others. Sharing your expertise, offering assistance, and providing support to your network fosters reciprocal relationships. Mentorship is not a one-sided transaction; it's a collaborative process. Be open to opportunities to mentor junior colleagues, providing support and guidance to those starting their AI journey. This act of mentorship not only benefits the mentee but strengthens your position within the community, fostering mutual respect and reciprocal support.

Building a robust network involves consistent effort, genuine engagement, and a commitment to reciprocal relationships. By actively participating in these activities and cultivating meaningful connections, you can create a supportive environment that will propel your career forward in the dynamic landscape of artificial intelligence. The ability to navigate this network, secure mentorship, and foster collaborative relationships is as critical as the technical skills themselves, ensuring long-term success and career fulfillment in the AI industry.

Online Communities and Forums for AI Professionals

The digital age has revolutionized how professionals connect and collaborate, and the AI field is no exception. Online communities and forums have become indispensable hubs for knowledge sharing, networking, and professional development. This section serves as a directory, guiding you through a selection of valuable online resources, categorized for ease of use and evaluated for their credibility and practical usefulness. Navigating this digital landscape effectively can significantly accelerate your career growth and keep you at the forefront of AI advancements.

Let's start with dedicated AI forums and discussion platforms.

Reddit, a vast online community, hosts several subreddits specifically focused on artificial intelligence. r/artificialintelligence is a popular choice, offering a broad range of discussions, from theoretical concepts to practical implementation challenges. The community is active, with daily posts covering a wide spectrum of topics, making it a great place to ask questions, share insights, and participate in ongoing debates. However, it's crucial to approach such forums with a critical eye, verifying information from multiple sources before accepting it as definitive truth. The diverse range of expertise within these communities means the quality of responses can vary; always prioritize well-reasoned and well-supported answers over those lacking substantial evidence or technical depth. Moreover, be mindful of the potential for misinformation, especially regarding cutting-edge research or emerging technologies.

Beyond Reddit, numerous specialized forums cater to specific AI subfields. For instance, those focused on natural language processing (NLP) might find valuable resources within forums dedicated to NLP tools, libraries, and research papers. Similarly, individuals working with computer vision will likely benefit from engaging with online communities focused on image processing, deep learning architectures tailored for vision tasks, and related topics. These specialized forums often foster deeper discussions and more targeted support, allowing for more in-depth exploration of niche areas within the broader field of AI. Look for forums with active moderators who actively manage and filter content, ensuring a high quality of discussion and minimizing the spread of misinformation. A strong moderator presence is a key indicator of a well-maintained and trustworthy online community.

Social media platforms have also become crucial spaces for AI professionals. LinkedIn, a professional networking platform, is invaluable for connecting with colleagues, potential employers, and industry experts. Joining relevant LinkedIn groups focusing on AI, machine learning, or specific AI applications can greatly expand your professional network. Participate actively in discussions, share relevant articles and insights, and engage respectfully with other members. Building a strong LinkedIn profile highlighting your skills and experience is essential for attracting attention from potential collaborators and employers. Remember to tailor your LinkedIn profile to your specific career goals, highlighting the skills and experience most relevant to the positions you seek.

Twitter (X), despite its brevity, serves as a powerful tool for staying abreast of the latest AI news and research. Following leading AI researchers, influential industry figures, and key AI companies allows you to receive timely updates on breakthroughs, conferences, and job opportunities. Engaging in relevant conversations using appropriate hashtags can increase your visibility and connect you with other active members of the AI community. However, be aware that Twitter's fast-paced environment can make it challenging to verify information quickly. Cross-reference information from various sources to avoid spreading misinformation inadvertently.

Beyond these established platforms, many companies and organizations maintain their own online forums or communities.

Some research institutions, for example, offer online discussion boards where researchers can collaborate, share data, and discuss findings. Many technology companies also host online communities for users of their AI tools or platforms, providing a space for users to help each other, troubleshoot issues, and suggest improvements.

These company-specific forums can be particularly useful for gaining deep insights into the specific tools and technologies relevant to your work. Actively participating in these forums can enhance your proficiency and demonstrate your expertise to potential employers.

GitHub, primarily known as a code repository, also acts as a substantial online community. Participating in open-source AI projects not only allows you to contribute to impactful initiatives but also connects you with developers worldwide, expanding your network and exposing you to diverse coding styles and best practices. Contributing to well-established projects can significantly boost your credibility, showcasing your technical proficiency to potential employers and collaborators. Reviewing and commenting on other developers' code can further improve your understanding of existing systems, highlighting your skills to those within the open-source community. Remember, consistent and high-quality contributions are paramount; merely registering an account and submitting sporadic contributions will not yield the same positive impact.

In addition to these general-purpose forums and platforms, numerous specialized online communities cater to particular AI applications or industries. For instance, communities focused on AI in healthcare often involve medical professionals, AI developers, and researchers, creating a unique and interdisciplinary environment. Similar niche communities exist for AI in finance, manufacturing, education, and other sectors. These focused groups offer opportunities for in-depth discussion and knowledge exchange relevant to specific industry applications. Participating in these tailored communities showcases your interest and expertise in specific domains, thereby attracting opportunities aligned with your preferred career path.

To maximize the benefits of these online communities, it's essential to follow certain best practices. Always verify information, especially regarding novel research or unverified claims. Engage respectfully, contributing constructively and thoughtfully to discussions. Avoid making unsubstantiated claims or engaging in aggressive debates. Remember that the goal is to collaborate, learn, and network effectively; maintaining a professional and respectful demeanor is paramount for building positive relationships within these online communities.

Finally, consider the time commitment involved. While online forums and communities offer invaluable resources, they demand careful management of your time and energy. Prioritize forums and groups that directly contribute to your professional development and career goals. Avoid spreading yourself too thin by engaging with every online community you come across. A focused and strategic approach to participation will yield far greater benefits than sporadic involvement in a multitude of unrelated platforms. By strategically engaging with the right online communities, you'll not only enhance your technical skills and knowledge but also cultivate a powerful network of professional contacts, significantly boosting your career prospects in the dynamic world of AI.

Staying Informed Key Publications and Industry News

Staying informed about the rapidly evolving landscape of AI and its impact on the workplace is paramount for anyone seeking to thrive in this new era. This requires a strategic approach to information gathering, focusing on credible sources that provide accurate, insightful, and timely updates. This section provides a curated list of key publications, industry news sources, and blogs that offer a comprehensive view of the field, categorized for easy navigation and evaluated for their reliability and relevance.

Let's begin with prominent academic journals and publications. These peer-reviewed journals provide rigorous analyses of cutting-edge AI research and its applications. *Journal of Artificial Intelligence Research (JAIR)* , for example, publishes original research across the breadth of AI, including machine learning, natural language processing, and robotics. Its articles delve into the theoretical foundations and practical implementations of AI algorithms, offering valuable insights for those seeking a deeper understanding of the field. Similarly, *Artificial Intelligence* is another leading journal featuring high-quality research articles, technical notes, and survey papers that cover a wide spectrum of AI topics. Its rigorous peer-review process ensures that only well-researched and rigorously validated findings are published, making it a trusted source for professionals seeking in-depth analysis.

Moving beyond highly technical publications, *Communications of the ACM* provides a broader perspective on AI, including its societal impact and ethical considerations. This journal covers a wide range of topics within computer science, with a significant portion dedicated to AI, featuring articles on applications in various sectors, along with discussions of ethical implications and policy considerations. Its accessibility, compared to highly specialized journals, makes it an excellent resource for those seeking a more balanced and comprehensive view. Further broadening our scope, publications like *MIT Technology Review* and *Wired* offer insightful analysis of the latest AI advancements and their potential impacts, often focusing on the business and societal implications rather than the technical details. These publications offer timely reporting and commentary, keeping readers abreast of major developments and their potential disruptions across various industries.

While academic publications provide rigorous in-depth analysis, industry news sources offer timely updates on market trends, technological advancements, and corporate strategies. News outlets dedicated to the tech industry, such as *TechCrunch*, *VentureBeat*, and *The Verge*, regularly feature articles on AI developments, including new product launches, acquisitions, funding rounds, and significant breakthroughs. These sources provide a valuable window into the business aspects of AI, informing professionals about emerging opportunities and potential market shifts. However, it's crucial to approach these sources with a discerning eye, recognizing the potential for bias in reporting, especially regarding company-specific announcements. Cross-referencing information from multiple sources is advisable to obtain a more objective understanding.

Specialized industry publications offer even greater depth and focus. For example, publications tailored to the financial industry, such as *American Banker* and *The Wall Street Journal*, often include sections dedicated to fintech and AI's growing role in financial services. Similarly, publications in the healthcare industry often discuss the application of AI in diagnostics, treatment, and drug discovery. These niche publications provide invaluable insights into how AI is transforming specific industries, offering a granular view of the challenges and opportunities facing those working within those fields. To ensure accuracy, it's crucial to focus on reputable publications with a demonstrated track record of journalistic integrity.

Blogs and online publications also provide valuable insights into the world of AI, often offering more informal and accessible commentary on the latest developments. Blogs by leading AI researchers, industry experts, and influential figures often share their insights, experiences, and opinions. However, the diversity of perspectives and lack of formal peer-review process means a critical evaluation of sources is essential. Look for blogs that cite verifiable sources and avoid those making unsubstantiated claims or exhibiting clear bias. A good indicator of credibility is a blog maintained by a respected individual or institution with a demonstrable background in the field.

Staying informed also involves actively engaging with the ethical and societal implications of AI. Publications such as *The AI Ethics Journal* , *Data & Society Research Institute reports* , and various publications from organizations like the World Economic Forum offer insightful analysis on the social, ethical, and legal ramifications of AI deployment. These sources are vital for understanding the broader context of AI and its impact on society, ensuring that technological advancements align with ethical principles and societal well-being. Engaging with these perspectives broadens the understanding of potential challenges and encourages responsible innovation.

To effectively utilize these numerous sources, a strategic approach is essential. Prioritize reputable publications and cross-reference information from multiple sources to ensure accuracy and avoid biased reporting. Develop a personalized reading list, tailoring it to your specific interests and career goals. Employ RSS feeds or email alerts to receive timely updates from your chosen publications. Use tools like content aggregators to consolidate news from various sources and filter out less relevant information. A structured and disciplined approach to staying informed will not only enhance your understanding of the AI landscape but also equip you with the knowledge necessary to navigate the challenges and seize the opportunities of this transformative technology.

Regular engagement with these resources will keep you at the forefront of the AI revolution and empower you to build a resilient and thriving career in the face of constant technological change. Remember that continuous learning is crucial in this rapidly evolving field; a commitment to staying informed is a crucial investment in your professional future.

Chapter 10: Actionable Steps for Career Advancement

Step-by-Step Guide to Upskilling in AI-Related Skills

Embarking on a journey of upskilling in AI requires a structured and personalized approach. It's not simply about accumulating knowledge; it's about strategically developing skills that are both relevant to your career aspirations and in high demand within the evolving AI landscape. This section outlines a step-by-step process to guide you effectively.

Step 1: Self-Assessment and Goal Setting

Before diving into specific courses or resources, a thorough self-assessment is crucial. This involves honestly evaluating your existing skills and knowledge, identifying areas of strength and weakness, and clarifying your career goals. Ask yourself: What are my current technical skills? What industries am I interested in? What are my long-term career aspirations? What specific roles within the AI field am I targeting (e.g., data scientist, AI engineer, AI ethicist, AI product manager)?

This introspection should inform the creation of a detailed learning plan. Define specific, measurable, achievable, relevant, and time-bound (SMART) goals. For example, instead of a vague goal like "learn more about AI," a SMART goal might be: "Complete the 'Machine Learning A-Z' course on Udemy and build a portfolio of three machine learning projects by December 2024." This level of specificity provides direction and helps track progress. Consider creating a timeline that outlines milestones and deadlines, making the learning process more manageable and motivating.

Step 2: Choosing the Right Learning Path

The AI field is vast, encompassing numerous specializations. Your chosen learning path should directly align with your career objectives. If you aim for a data science role, focusing on statistical modeling, machine learning algorithms, and data visualization tools is essential. Aspiring AI engineers might prioritize programming languages like Python, experience with cloud computing platforms (AWS, Azure, GCP), and familiarity with deep learning frameworks such as TensorFlow or PyTorch. Those interested in AI ethics should explore courses on responsible AI, algorithmic bias, and the societal impact of AI technologies.

Several pathways exist to acquire these skills:

Formal Education: A master's degree or Ph.D. in computer science, data science, or a related field provides a strong foundational understanding of AI principles. However, this requires a significant time investment. Specialized bootcamps and certificate programs offer more focused, intensive training, often leading to quicker career transitions. These programs usually cover practical skills in high demand, and some offer career placement services. Carefully research program accreditation and curriculum to ensure alignment with your goals.

Online Courses and Platforms: Platforms like Coursera, edX, Udacity, and Udemy offer a wide variety of AI-related courses, catering to different skill levels and interests. These platforms often partner with top universities and companies, providing access to high-quality educational materials at a more affordable price than traditional education. Many courses offer flexible learning schedules, accommodating busy professionals. However, self-discipline is essential to complete these courses successfully.

Workshops and Conferences: Attending workshops and conferences offers valuable networking opportunities and exposure to the latest advancements in the field. These events frequently feature presentations by leading experts, providing insights into cutting-edge research and industry best practices. Participating in workshops provides hands-on experience, enhancing practical skills and allowing you to connect directly with peers and professionals.

Self-Learning and Resources: The sheer volume of online resources available facilitates self-learning. Utilizing online documentation, tutorials, and open-source projects allows for exploration at your own pace. Engaging with online communities, forums, and social media groups dedicated to AI expands your network and allows access to diverse perspectives and support. However, effective self-learning necessitates a disciplined approach and a structured learning plan.

Step 3: Building a Strong Portfolio

A portfolio showcasing practical projects is crucial for demonstrating your skills to potential employers. This portfolio serves as tangible evidence of your abilities, allowing recruiters and hiring managers to assess your expertise firsthand. Choose projects that are relevant to your career goals and highlight your acquired skills. Contribute to open-source projects, participate in Kaggle competitions (a platform hosting data science competitions), or create your own personal projects addressing real-world problems.

These projects should not merely replicate course exercises; they should demonstrate your ability to apply learned skills creatively and solve complex problems. Document your projects thoroughly, clearly explaining your approach, methodologies, and results.

Step 4: Networking and Mentorship

Building a professional network within the AI field is vital for career advancement. Attend industry events, join online communities, and connect with professionals on LinkedIn. Seek mentorship from experienced individuals in your chosen area of specialization. A mentor can offer guidance, advice, and support, accelerating your professional growth.

Step 5: Continuous Learning

The AI field is constantly evolving, so continuous learning is not merely beneficial; it's essential. Stay updated on the latest research, technological advancements, and industry trends. Regularly revisit your learning plan, adjusting it as necessary to remain relevant and competitive.

Examples of Upskilling Paths:

Let's consider three distinct career paths and illustrate how upskilling can be tailored to each:

Path 1: Transitioning from Marketing to AI-Driven Marketing:

Self-Assessment: Strong marketing background but limited technical skills. Goal: become a marketing analyst leveraging AI tools for better campaign optimization.

Learning Path: Focus on online courses covering data analysis, machine learning basics, and marketing analytics using tools like Google Analytics and marketing automation platforms. Develop projects using marketing datasets to predict customer behavior or optimize ad spending.

Portfolio: Include projects demonstrating A/B testing optimization using machine learning, customer segmentation using clustering algorithms, or predictive modeling for campaign performance.

Path 2: Shifting from Finance to Algorithmic Trading:

Self-Assessment: Strong financial knowledge; needs programming and quantitative skills. Goal: become a quantitative analyst involved in algorithmic trading.

Learning Path: Prioritize programming in Python, learning libraries like Pandas and NumPy for data manipulation, and mastering statistical modeling and time series analysis. Explore online courses and workshops dedicated to algorithmic trading strategies and risk management.

Portfolio: Create projects involving backtesting trading algorithms, developing automated trading strategies, and analyzing financial market data using machine learning techniques.

Path 3: Moving from Software Engineering to AI Engineering:

Self-Assessment: Strong programming skills; needs expertise in machine learning and deep learning. Goal: become an AI engineer specializing in natural language processing (NLP).

Learning Path: Focus on deep learning frameworks like TensorFlow and PyTorch, NLP techniques (sentiment analysis, named entity recognition), and cloud computing platforms. Engage in projects involving building chatbots, sentiment analysis tools, or machine translation systems.

Portfolio: Demonstrate projects involving building and deploying NLP models, using cloud services for model training and deployment, and showcasing proficiency in deep learning architectures.

This detailed step-by-step guide provides a framework. Your specific journey will be unique, reflecting your individual skills, interests, and career aspirations. Remember, upskilling is an ongoing process, demanding dedication and persistence. But the rewards—increased career opportunities, higher earning potential, and a future-proof career—make the effort worthwhile. Embrace the challenge, and the AI revolution will not only be navigated but mastered.

Strategies for Networking and Building Relationships in the AI Industry

Building a robust network within the rapidly evolving AI industry is paramount for career advancement. It's no longer sufficient to simply possess the technical skills; you must also cultivate relationships that open doors to opportunities, mentorship, and collaboration. This section outlines practical strategies to help you effectively network and build meaningful relationships within the AI community.

The AI industry is characterized by its dynamic nature, constantly shifting technological landscapes, and a community of passionate professionals. Effective networking in this context requires a proactive and multifaceted approach. Passive observation won't suffice; you need to actively engage, build relationships, and establish yourself as a valuable member of the community. This involves more than simply collecting business cards; it's about creating genuine connections that foster mutual respect, collaboration, and long-term professional growth.

Attending Industry Events: More Than Just a Badge

Conferences, workshops, meetups, and hackathons provide unparalleled opportunities to connect with industry leaders, peers, and potential collaborators. The key here is not merely to attend; it's to actively participate. Prepare in advance by reviewing the speaker list, identifying individuals whose work resonates with your interests, and formulating insightful questions to engage them in conversation. Don't just stand at the periphery; actively participate in Q&A sessions, contribute to discussions, and network during breaks and social events. Attend workshops and hands-on sessions to enhance your practical skills and showcase your abilities to others. These events often foster informal networking opportunities, making them ideal environments to build genuine connections.

After the event, follow up with the people you met, sharing your insights from the conference and expressing your interest in staying connected.

Beyond large-scale conferences, consider attending smaller, more specialized meetups and workshops focused on specific areas within AI, like natural language processing or computer vision. These niche events offer a more intimate setting for building deeper connections with individuals who share similar interests and expertise. They're less overwhelming than larger conferences and allow for more focused conversations. Look for online communities or professional groups associated with your field and check their event calendars regularly.

Leveraging Online Networking Platforms: Beyond LinkedIn Profiles

While LinkedIn remains a critical tool for professional networking, it's crucial to use it strategically. A well-crafted profile highlighting your skills, experience, and aspirations is essential. Don't just list your accomplishments; showcase them with quantifiable results whenever possible. Engage actively with relevant content, participate in group discussions, and share your own insightful articles or perspectives. This establishes you as a thought leader and increases your visibility within the AI community.

Go beyond a static LinkedIn profile. Explore other platforms frequented by AI professionals, such as GitHub, where you can showcase your coding skills through contributions to open-source projects or personal repositories. This provides potential employers and collaborators with concrete evidence of your abilities and working style. Also, consider engaging with online forums and discussion groups dedicated to AI-related topics. Contributing your expertise and participating in thoughtful discussions helps build your reputation and establishes you as a valuable resource within the community.

Joining Relevant Organizations: Expanding Your Network's Reach

Many professional organizations focus on artificial intelligence and related fields. Membership provides access to exclusive networking events, resources, and opportunities. These organizations often host conferences, workshops, and mentorship programs, furthering your professional development while expanding your network. Explore organizations like the Association for the Advancement of Artificial Intelligence (AAAI), the Institute of Electrical and Electronics Engineers (IEEE), or specialized groups focused on specific AI applications. Active participation, such as volunteering for committees or contributing to publications, increases your visibility and allows for deeper engagement with the organization's members.

Developing Relationships with Mentors and Key Players:

Seeking mentorship from experienced professionals in the AI field can be incredibly beneficial. A mentor can provide guidance, advice, and insights into navigating the industry's complexities. They can offer valuable perspectives on career progression, provide feedback on your projects, and introduce you to their network of contacts. Identifying potential mentors can be accomplished by attending industry events, engaging in online communities, or reaching out to individuals whose work you admire. Remember that building a mentorship relationship requires mutual respect and a commitment to ongoing communication and learning.

Networking doesn't end with initial connections. Cultivate relationships by staying in touch, sharing relevant articles or insights, offering assistance when appropriate, and celebrating others' successes. This fosters goodwill and strengthens professional bonds, making you a valued member of the AI community.

Networking Techniques: Strategies for Success

Beyond attending events and using online platforms, there are specific techniques to improve your networking effectiveness. The art of conversation is crucial. Practice engaging in meaningful conversations, asking open-ended questions that encourage others to share their experiences and perspectives. Listen actively, demonstrate genuine interest in what others have to say, and remember details about their work and aspirations. Following up after conversations is equally important. Send a personalized email reiterating your interest in connecting and highlighting something specific you discussed.

Maintaining Your Network: Long-Term Engagement

Networking isn't a one-time activity; it's an ongoing process.

Regularly update your online profiles to reflect your achievements and evolving skills. Continuously engage in online communities, share your knowledge and insights, and support others' work.

Nurture your relationships by staying in touch, celebrating milestones, and offering help whenever possible. This approach builds trust and strengthens the connections that can significantly impact your career trajectory. Regularly revisit your network, identifying new individuals to connect with and maintaining strong relationships with existing contacts. Your network is a valuable asset, and its growth and maintenance are crucial for long-term success in the dynamic AI landscape. Think of it as a living, breathing entity that requires ongoing attention and nurturing.

The AI industry is built on collaboration and knowledge sharing. By actively participating in the community, building genuine relationships, and leveraging available resources, you will not only advance your career but also contribute to the growth and innovation of the field. Remember, your network is your net worth, particularly in a rapidly evolving field like AI. Invest wisely in nurturing it, and the returns will be significant. The effort you dedicate to building and maintaining your professional network will directly influence your success in securing promotions, attracting high-paying opportunities, and achieving your career aspirations.

Crafting a Compelling Personal Brand to Attract Recruiters

In the rapidly evolving landscape of artificial intelligence, possessing technical skills is no longer enough to secure career advancement. Recruiters are increasingly seeking individuals who possess a strong personal brand—a unique and compelling narrative that showcases their skills, experience, and value proposition within the AI industry. Crafting such a brand is a strategic process that requires thoughtful planning and consistent effort. It's about more than just listing accomplishments; it's about telling a story that resonates with recruiters and positions you as a desirable candidate.

Building a strong online presence is paramount. While LinkedIn remains the cornerstone of professional networking, a well-crafted profile is merely the starting point. Your profile shouldn't be a static document; it should dynamically reflect your evolving expertise and accomplishments. Quantifiable results are key. Instead of simply stating "improved efficiency," quantify the improvement: "improved efficiency by 15% through the implementation of a new AI-powered system." This level of detail demonstrates a tangible impact and showcases your abilities to potential employers.

Beyond the numerical achievements, highlight the impact of your work. Recruiters want to understand the "why" behind your accomplishments. Did your project lead to increased revenue, cost savings, or improved customer satisfaction? Articulating this impact paints a more comprehensive picture of your contributions and makes your achievements more relatable and memorable.

Furthermore, incorporate keywords relevant to the AI industry, ensuring your profile appears in relevant search results. This subtle SEO optimization significantly improves your visibility to recruiters actively searching for candidates with your specific skill set.

Go beyond LinkedIn. Establish a presence on platforms frequented by AI professionals, such as GitHub. This platform is invaluable for showcasing technical expertise through contributions to open-source projects or personal repositories. Publicly accessible code demonstrates your coding skills, problem-solving abilities, and collaboration style.

Consider creating a personal website or blog where you can share your thoughts, insights, and expertise on AI-related topics. This demonstrates your passion for the field and establishes you as a thought leader, increasing your visibility among potential employers and collaborators. Consistency is key; regular updates to your online profiles and content creation keep your brand fresh and relevant.

Develop a unique value proposition. What makes you stand out from other candidates? What unique skills, experience, or perspectives do you bring to the table? Identifying your unique selling points (USPs) is crucial. Perhaps you possess a unique combination of technical expertise and business acumen, or maybe you have a proven track record of successfully implementing AI solutions in a specific industry. Clearly articulate these USPs in your online profiles, resume, and cover letters. Tailor your message to each job application, highlighting the aspects of your brand most relevant to the specific role and company. This personalized approach demonstrates your genuine interest and understanding of their needs.

Use storytelling to your advantage. Instead of simply listing your skills and experience, weave them into a compelling narrative. Recruiters are more likely to remember a story than a list of bullet points. Share anecdotes that illustrate your accomplishments, challenges overcome, and lessons learned. This approach makes your profile more engaging and memorable, helping you stand out from the competition. For example, instead of simply listing "experience with deep learning," describe a project where you applied deep learning techniques to solve a challenging problem, highlighting the positive impact of your solution.

Actively participate in online communities. Engage in relevant discussions, share your insights, and respond to questions. This demonstrates your expertise and establishes you as a valuable member of the AI community. Furthermore, networking with industry professionals helps expand your professional network, providing valuable connections and opportunities for collaboration.

Sharing insightful articles or blog posts on your social media platforms also increases your visibility and solidifies your position as a thought leader within the field.

Seek feedback on your personal brand. Ask trusted colleagues, mentors, and career advisors for feedback on your online presence, resume, and cover letters. They can offer valuable insights and help you identify areas for improvement. Consider having a professional resume review conducted by a service or mentor specifically focused on the technology sector; they often possess insights into current industry trends. Their objective assessment can help you fine-tune your brand and ensure it resonates with recruiters.

Continuously refine your personal brand. The AI industry is Constantly evolving, so your brand must adapt accordingly.

Continuously learn new skills, stay abreast of industry trends, and update your online profiles to reflect your progress. Your personal brand is a living document, constantly evolving to reflect your experiences and achievements. It's a dynamic representation of your career progression and commitment to the field.

By diligently crafting a compelling personal brand and showcasing your skills, experience, and unique value proposition, you can significantly improve your chances of attracting recruiters in the highly competitive AI industry. Remember, personal branding isn't a one-time task; it's an ongoing process that requires consistent effort and adaptation to remain relevant and competitive. The time and effort invested in cultivating a strong personal brand will yield significant returns in securing promotions, attracting high-paying opportunities, and achieving your career aspirations within the exciting and rapidly changing world of artificial intelligence. The investment in refining your personal brand is a direct investment in your professional future.

Beyond the digital landscape, consider attending industry events and conferences. These gatherings provide valuable opportunities to network with potential employers and colleagues. Prepare in advance by researching the attendees and identifying individuals whose work aligns with your interests. Actively participate in discussions, ask insightful questions, and follow up after the event with personalized emails. These interactions help establish relationships and solidify your presence within the industry.

Remember, your personal brand is your professional reputation. It's the perception others have of you and your capabilities. By proactively managing your brand, you can control how you're perceived, attracting the attention of recruiters and solidifying your position as a desirable candidate. It's a long-term strategy that requires continuous nurturing and refinement, but the rewards far outweigh the investment. It's a strategy that positions you for success not just in today's job market but also in the ever-shifting landscape of the future AI-driven economy. Your brand is your most valuable asset; invest in it wisely.

Consider creating a portfolio showcasing your best work. This is especially relevant for roles requiring practical skills and tangible results. A portfolio demonstrates your capabilities and allows potential employers to assess your work firsthand. Include a brief description of each project, highlighting the challenges, solutions, and outcomes. Choose projects that showcase your unique skills and highlight your achievements effectively. The visual representation of your accomplishments further strengthens your personal brand and creates a lasting impression on potential recruiters.

Develop a strong elevator pitch. This concise summary of your skills and experience is essential for networking events and interviews.

Practice delivering your pitch smoothly and confidently, highlighting your unique value proposition. Tailor the pitch to the specific audience and situation. A well-crafted elevator pitch can significantly impact your initial interactions and leave a lasting positive impression. It's a key tool for making those crucial first connections and seizing opportunities.

Finally, embrace continuous learning. The AI industry is dynamic, with new technologies and advancements emerging constantly. Stay updated with the latest trends and technologies through online courses, conferences, and industry publications. Demonstrate your commitment to lifelong learning in your brand, showcasing your adaptability and willingness to embrace new challenges. This continuous growth and adaptation are crucial to maintaining a strong and relevant personal brand within the rapidly changing landscape of the AI industry. It signals your readiness to take on future roles and challenges in this exciting and evolving domain.

Tactics for Successfully Negotiating a Higher Salary and Better Benefits

Negotiating a higher salary and comprehensive benefits in the competitive AI landscape requires a strategic approach that goes beyond simply stating your desired compensation. It involves thorough preparation, a confident presentation of your value, and a skillful understanding of negotiation dynamics. Successfully navigating this process can significantly impact your long-term financial well-being and career trajectory.

Begin by conducting thorough market research. Utilize online resources like Glassdoor, Salary.com, and Payscale to gain insights into salary ranges for similar roles in your geographic location and industry. Consider factors like your experience level, specific skills (e.g., proficiency in TensorFlow, PyTorch, or specific AI algorithms), education, and the company's size and financial standing. Don't solely rely on averages; analyze the data to identify the upper quartile – the range where top performers are compensated. This provides a realistic benchmark for your target salary. Supplement your online research with networking. Reach out to your professional contacts within the AI field, including recruiters, colleagues, and mentors, to gather information about current salary trends and compensation packages. These informal conversations often yield valuable insights not readily available online. The more data you collect, the stronger your negotiating position will be.

Once you have a solid understanding of market rates, it's crucial to articulate your value proposition effectively. This goes beyond listing your skills and experience; it requires showcasing the tangible impact you've made in previous roles. Quantify your achievements whenever possible. Instead of saying "improved efficiency," state "improved model accuracy by 12%, resulting in a 15% reduction in error rates and a $50,000 annual cost savings." Similarly, if you led a team, highlight the team's successes and your contribution to those achievements. Focus on results that demonstrate your contribution to the bottom line – increased revenue, cost reduction, improved customer satisfaction, or accelerated product development. These demonstrable results are far more persuasive than general statements of competence.

Preparing for the negotiation process is paramount. This involves not only researching salary ranges but also anticipating potential counter-offers and developing counterarguments. Think about the aspects of the job that are most important to you beyond salary. This might include benefits like comprehensive health insurance, professional development opportunities (conferences, training courses), flexible work arrangements (remote work options, flexible hours), stock options, or generous paid time off. Knowing your priorities allows you to strategically trade off certain aspects to achieve your overall compensation goals.

During the negotiation itself, project confidence and maintain a professional demeanor. Avoid immediately stating your desired salary; instead, let the employer make the first offer. This provides valuable information about their budget and expectations. Once they present their offer, carefully consider the total compensation package, not just the base salary. Analyze the benefits package, stock options (if applicable), and any bonuses or incentives offered.

If the initial offer is below your target range, express your appreciation for the offer while respectfully stating your expectation based on your research and experience. You can phrase this by saying something like, "I appreciate the offer, however, based on my research and my experience in delivering X, Y, and Z results, I was targeting a compensation package in the range of $X to $Y, reflecting the market value for a candidate with my skillset and achievements."

Be prepared to justify your requested compensation. Have specific examples ready to support your claims. Reference your quantifiable accomplishments and the value you bring to the organization.

Maintain a collaborative rather than confrontational approach.

Negotiation should be a dialogue, not a battle. Avoid making demands; instead, present your requests as preferences and be open to compromise. If the employer pushes back on your salary expectations, explore alternative areas of negotiation. Perhaps you can negotiate a higher starting bonus, accelerated promotion timelines, or additional professional development opportunities.

These concessions might help you reach a mutually agreeable outcome.

Remember that benefits are a significant component of the overall compensation package. Don't overlook the value of health insurance, retirement plans (401k matching, pension), paid time off, and other perks. These benefits often add considerable value to your overall compensation and contribute to your long-term financial security. During the negotiation, thoroughly examine each benefit component to ensure it aligns with your needs and expectations.

In the AI industry, continuous learning and skill development are essential for career advancement. Therefore, actively seek opportunities for professional development, such as conferences, workshops, or online courses. During negotiations, emphasize your commitment to lifelong learning and inquire about the company's support for professional development initiatives. This demonstrates your proactive approach to maintaining your skills and your dedication to staying ahead of the curve in the rapidly evolving AI field. This eagerness to learn and adapt is a highly valued trait in the AI industry, making you a more attractive and valuable asset to the company.

Negotiating a higher salary and comprehensive benefits requires practice and confidence. Don't be discouraged if the process feels challenging. With thorough preparation, a clear understanding of your value, and a strategic negotiation approach, you can significantly improve your chances of securing the compensation package you deserve in this dynamic and highly competitive field.

By mastering these negotiation tactics, you can not only secure a higher salary but also establish a strong foundation for continued career growth and success in the AI industry. Remember that your skills and experience are valuable assets, and it is crucial to advocate for your worth. This process strengthens your professional standing and positions you for continued success in your AI career journey. The investment you make in learning these skills will pay off handsomely over the course of your career.

Long Term Career Planning in the Age of AI

The rapid advancements in artificial intelligence are reshaping the professional landscape at an unprecedented pace. While the previous section focused on immediate salary negotiations, securing your long-term career success requires a more holistic and forward-thinking approach. This demands a proactive and adaptable strategy that goes beyond reacting to immediate changes and instead anticipates and shapes your future career trajectory within this evolving technological environment.

The cornerstone of successful long-term career planning in the age of AI is continuous learning. This isn't simply about attending the occasional workshop; it's a commitment to lifelong learning, constantly updating your skillset and knowledge base to stay ahead of the technological curve. The AI field is characterized by rapid innovation, with new algorithms, tools, and applications emerging consistently. Failing to adapt to these changes will quickly render your skills obsolete, leaving you vulnerable in the job market.

To effectively engage in continuous learning, you must become a proactive and discerning learner. Don't passively wait for training opportunities to arise; actively seek them out. This involves regularly exploring online courses offered by platforms like Coursera, edX, Udacity, and fast.ai. These platforms offer a wide range of courses covering various aspects of AI, from fundamental concepts to advanced techniques. Look for courses focusing on areas relevant to your field and career goals, enabling you to specialize in high-demand skills within AI.

Beyond online courses, consider attending industry conferences and workshops. These events provide invaluable networking opportunities, allowing you to connect with leading experts, learn about the latest advancements, and gain insights into future trends.

Participating in these events helps you stay abreast of the latest developments and exposes you to diverse perspectives and approaches within the field. Networking with peers and industry leaders opens doors to potential collaborations, mentorship, and job opportunities.

Furthermore, engaging in self-directed learning is crucial. Explore online resources, research papers, and industry publications to expand your understanding of AI and its applications. Develop a habit of reading industry blogs, following influential figures on social media, and actively participating in online forums and communities related to AI. This continuous engagement with the field helps you stay current with emerging technologies and industry trends, giving you an edge in your career advancement.

Beyond technical skills, the ability to adapt is paramount in the age of AI. Technological advancements will undoubtedly lead to changes in job descriptions and the required skills. Cultivating adaptability requires a growth mindset, embracing new challenges, and viewing changes as opportunities for growth rather than threats to your career security. This involves willingly embracing new technologies, learning new methods, and being open to reskilling or upskilling as needed.

A crucial component of adaptability is embracing AI tools to augment your productivity and efficiency. Rather than viewing AI as a threat, recognize its potential to enhance your capabilities. Learn how to effectively utilize AI-powered tools relevant to your profession, mastering them to improve your workflow and output. This demonstrates your willingness to adopt new technologies and improve your efficiency, showcasing your adaptability and readiness to work alongside AI.

Proactive career transitions are another critical element of long-term planning. The rapid evolution of the AI landscape means that staying in the same role for an extended period might not be the most strategic path for long-term career success. Regularly assess your skills, the market demands, and your career aspirations. Be open to exploring new opportunities and making strategic transitions to align your career with the evolving technological demands.

This proactive approach requires careful planning and execution. Assess your current skill set and identify areas where upskilling or reskilling is necessary to make yourself a competitive candidate in a future role. Network with individuals in the desired field to gain insights into the necessary qualifications and expectations. Develop a targeted job search strategy that focuses on opportunities aligned with your updated skill set and career goals. This might include tailoring your resume and cover letter to highlight the relevant skills, preparing for interviews by practicing your responses to common questions, and actively reaching out to potential employers through networking and online applications.

Developing a long-term vision for your career is essential. This requires self-reflection on your goals, aspirations, and values. Consider your short-term, mid-term, and long-term career objectives, identifying milestones and strategies to help you achieve them. This long-term perspective will guide your decisions regarding learning opportunities, career transitions, and skill development. It provides a framework for evaluating opportunities and ensuring your actions are aligned with your overall career aspirations.

Regularly reviewing and updating your long-term career plan is also crucial. The technological landscape changes rapidly, so your plan needs to evolve alongside it. Periodically review your progress, considering any unforeseen challenges or opportunities that might require adjustments to your plan. Seek feedback from mentors, colleagues, and industry professionals to gain external perspectives and ensure your plan remains aligned with the evolving market demands and your evolving aspirations.

Networking plays a critical role in navigating the complexities of long-term career planning. Building and maintaining strong professional relationships can open doors to new opportunities and provide invaluable support during transitions. Engage actively in your professional network, attending industry events, participating in online communities, and proactively seeking out mentors and advisors. This network can provide crucial insights, guidance, and support throughout your career journey.

In conclusion, long-term career planning in the age of AI necessitates a proactive, adaptive, and future-oriented approach. By embracing continuous learning, actively navigating career transitions, and developing a well-defined long-term vision, you can not only survive but thrive in this rapidly changing environment.

The proactive steps outlined above provide a framework for securing your long-term career success in the exciting and evolving world of AI. Remember, your career journey is a continuous evolution, requiring constant adaptation and strategic planning to secure a fulfilling and successful future. The commitment to lifelong learning and adaptability will be the defining factors in determining your success in the age of AI.

Chapter 11: Overcoming Challenges and Obstacles

Addressing Fear and Anxiety Around AI-Driven Job Displacement

The previous sections have focused on proactive strategies for navigating the evolving job market shaped by AI. However, the rapid pace of technological change can understandably trigger fear and anxiety, particularly concerning job security. It's crucial to acknowledge these feelings as legitimate responses to a significant shift in the professional landscape. Ignoring or suppressing these anxieties won't make them disappear; instead, it's essential to develop healthy coping mechanisms and cultivate a resilient mindset.

One of the most effective strategies for managing anxiety surrounding AI-driven job displacement is to acknowledge and validate your feelings. Allow yourself to experience the fear, sadness, or uncertainty without judgment. Suppressing these emotions only intensifies them. Journaling can be a powerful tool for processing these feelings, providing a safe space to articulate your anxieties and explore your thoughts and concerns. Regularly writing down your worries can help you gain perspective, identify patterns in your thinking, and develop strategies for managing your emotions more effectively.

Beyond journaling, engaging in self-care practices is paramount.

Stress management techniques like mindfulness meditation, deep breathing exercises, and yoga can significantly reduce anxiety levels. These practices help calm your nervous system, promote relaxation, and improve your overall well-being. Even short periods of mindfulness meditation can have a profoundly positive impact on your mental state, helping you approach challenges with greater clarity and composure. Finding activities that you find calming and enjoyable, such as spending time in nature, listening to music, or engaging in hobbies, is also crucial for managing stress and maintaining emotional balance during periods of uncertainty.

It's also vital to reframe your thinking. Instead of focusing solely on the potential threats posed by AI, actively seek out opportunities. Consider how AI can augment your skills and enhance your productivity rather than replace your role entirely. Many jobs will not be entirely automated but will instead evolve to incorporate AI tools. By embracing AI and learning to utilize these technologies effectively, you can position yourself as a valuable asset in this changing environment. Focus on developing skills that are uniquely human and difficult to automate, such as critical thinking, creativity, emotional intelligence, complex problem-solving, and interpersonal communication. These skills are essential in navigating the complexities of the modern workplace and will become increasingly valuable in an AI-driven economy.

Building a strong support network is also critical during periods of uncertainty. Surround yourself with positive and supportive individuals who can provide encouragement and guidance. Talking to friends, family, mentors, or career counselors can help you process your anxieties, gain different perspectives, and develop strategies for overcoming challenges. Consider joining professional organizations or online communities related to your field to connect with others who share similar concerns and experiences. These networks offer opportunities for peer support, mentorship, and collaboration, providing a sense of community and shared purpose.

Sharing your experiences and anxieties can help you feel less isolated and more empowered to face the challenges ahead.

Seeking professional help is a sign of strength, not weakness. If your anxiety is overwhelming or interfering with your daily life, don't hesitate to seek support from a mental health professional.

Therapists and counselors can provide evidence-based strategies for managing anxiety, such as cognitive behavioral therapy (CBT) or other coping techniques. CBT can help you identify and challenge negative thought patterns that contribute to anxiety, replacing them with more realistic and positive perspectives. This approach helps you develop a more resilient mindset, enabling you to better handle stress and uncertainty. Don't underestimate the value of professional support; it can make a significant difference in navigating the challenges of a changing job market.

Focusing on continuous learning and skill development is also a powerful antidote to anxiety. By actively pursuing new knowledge and skills, you're taking control of your career trajectory, demonstrating proactivity, and building your confidence. This focus shifts your attention from the potential threats of AI to the opportunities for growth and advancement. When you're actively engaged in learning, you're less likely to dwell on anxieties about the future. The sense of accomplishment and progress achieved through continuous learning boosts self-esteem and confidence, making you better equipped to handle uncertainty.

Developing a proactive career plan is essential for mitigating anxiety. By anticipating future job market trends, identifying potential skill gaps, and developing strategies for acquiring new skills, you create a sense of control and direction. This plan should encompass short-term, mid-term, and long-term goals, providing a roadmap for your career progression. Having a clear plan allows you to focus your efforts, minimizing feelings of helplessness and uncertainty. Regularly reviewing and updating your plan is essential, adapting to changing market conditions and emerging opportunities. This iterative process reinforces a sense of control and reduces the likelihood of being caught off guard by unexpected changes.

Moreover, it's important to cultivate a growth mindset. A growth mindset focuses on the potential for learning and improvement, recognizing that skills and abilities can be developed over time. This contrasts with a fixed mindset, which views abilities as innate and unchanging. Adopting a growth mindset allows you to embrace challenges, view setbacks as learning opportunities, and persist in the face of difficulties. This resilience is crucial in navigating the unpredictable nature of the job market, particularly in the age of AI.

By focusing on continuous learning and development, you are constantly expanding your capabilities, making you more adaptable and resilient to change.

Remember that the fear of job displacement is a shared experience. Many professionals are grappling with similar anxieties. Connecting with others who share your concerns can provide validation, support, and a sense of community. Online forums, professional organizations, and networking events offer opportunities to connect with peers, share experiences, and exchange strategies for coping with these anxieties. This shared experience can significantly reduce feelings of isolation and empower you to approach the challenges ahead with greater confidence and resilience.

Finally, consider volunteering or engaging in pro bono work. This allows you to explore new fields, develop new skills, and expand your network while also contributing positively to society. The experience can be incredibly rewarding, enhancing your confidence and self-esteem. Additionally, it provides opportunities to learn new technologies and build valuable experience in different settings, making you a more adaptable and desirable candidate for future employment. These actions can also demonstrate your versatility and adaptability to prospective employers.

In conclusion, addressing the fear and anxiety surrounding AI-driven job displacement requires a multi-faceted approach. By integrating stress management techniques, positive self-talk, proactive career planning, continuous learning, building support networks, seeking professional help when needed, and embracing a growth mindset, you can not only manage your anxieties but also leverage the opportunities presented by the AI revolution. The journey may be challenging, but by embracing these strategies, you can navigate this transformative period and position yourself for success in the future. Remember that adaptability, resilience, and a commitment to lifelong learning will be your most valuable assets in this evolving landscape.

Managing Resistance to Change in the Workplace

The previous sections have focused on the individual's journey through the AI revolution, equipping you with the tools and mindset to navigate this evolving landscape. However, the successful integration of AI into the workplace isn't solely dependent on individual adaptation; it hinges on effective organizational change management. The reality is that introducing AI into established workflows often meets resistance. This resistance isn't necessarily rooted in malice or ignorance; it frequently stems from valid concerns about job security, the perceived complexity of new technologies, and the disruption of established routines.

Effectively managing this resistance is critical to a smooth and successful AI implementation, ensuring both productivity gains and employee well-being.

One of the primary challenges is effective communication. Too often, the introduction of AI is framed solely in terms of cost savings and increased efficiency, leaving employees feeling like mere cogs in a machine, expendable in the face of technological advancements. This approach inevitably breeds resentment and resistance. A more effective strategy involves transparent and empathetic communication, emphasizing the collaborative nature of AI integration. Instead of portraying AI as a replacement for human workers, position it as a tool to augment human capabilities, freeing employees from repetitive tasks and allowing them to focus on higher-value work requiring creativity, critical thinking, and complex problem-solving. This reframing requires a shift in narrative from a "cost-cutting" measure to an "employee empowerment" strategy.

This shift necessitates a proactive approach to communication. Begin early, long before the AI implementation commences. Regular town hall meetings, departmental briefings, and individual consultations should be utilized to keep employees informed throughout the process. Provide clear, concise information about the purpose of AI integration, its potential benefits for the organization and individual employees, and the timeline for implementation. Addressing employees' concerns directly, openly, and honestly is crucial. Open forums where employees can voice their anxieties, ask questions, and receive direct answers from leadership demonstrate transparency and create a space for dialogue. This proactive approach helps mitigate misunderstandings and prevents rumors from spreading, fostering a more collaborative and trusting environment.

Furthermore, effective communication requires tailored messages.

Different departments, roles, and individuals will have different concerns and levels of technological literacy. Therefore, communication strategies must be tailored to specific audiences, using language and examples that resonate with each group. For example, a highly technical explanation of machine learning algorithms would be inappropriate for a non-technical department. Conversely, a simplistic overview might not satisfy highly technical employees who require a deeper understanding of the technology. Employing diverse communication channels – videos, infographics, presentations, written materials – can also enhance understanding and engagement.

Beyond communication, addressing employee concerns directly is paramount. Concerns about job displacement are often at the forefront, and ignoring or dismissing these anxieties is counterproductive. Instead, organizations should proactively address these concerns through retraining programs, skill development initiatives, and career transition support. Offering opportunities for employees to upskill or reskill, ensuring they can adapt to the changing job landscape, shows a commitment to their professional development and demonstrates that they are valued assets. This proactive approach fosters a sense of security and empowers employees to embrace the changes rather than resist them.

Investing in comprehensive training programs is essential.

Employees may be apprehensive about working with new technologies, and inadequate training only exacerbates these fears.

The training should be practical, hands-on, and tailored to individual needs and skill levels. Offering multiple training formats– online courses, workshops, mentorship opportunities – can cater to different learning styles and preferences. Furthermore, ongoing support and access to technical experts should be provided to address any challenges employees may encounter post-training. This ongoing support reinforces the message that the organization is committed to their success in the new AI-driven environment.

Fostering a culture of collaboration and adaptability is also essential. AI integration isn't just about implementing new technologies; it's about changing the way work gets done. This transformation requires a shift in organizational culture, embracing adaptability, continuous learning, and collaboration. One way to achieve this is through cross-functional teams, which bring together individuals with diverse skillsets and perspectives. These teams can collaborate to solve problems, develop new processes, and integrate AI effectively. This not only enhances problem-solving but also promotes teamwork and a sense of shared responsibility for the successful AI implementation.

Embracing a culture of continuous learning is vital. The rapid pace of technological change requires a commitment to lifelong learning, both for individual employees and the organization as a whole.

Establishing a learning culture that encourages experimentation, embraces failure as a learning opportunity, and provides resources for continuous professional development is crucial for success in the age of AI. This may involve internal training programs, external courses, conferences, and mentorship opportunities, fostering a mindset of continuous improvement and adaptability.

Moreover, recognizing and rewarding employees who embrace change and contribute positively to AI implementation is critical.

Acknowledging their efforts and showcasing successes through internal communication channels helps reinforce positive behaviors and builds a sense of collective accomplishment. This recognition can take many forms, including bonuses, promotions, public acknowledgement, and opportunities for leadership roles in AI-related projects. Rewarding adaptability and collaboration incentivizes further adoption and contributes to a more positive and productive work environment.

Finally, recognizing the emotional toll of change is essential. The introduction of AI can be unsettling for employees, even with the best communication and training. Providing access to employee assistance programs (EAPs), stress management workshops, and mental health resources can help employees cope with anxieties and concerns. This demonstrates a commitment to employee well-being, fostering a supportive and compassionate work environment. The focus should be on supporting employees through this transition, ensuring a humane and empathetic approach to change management.

In conclusion, managing resistance to change in an AI-driven transformation requires a comprehensive strategy that goes beyond simply introducing new technology. It demands proactive communication, tailored training, a supportive work environment, and a genuine commitment to employee well-being. By focusing on empathy, transparency, and continuous support, organizations can successfully navigate the challenges of AI integration, fostering a productive and collaborative workforce capable of thriving in the new era of work. Ignoring resistance only serves to amplify it; actively managing it through these strategies is key to reaping the benefits of AI implementation while preserving the valuable human element that underpins organizational success.

Navigating Ethical Dilemmas in the Age of AI

The seamless integration of AI into the workplace, while promising increased efficiency and productivity, also presents a complex tapestry of ethical dilemmas. These dilemmas aren't merely theoretical exercises; they are real-world challenges that demand careful consideration and proactive solutions. Failing to address these ethical concerns can lead to significant reputational damage, legal repercussions, and a fractured workforce. This section provides a framework for understanding and navigating these complexities, offering practical strategies for ethical decision-making in the age of AI.

One of the most prevalent ethical dilemmas centers around **algorithmic bias** . AI systems are trained on data, and if that data reflects existing societal biases—be it racial, gender, or socioeconomic—the AI system will perpetuate and even amplify those biases. For example, a recruiting AI trained on historical hiring data from a company with a predominantly male workforce might inadvertently discriminate against female applicants, even if gender is not explicitly included as a selection criterion. The AI might identify seemingly neutral factors, such as preferred extracurricular activities or even word choice in resumes, that correlate with past hiring decisions and ultimately disadvantage women.

This is a critical ethical challenge, as it not only perpetuates inequality but also undermines the principles of fairness and equal opportunity. Addressing this requires careful auditing of training data, ensuring diversity and representativeness, and employing techniques to mitigate bias in the algorithm itself. This includes the use of fairness-aware algorithms and rigorous testing for bias throughout the AI lifecycle. Furthermore, human oversight remains crucial, enabling human intervention to correct for biases that may escape detection.

Another significant ethical dilemma arises from **data privacy and security** . AI systems often rely on vast amounts of data, including sensitive personal information. The collection, storage, and use of this data must adhere to strict ethical and legal guidelines, ensuring compliance with regulations like GDPR and CCPA. A failure to protect employee data can lead to significant legal penalties, reputational damage, and a loss of employee trust. Ethical data handling practices require organizations to be transparent about what data they collect, how they use it, and the measures they take to protect it. This includes obtaining informed consent from employees, implementing robust security protocols, and regularly auditing data practices to ensure compliance with relevant regulations and ethical standards. Anonymization and data minimization techniques can also be employed to reduce the risk of data breaches and protect employee privacy.

The question of **job displacement and its ethical implications** is a persistent concern. While AI can automate many tasks, it also has the potential to create new jobs and enhance existing ones.

However, the transition can be disruptive, and organizations have an ethical responsibility to mitigate the negative impact on their workforce. This requires proactive measures such as retraining programs, reskilling initiatives, and career transition support.

Organizations must actively invest in their employees' future, ensuring they have the skills needed to thrive in the evolving job market.

Moreover, open and honest communication about the potential impact of AI on jobs is crucial to fostering trust and addressing employee anxieties. Ethical considerations here extend beyond mere compliance; they necessitate a commitment to social responsibility and a focus on mitigating the human cost of technological advancement. This might involve partnering with educational institutions or offering stipends for employees pursuing new certifications.

The use of AI in **surveillance and monitoring** also raises significant ethical questions. While AI can improve security and productivity, it can also be used to intrude on employee privacy. For instance, AI-powered monitoring systems that track employee keystrokes, screen activity, or even facial expressions can create a sense of unease and distrust, fostering a culture of surveillance rather than collaboration. The ethical use of AI in this context necessitates establishing clear guidelines, ensuring transparency with employees about the scope of monitoring, and prioritizing the protection of their privacy. A balance needs to be struck between security needs and employee rights. This might involve using AI to detect security threats but avoiding the continuous monitoring of individual work behaviors.

Furthermore, the issue of **algorithmic accountability** is paramount. When an AI system makes a decision that has significant consequences— such as denying a loan application or misdiagnosing a patient— determining who is responsible for that decision can be complex. Establishing clear lines of accountability for the outcomes of AI systems is crucial. This means establishing robust processes for oversight, auditing, and redress, ensuring there are mechanisms in place for resolving disputes and holding individuals or organizations accountable for any unethical or harmful outcomes. This requires clear guidelines about human intervention points, and well-defined procedures for investigating and addressing errors.

The ethical use of AI also depends on **ensuring fairness and transparency**. Decisions made by AI systems should be explainable and justifiable. "Black box" AI systems, whose decision-making processes are opaque, are ethically problematic because they make it impossible to identify and rectify biases or errors. Strive for transparency in algorithmic design and decision-making, allowing for the review and scrutiny of the AI's processes. This promotes accountability and allows for the identification and correction of biases.

Navigating these ethical dilemmas requires a multi-pronged approach. First, **establish a clear code of ethics** specifically addressing the use of AI in the workplace. This code should be developed collaboratively, involving employees, management, and relevant stakeholders. Second, **invest in training and education** to raise awareness of ethical issues related to AI and best practices.

Third, **establish mechanisms for reporting and addressing ethical concerns**. This might involve an ethics committee or a dedicated reporting line. Finally, **engage in ongoing dialogue and review**. The field of AI is constantly evolving, and ethical guidelines must adapt accordingly. Regular review and updates are critical to maintaining alignment with evolving ethical standards and technological advances.

In conclusion, the successful and ethical integration of AI into the workplace is not solely about technological advancements; it is fundamentally about upholding ethical principles and safeguarding human values. By proactively addressing these ethical dilemmas through transparent communication, robust policies, and a commitment to accountability, organizations can harness the power of AI while fostering a just, equitable, and thriving work environment. This requires a continuous commitment to ethical reflection and adaptation, ensuring that AI serves humanity, rather than the other way around. The ethical considerations presented here are not static; they require ongoing attention and a willingness to adapt as AI technologies continue to evolve and their applications expand. The future of work depends on not only embracing AI but also ensuring its ethical implementation.

Dealing with Job Loss Due to Automation

The previous section explored the ethical complexities inherent in integrating AI into the workplace. However, the reality of AI's rapid advancement is that job displacement, while potentially creating new opportunities, also causes significant disruption for individuals and families. This section focuses on providing support and practical strategies for navigating the emotional and professional challenges of job loss due to automation. Facing unemployment, especially when it stems from technological change, can be a deeply unsettling experience. It's crucial to acknowledge the emotional toll this can take, allowing yourself time to process the feelings of loss, frustration, and uncertainty that are completely natural and valid.

Denial, anger, bargaining, depression, and acceptance—these stages of grief aren't just for bereavement; they're a common framework for understanding the emotional journey following job loss. Allow yourself to feel these emotions without judgment. Don't minimize your experience or try to rush through the process. Seeking support during this time is paramount. Lean on your support network—family, friends, mentors—for emotional sustenance. They can provide a listening ear, a shoulder to cry on, and practical assistance as you navigate this transition.

Consider professional support as well. Therapists specializing in career transitions can provide guidance and coping mechanisms to navigate the emotional challenges of unemployment. They can help you identify and address negative thought patterns, build resilience, and develop strategies for managing stress and anxiety. Group therapy or support groups for individuals facing job displacement can also offer a sense of community and shared experience, reducing feelings of isolation. Many online forums and communities are dedicated to providing mutual support in these situations.

Once you've allowed yourself time to process the emotional impact, it's time to shift your focus to developing a proactive job search strategy. This requires a realistic assessment of your skills and experience, coupled with a deep understanding of the evolving job market. Start by identifying your transferable skills—those abilities that are applicable across various industries and roles. These skills are often overlooked during initial moments of panic and loss, so careful reflection is key.

Many skills honed in previous roles may be highly valuable in the AI-driven economy. For instance, critical thinking, problem-solving, creativity, and emotional intelligence are skills that AI currently struggles to replicate effectively. Highlight these transferable skills prominently in your resume and cover letter, demonstrating how they align with the requirements of new positions. Consider taking online courses or workshops to update your skills and gain familiarity with new technologies. Many organizations offer free or subsidized training programs to help displaced workers re-skill or upskill, including resources that are government-funded.

Networking is a crucial aspect of any successful job search, but it is particularly essential in the context of AI-driven job displacement.

Reach out to your former colleagues, supervisors, and industry contacts. Inform them about your situation and let them know you're open to exploring new opportunities. Attend industry events and conferences to meet new people and learn about emerging trends. Leverage LinkedIn and other professional networking platforms to connect with potential employers and recruiters.

Tailor your resume and cover letter to each specific job application, highlighting the skills and experiences that are most relevant to the position. Generic applications are less likely to succeed, especially in a competitive job market. Demonstrate your understanding of AI and its implications for the industry you're targeting. Consider adding a section to your resume that showcases any experience or training you have with AI tools or technologies, even if it's from personal projects or online courses. This indicates a proactive approach to adapting to the changing job market.

Exploring new career paths may be necessary, especially if your previous role was highly susceptible to automation. Don't limit your search to jobs that are similar to your previous role. Instead, broaden your horizons and consider opportunities in fields that are less susceptible to automation or that require uniquely human skills. Careers in healthcare, education, social work, and the creative arts often rely on empathy, interpersonal skills, and critical thinking that AI currently cannot effectively replicate.

The growth of AI has also created new roles and industries.

Consider pursuing careers related to AI development, data science, AI ethics, or AI training and implementation. Many of these roles require specialized skills, but there are numerous training programs and boot camps available to help you acquire the necessary qualifications. Remember, acquiring new skills is an investment in your future. It requires time, dedication, and potentially some financial resources, but it's an investment that will pay off in the long run.

Financial planning is a crucial element of managing job loss.

Review your budget, identify areas where you can cut expenses, and explore potential sources of financial assistance. Unemployment benefits, severance packages, and other government assistance programs can provide temporary financial support. Consider consulting with a financial advisor to create a budget that aligns with your circumstances and to explore options for managing debt and saving for the future.

Don't underestimate the importance of maintaining a healthy lifestyle during this challenging period. Prioritize physical activity, mindfulness practices, and sufficient sleep to manage stress and maintain your overall well-being. Engage in activities you enjoy to maintain a sense of purpose and prevent burnout. Taking care of your physical and mental health is critical to successfully navigating job loss and embarking on a new career path.

Government agencies and non-profit organizations offer various resources to help individuals facing job displacement. Many offer career counseling, job search assistance, and training programs.

Look into local community colleges or vocational schools that provide retraining opportunities and access to online resources, often free or at a reduced cost. These resources aren't always well advertised, so proactive research is vital. Don't hesitate to seek assistance from these organizations; they can provide valuable support and guidance as you navigate this transition.

The transition from job loss to a new career path may be long and challenging, but it's also an opportunity for growth and personal development. Embrace the challenge, utilize the resources available, and remember that you are not alone in this experience. Many people have successfully navigated job loss due to automation and gone on to build fulfilling and successful careers. By adopting a proactive mindset, developing a strong job search strategy, and seeking appropriate support, you can overcome this obstacle and secure a brighter future in the age of AI. The future of work is evolving, and your ability to adapt and acquire new skills will be your greatest asset. Your resilience, adaptability, and transferable skills will be your keys to future success. This transition is a journey, not a race, and patience and self-compassion will be essential allies in your path to re-employment and career fulfillment.

Building Resilience and Adaptability in the Face of Uncertainty

The previous section detailed the practical steps to navigate job displacement caused by AI-driven automation. However, the evolving nature of the workplace requires more than just reactive responses; it demands proactive strategies for building resilience and adaptability. The uncertainty inherent in this rapidly changing landscape can be daunting, but by cultivating a growth mindset and embracing continuous learning, individuals can not only survive but thrive in the age of AI.

The foundation of resilience in the face of technological disruption lies in embracing a growth mindset. This isn't simply about positive thinking; it's about fundamentally shifting your perspective on challenges. Instead of viewing job displacement as a failure, consider it a pivotal moment, an opportunity to re-evaluate your skills, explore new passions, and embark on a potentially more fulfilling career path. This perspective shift requires actively challenging negative self-talk and replacing it with constructive self-affirmations. When faced with setbacks, focus on the lessons learned rather than dwelling on the disappointments.

Continuous learning is the lifeblood of adaptability in a rapidly evolving job market. The skills that are in demand today may be obsolete tomorrow. Therefore, a commitment to lifelong learning is no longer a desirable trait; it's a necessity. This doesn't necessarily mean pursuing a formal degree every few years. Instead, it involves actively seeking out opportunities to enhance existing skills and acquire new ones. Online courses, workshops, webinars, and industry conferences provide readily accessible avenues for professional development. Many platforms offer free or affordable resources, making continuous learning accessible to everyone, regardless of their financial situation.

Focusing on transferable skills is crucial in this context. These are the skills that are applicable across various roles and industries, making them less susceptible to automation. Critical thinking, problem-solving, communication, emotional intelligence, and creativity are examples of transferable skills that are highly valued in the AI-driven economy. Identify your transferable skills and actively highlight them in your resume and cover letter, demonstrating how they align with the requirements of the jobs you're applying for. Consider documenting your skills through projects, portfolios or volunteer work, demonstrating real-world application of these skills.

Proactive career planning is another critical component of building resilience. Instead of waiting for job displacement to force a career change, proactively evaluate your current career trajectory and identify potential areas of vulnerability to automation. Research emerging trends in your industry and explore potential career paths that are less susceptible to automation or that leverage uniquely human skills. Develop a long-term career plan that incorporates continuous learning, skill development, and adaptability. Regularly review and update this plan to reflect the evolving job market and your own evolving interests and goals. This proactive approach allows for a more controlled and less stressful transition should job displacement occur.

Networking plays a vital role in navigating uncertainty. Building and maintaining strong professional relationships can provide invaluable support and opportunities during times of transition. Attend industry events, join professional organizations, and actively engage on professional networking platforms like LinkedIn.

Regularly connect with your network, keeping them informed about your career goals and seeking their advice and support. A strong network can provide insights into emerging job opportunities, offer mentorship, and provide emotional support during challenging times. The value of strong networking should not be underestimated, particularly when adapting to an evolving job market.

Building resilience also involves cultivating a support system.

Having a network of family, friends, and mentors who provide emotional support and practical advice can be invaluable during times of uncertainty. Don't hesitate to seek professional help if needed. Career counselors and therapists can provide guidance and support in navigating career transitions and managing stress. Remember, seeking help is a sign of strength, not weakness.

Support groups can offer valuable insight and camaraderie, helping individuals feel less alone in their experiences.

Mastering the art of effective communication is critical in the AI age. While AI can automate many tasks, it cannot replicate the nuance and complexity of human communication. Therefore, honing your communication skills – both written and verbal – is crucial for success in virtually any field. Practice your ability to articulate complex ideas clearly and concisely, actively listening to others, and effectively conveying both technical and emotional information.

Developing emotional intelligence is another key skill that can enhance resilience and adaptability. Emotional intelligence encompasses self-awareness, self-regulation, empathy, and social skills. These skills enable individuals to navigate complex interpersonal dynamics, build strong relationships, and effectively manage stress and conflict. Emotional intelligence can be developed through self-reflection, mindfulness practices, and active listening.

These are skills that are increasingly valuable in the workplace, where human interaction and collaboration remain essential, even in increasingly automated environments.

Finally, remember that setbacks are inevitable, and that learning from mistakes is crucial to navigating any career path, especially one as dynamic as the AI-driven landscape. View every challenge as an opportunity for growth, focusing on continuous learning and self-improvement. By embracing uncertainty, cultivating resilience, and developing a proactive approach to career planning, individuals can not only weather the storm of technological disruption, but also harness the opportunities it presents to create a more fulfilling and successful career. The future of work is changing, but with the right mindset and strategies, individuals can adapt and thrive in this new reality. This adaptation requires continuous effort and attention, but the rewards of mastering these skills will be valuable throughout your entire career.

Chapter 12: The Role of Education and Training

The Importance of STEM Education in the Age of AI

The previous sections focused on individual strategies for navigating the AI revolution in the workplace. However, individual preparedness is only one piece of the puzzle. The broader societal response, particularly in education, will significantly determine the success and equitable distribution of opportunities in this new era.

This section emphasizes the crucial role of STEM (Science, Technology, Engineering, and Mathematics) education in mitigating the potential negative impacts of AI and maximizing its potential benefits. Without a robust STEM foundation, societies risk exacerbating existing inequalities and failing to capitalize on the innovative potential of AI.

The transformative power of AI extends far beyond the automation of routine tasks. It's reshaping entire industries, creating new roles, and requiring a fundamentally different skill set from the workforce. While some jobs are indeed at risk of automation, the reality is more nuanced than a simple displacement narrative. The AI revolution creates a far greater number of new roles demanding specialized skills and knowledge, many of which lie within the STEM fields. The development, implementation, maintenance, and ethical oversight of AI systems all require individuals with strong backgrounds in science, technology, engineering, and mathematics.

Consider the booming field of data science, a direct product of the AI boom. Data scientists are crucial for collecting, cleaning, analyzing, and interpreting massive datasets, the raw material that fuels many AI applications. This requires not only a deep understanding of statistics and computer science but also a strong foundation in mathematics, particularly linear algebra and calculus, to understand the underlying algorithms and models. Similarly, machine learning engineers require expertise in software engineering, algorithms, and statistical modeling. They are the architects of the AI systems themselves, building and optimizing the algorithms that power everything from self-driving cars to medical diagnoses.

Beyond these directly AI-related roles, STEM skills are becoming increasingly vital across all sectors. Even seemingly unrelated fields like marketing and finance are integrating AI-powered tools, requiring professionals with the ability to understand and utilize these technologies effectively. A marketer who can interpret AI-driven customer segmentation analysis will have a significant advantage over one who cannot. A financial analyst who understands the algorithms behind automated trading systems will be better equipped to make informed decisions. In short, STEM literacy is becoming a fundamental requirement for success in the modern workplace, regardless of specific career path.

The education system has a critical role to play in ensuring that individuals are equipped with the necessary STEM skills. This requires a multi-faceted approach, beginning at the foundational levels of education. Early exposure to STEM concepts, through engaging and interactive learning experiences, can spark an interest in these fields from a young age. Schools need to move beyond rote memorization and embrace more hands-on, project-based learning that encourages critical thinking, problem-solving, and collaboration—skills highly valued in the AI-driven workplace.

Beyond primary and secondary education, higher education institutions must adapt their curricula to reflect the demands of the AI era. This includes investing in programs that focus on AI-related fields, such as data science, machine learning, artificial intelligence ethics, and cybersecurity. Furthermore, it's crucial to integrate AI concepts and tools into existing STEM disciplines, preparing students in fields like engineering, biology, and chemistry to leverage AI in their respective domains. This interdisciplinary approach will be essential for fostering innovation and addressing the complex challenges posed by the rapid advancement of AI.

However, simply increasing the number of STEM graduates isn't enough. The quality of STEM education must also be significantly improved. This means focusing on developing critical thinking skills, problem-solving abilities, and creativity, rather than simply teaching technical skills. AI systems can automate many routine tasks, but they cannot yet replicate the uniquely human abilities of creativity, critical thinking, and complex problem-solving.

Cultivating these abilities is crucial for ensuring that human workers remain valuable assets in an increasingly automated world.

Furthermore, inclusivity and equity within STEM education are paramount. The benefits of AI should be accessible to all members of society, not just a privileged few. This requires addressing systemic barriers that prevent underrepresented groups from pursuing STEM careers. This includes tackling gender disparities in STEM fields, increasing access to quality STEM education for students from disadvantaged backgrounds, and fostering inclusive learning environments that welcome diverse perspectives and experiences. The future of AI and its impact on the workforce will be significantly shaped by the diversity of its developers and users.

The role of governments and industry in supporting STEM education cannot be overstated. Increased funding for research and development in AI, coupled with supportive policies that incentivize investment in STEM education, are crucial for fostering innovation and preparing the workforce for the future. Government initiatives should also focus on promoting STEM literacy among the broader public, fostering a greater understanding of AI and its societal implications. This public understanding is key to informing policy decisions and ensuring that AI is developed and deployed ethically and responsibly.

Industry plays a critical role as well. Companies involved in AI development and implementation can collaborate with educational institutions to develop curricula and training programs that meet the needs of the workforce. They can also provide internships, apprenticeships, and mentorship opportunities for students interested in AI-related careers. Such partnerships between academia and industry are essential for creating a talent pipeline that ensures a sufficient supply of qualified AI professionals. This includes not only the highly specialized roles, but also those who can critically evaluate and use AI technology effectively in various contexts.

Finally, continuous professional development is a necessity for anyone hoping to thrive in the age of AI. The rapid pace of technological change necessitates lifelong learning, requiring individuals to continually update their skills and knowledge. Online courses, workshops, and conferences offer numerous avenues for professional development, allowing individuals to acquire new skills and stay abreast of the latest advances in AI. Educational institutions, too, can play a role here, offering continuing education programs for professionals seeking to upskill or transition into AI-related roles. This need for lifelong learning should not be considered a burden, but as an opportunity to continuously adapt and grow, remaining competitive in an ever-evolving landscape.

In conclusion, the importance of STEM education in the age of AI cannot be overstated. It is not merely about producing a workforce capable of developing and implementing AI systems; it's about fostering a society that can critically evaluate, understand, and responsibly utilize this transformative technology. By investing in quality STEM education, promoting inclusivity, and encouraging lifelong learning, we can mitigate the potential negative impacts of AI while harnessing its transformative power to create a more equitable and prosperous future for all. This requires a concerted effort from educational institutions, governments, industry, and individuals alike, but the rewards of such investment will be immeasurable.

Reskilling and Upskilling Initiatives for AI Literacy

The previous discussion highlighted the critical role of STEM education in preparing the workforce for the age of AI. However, simply bolstering STEM education at the foundational level is insufficient. The existing workforce, possessing valuable experience and expertise in various fields, also requires strategic reskilling and upskilling initiatives to remain relevant and competitive in the evolving landscape. This necessitates a multifaceted approach involving governments, educational institutions, and corporations, all working in concert to bridge the skills gap and foster AI literacy across diverse sectors.

Government initiatives play a crucial role in driving large-scale reskilling and upskilling efforts. Many countries are already investing heavily in programs designed to equip workers with AI-related skills. These initiatives often take the form of grants, subsidies, and tax breaks for companies offering AI-related training programs. For example, the European Union's Digital Skills and Jobs Coalition promotes digital literacy and skills development across the continent, with a significant focus on AI. Similarly, many national governments are funding boot camps and intensive short courses focusing on practical AI applications, aiming to quickly upskill individuals for in-demand roles. The success of these programs hinges on careful curriculum design, ensuring that training aligns with actual industry needs and avoids creating a mismatch between skills taught and those demanded by employers.

A key aspect is evaluating the efficacy of these programs and adapting them based on real-world outcomes. Continuous monitoring and adjustment based on feedback from both trainees and employers are crucial to their long-term success. Furthermore, accessibility is paramount. Government-funded programs should ensure equitable access for workers from diverse backgrounds, including those from marginalized communities or those lacking prior educational opportunities. This necessitates addressing socioeconomic barriers and ensuring geographical accessibility of training resources.

Educational institutions are also pivotal in providing reskilling and upskilling opportunities for AI literacy. Universities and colleges are expanding their offerings to incorporate AI-related courses and certifications into existing degree programs and offering specialized certificates and micro-credentials for professionals seeking focused training. These institutions can adapt their traditional continuing education programs to incorporate AI-focused content, delivering both theoretical knowledge and practical, hands-on skills development. Online learning platforms, often in partnership with universities and colleges, are gaining significant traction, providing flexible and accessible options for professionals juggling work and personal commitments. These platforms offer a wide array of courses, from introductory overviews to advanced specializations, catering to various levels of prior knowledge and expertise. The key to success here is ensuring the quality and relevance of online materials. This involves collaboration with industry experts to maintain up-to-date curriculum and incorporating interactive learning modules and real-world case studies to facilitate deeper understanding and knowledge retention. Regular updates are essential to stay abreast of rapid technological advancements in the field.

Corporate training programs are another critical component of AI literacy initiatives. Forward-thinking companies are investing in internal training programs to upskill their existing workforce, anticipating the transformative impact of AI on their operations. These programs can range from introductory workshops on basic AI concepts to specialized training for specific roles such as data scientists or machine learning engineers. Successful corporate training programs often leverage internal expertise, using experienced employees as instructors to share their knowledge and practical experience. This fosters a culture of internal knowledge sharing and empowers employees to take ownership of their professional development. Furthermore, companies are increasingly partnering with external training providers, leveraging their expertise and resources to enhance their internal programs.

Mentorship programs within the company, pairing experienced employees with those undergoing training, provide crucial guidance and support, facilitating a smoother transition to AI-related roles.

However, the effectiveness of these programs depends on commitment from senior leadership, allocating sufficient resources and time for employees to engage in training activities without negatively impacting their daily responsibilities.

Examples of successful reskilling and upskilling initiatives abound.

For instance, many tech companies offer comprehensive internal training programs for employees wishing to transition into data science or AI engineering roles. These programs typically involve a combination of classroom instruction, online learning modules, and hands-on projects, culminating in a practical assessment to demonstrate competency. Several non-profit organizations and government agencies have partnered to provide free or subsidized training for workers in industries significantly affected by automation. These initiatives often focus on equipping individuals with transferable skills, such as critical thinking, problem-solving, and communication, enhancing their adaptability to changing job markets. Moreover, successful programs often provide career counseling and job placement support to assist participants in transitioning into new roles once they complete their training. The long-term success of such initiatives is typically measured by employment outcomes, wage increases, and overall career satisfaction among participants.

A crucial aspect of successful reskilling and upskilling is tailoring programs to the specific needs of different industries and worker profiles. A one-size-fits-all approach is ineffective. Programs should be designed to recognize the varying levels of prior knowledge and expertise, offering entry-level training for those with limited technical backgrounds and advanced specialization for those seeking to enhance their existing skills. Consider the contrasting training needs of a marketing professional versus a manufacturing worker; both may benefit from AI literacy, but the specific skills required differ significantly. Successful programs proactively anticipate future skill demands by staying abreast of industry trends and incorporating emerging technologies into their curriculum. Continuous evaluation and adjustment are vital; gathering feedback from employers, trainers, and participants ensures the programs remain relevant and effective in the long run.

Beyond the technical skills themselves, reskilling and upskilling initiatives should also focus on developing uniquely human skills that complement AI capabilities. Emotional intelligence, critical thinking, complex problem-solving, and creative thinking are vital for navigating the AI-driven workplace. AI can process data and automate tasks, but it cannot yet replicate human creativity, empathy, and the ability to understand nuanced situations.

Programs should incorporate modules that cultivate these skills, highlighting their importance in a collaborative human-AI work environment. This involves designing training exercises that encourage collaboration, communication, and the ability to navigate ambiguous situations, aspects critical for success in the age of AI.

The challenge of AI literacy extends beyond simply acquiring technical skills; it also necessitates fostering a societal understanding of AI's ethical implications and potential societal impact. Reskilling and upskilling programs should incorporate modules addressing ethical considerations, bias in algorithms, and the responsible use of AI. A workforce versed in both technical and ethical aspects of AI is crucial for ensuring responsible development and deployment of AI technologies, promoting fairness, and mitigating potential risks. This includes developing awareness of the impact of AI on employment, social structures, and individual privacy, creating a more informed and engaged citizenry.

In conclusion, successful reskilling and upskilling initiatives for AI literacy require a concerted effort from governments, educational institutions, and corporations. These programs must be flexible, adaptable, and accessible, catering to the diverse needs of the workforce. They should prioritize not only technical skills but also the uniquely human skills that complement AI's capabilities. A focus on ethical considerations is also vital, ensuring responsible development and deployment of AI technologies. By strategically investing in these initiatives, society can effectively navigate the AI revolution, ensuring a future where humans and AI collaborate to create a more equitable and prosperous world. The ongoing nature of technological advancement means continuous learning and adaptation are not just desirable, but essential for navigating this dynamic environment successfully.

The Need for Lifelong Learning in the Age of AI

The relentless pace of technological advancement, particularly in the realm of artificial intelligence, necessitates a fundamental shift in our approach to education and career development. The traditional model of acquiring skills early in one's career and relying on those skills for a lifetime is no longer sustainable. In the age of AI, lifelong learning isn't merely advantageous; it's essential for survival and prosperity. The very nature of work is evolving, with AI automating tasks across various sectors, rendering certain skill sets obsolete while creating demand for entirely new ones. This dynamic necessitates a proactive and continuous approach to learning, equipping individuals with the adaptability needed to navigate the ever-changing landscape of the future workplace.

This need extends beyond acquiring specific technical skills related to AI. While proficiency in data science, machine learning, or AI-related programming languages is crucial for some roles, the benefits of lifelong learning encompass a broader spectrum of competencies. The ability to learn quickly, adapt to new technologies, and continuously update one's knowledge base is arguably more important than possessing any single, specific skill set. AI's rapid evolution means that even highly specialized skills can become outdated relatively quickly. Therefore, the emphasis should shift from acquiring static knowledge to cultivating a growth mindset – a belief that one's abilities and intelligence are malleable and can be developed through dedication and hard work.

This shift requires a paradigm change in both individual attitudes and institutional support. Individuals need to actively embrace a culture of continuous learning, viewing professional development not as an occasional endeavor but as an ongoing process integrated into their daily lives. This involves dedicating time for self-directed learning, actively seeking out new opportunities to expand their knowledge and skills, and demonstrating a willingness to embrace new technologies and methodologies. This proactive approach translates to a greater sense of control over one's career trajectory, empowering individuals to navigate technological disruptions rather than being passively swept along by them.

The responsibility for fostering lifelong learning extends beyond the individual. Educational institutions, from primary schools to universities, must adapt their curricula to emphasize critical thinking, problem-solving, and adaptability – skills that are less susceptible to automation. Traditional rote learning should be replaced with more engaging and interactive learning methods that encourage active participation and the development of higher-order thinking skills.

Furthermore, educational institutions need to provide access to continuous learning opportunities, offering diverse pathways for upskilling and reskilling throughout an individual's working life. This might involve offering modular courses, micro-credentials, or certificate programs focused on specific technologies or skill sets, allowing individuals to tailor their learning to their specific career aspirations.

The role of employers in promoting lifelong learning is equally critical. Forward-thinking companies understand that investing in their employees' professional development is not just a cost, but an investment in their long-term success. Companies should actively support employees in acquiring new skills, providing opportunities for training, mentoring, and professional development. This might include offering subsidized tuition for relevant courses, providing access to online learning platforms, or creating internal mentorship programs where experienced employees can share their knowledge and expertise with their colleagues. Furthermore, companies should create a culture that values continuous learning, recognizing and rewarding employees who actively seek out new knowledge and skills.

Government initiatives also play a vital role in fostering lifelong learning. Governments can provide financial incentives for individuals and organizations to engage in continuous learning, such as tax credits for professional development expenses or subsidies for training programs. Furthermore, governments can invest in the development of high-quality online learning resources and make them accessible to all citizens, regardless of their socioeconomic background. This ensures that everyone has the opportunity to participate in the digital economy and benefit from the opportunities presented by AI.

However, the effective implementation of lifelong learning initiatives requires careful consideration of various factors.

Curriculum design must be rigorous, ensuring that training programs are aligned with actual industry needs and that the skills taught are directly applicable to real-world scenarios. Furthermore, accessibility is crucial. Training programs should be designed to cater to diverse learning styles and accommodate individuals with different levels of prior knowledge and experience. Equitable access to learning opportunities is paramount, addressing potential barriers faced by marginalized communities and ensuring that the benefits of lifelong learning are shared by all.

Successfully integrating lifelong learning into the fabric of our society requires a collaborative effort from governments, educational institutions, employers, and individuals themselves. It demands a significant paradigm shift, moving away from a static view of education and career development toward a dynamic and adaptive model that embraces change and continuous growth. In an era defined by the rapid advancements of AI, the ability to learn continuously is not simply an asset; it is the cornerstone of personal and professional success, ensuring not only survival but indeed, the thriving of individuals and society in the face of technological transformation. The future of work is not about resisting change, but about embracing it – and lifelong learning is the key to navigating this future successfully. It's a commitment that extends beyond simply acquiring new skills; it involves cultivating an adaptable mindset, fostering a love for learning, and understanding that growth is a continuous journey, not a destination.

The integration of AI into various aspects of our lives is not just changing the nature of work; it's altering the very definition of skill and competency. The demand for traditional, highly specialized skills may diminish in certain areas, but the demand for adaptability, problem-solving, and critical thinking will only intensify. Lifelong learning becomes the essential skill in this context – the meta-skill that empowers individuals to navigate the ever-shifting landscape of the job market.

Consider the example of a marketing professional. Ten years ago, their core skills may have revolved around traditional advertising methods, print media, and perhaps early forms of digital marketing. Today, a successful marketing professional needs to be proficient in data analysis, AI-powered marketing automation tools, and social media strategies, all while understanding the ethical implications of using AI in advertising. Similarly, a manufacturing worker may need to master the operation and maintenance of robotic systems, data analysis techniques to optimize production lines, and perhaps even programming skills to interact with automated equipment.

These examples illustrate that lifelong learning isn't just about acquiring new skills; it's about constantly updating and re-evaluating existing skill sets in light of technological advancements.

This continuous adaptation requires a deep understanding of the nature of AI itself – not just its technical applications, but its broader societal impact. Individuals need to grasp the potential benefits and risks of AI, its ethical implications, and its potential to reshape various industries. Understanding the evolving relationship between humans and AI is crucial for effective collaboration and for navigating the ethical complexities of an increasingly automated world. Furthermore, a nuanced understanding of AI can empower individuals to critically evaluate the information they encounter, distinguishing between reliable sources and biased or misleading narratives.

This emphasis on lifelong learning necessitates a re-evaluation of our educational systems. They need to move beyond the confines of traditional degree programs and offer flexible, modular learning opportunities that can be accessed throughout one's life. This could involve micro-credentials, online courses, boot camps, and other forms of alternative education that cater to diverse learning styles and allow individuals to focus on specific skills relevant to their career aspirations. Such flexibility also accommodates the evolving demands of the job market, allowing individuals to quickly adapt and acquire the skills needed for emerging roles.

The responsibility for promoting lifelong learning doesn't rest solely on individuals and educational institutions. Governments play a critical role in creating an ecosystem that supports continuous learning. This involves investing in accessible and high-quality educational resources, providing financial incentives for individuals and businesses to invest in training and development, and creating policies that encourage employers to support their employees'professional growth. Government initiatives focused on digital literacy, reskilling, and upskilling are crucial steps in ensuring that the workforce is equipped to thrive in the age of AI.

In conclusion, the need for lifelong learning in the age of AI is not a matter of choice, but of necessity. It requires a fundamental shift in mindset, a commitment to continuous adaptation, and a collaborative effort from individuals, educational institutions, businesses, and governments. By embracing lifelong learning, we can empower individuals to not just survive, but thrive in the rapidly evolving world of artificial intelligence, harnessing its potential for progress while mitigating its risks. The future belongs to those who continuously learn, adapt, and innovate, shaping their own destinies in the face of technological change.

Bridging the Skills Gap Addressing the Shortage of AI Talent

The previous discussion highlighted the critical importance of lifelong learning in the face of accelerating AI integration across all industries.

However, a significant challenge emerges: the burgeoning skills gap in the field of artificial intelligence itself. The rapid advancements in AI are outpacing the supply of qualified professionals capable of developing, implementing, and managing these technologies. This shortage isn't confined to highly specialized roles like AI researchers or data scientists; it extends to a broader range of professions requiring even a basic understanding of AI's implications and applications. Marketing professionals need to leverage AI-powered tools, finance professionals require AI literacy for risk management and predictive modeling, and even leadership roles demand an understanding of how AI is reshaping organizational structures and workflows. This widespread need for AI literacy underscores the urgency of addressing the current talent shortage.

The core issue lies in the mismatch between the rapidly evolving demands of the AI industry and the current educational infrastructure. Traditional academic programs often struggle to keep pace with the breakneck speed of technological innovation.

Curricula can become outdated quickly, leaving graduates with skills that are already partially or entirely obsolete upon entering the workforce.

This necessitates a more agile and responsive approach to education, one that prioritizes continuous updating and adaptation to the ever-changing needs of the industry. This isn't simply a matter of adding a few AI-related courses to existing programs; it demands a fundamental rethinking of the entire educational ecosystem.

Bridging this skills gap requires a concerted, multi-pronged effort involving educational institutions, industry, and government.

Educational institutions need to revamp their curricula, incorporating practical, hands-on experience alongside theoretical knowledge. This means integrating real-world projects, internships, and collaborations with industry partners to provide students with exposure to the latest AI technologies and methodologies.

Universities and colleges should invest in state-of-the-art facilities and equipment, ensuring that students have access to the computational resources necessary for advanced AI research and development. Furthermore, fostering an environment that encourages interdisciplinary collaboration is essential. AI is not a standalone field; its applications cross numerous domains, demanding expertise in mathematics, computer science, engineering, business, and the social sciences. Educating students in an interdisciplinary setting can create a more holistic and adaptable workforce.

Industry plays a crucial role in shaping the educational pipeline.

Companies must actively engage with educational institutions, providing feedback on curriculum development, offering internships and mentorship opportunities, and creating pathways for graduates to transition into meaningful AI-related roles. This partnership ensures that the skills taught in educational institutions directly align with the actual needs and demands of the industry, reducing the risk of graduates entering the workforce with outdated or irrelevant skills. Companies should also invest in their existing employees' training and development, offering upskilling and reskilling programs to equip their workforce with the necessary AI literacy. This commitment demonstrates a long-term investment in their human capital and strengthens their competitive advantage in an increasingly AI-driven market.

The role of government in fostering AI talent extends beyond simple funding. Governments can play a pivotal role in creating an ecosystem that supports the development and growth of AI talent.

This includes creating and supporting national AI strategies, investing in research and development initiatives, and offering financial incentives for companies and individuals to participate in AI-related training and education. Government support can facilitate the establishment of national centers for AI research and education, providing resources and infrastructure for collaboration between industry and academia. Furthermore, governments can play a critical role in promoting digital literacy and STEM education at the primary and secondary levels, cultivating an interest in technology from an early age and increasing the pipeline of future AI professionals. Policy initiatives aimed at increasing the diversity of the AI workforce are crucial as well, as it is essential to ensure inclusive access to educational opportunities and to avoid perpetuating existing biases in the field.

Addressing the shortage of AI talent requires a comprehensive strategy that focuses on multiple aspects of education and training. One critical approach is to create more accessible pathways into AI-related fields. Boot camps, online courses, and micro-credential programs offer flexible and shorter-term learning options that can equip individuals with specific AI-related skills, regardless of their prior background. These programs can provide an alternative route for individuals seeking to transition into AI roles, allowing them to quickly acquire practical skills and enter the job market without the significant time commitment of a traditional degree program.

The focus should shift from purely technical skills to a broader emphasis on critical thinking, problem-solving, and ethical awareness. AI systems are increasingly integrated into decision-making processes, necessitating a workforce that understands the implications of these technologies and can critically evaluate their outputs. This requires not just technical proficiency, but also a deep understanding of the ethical considerations surrounding AI, including bias detection, fairness, accountability, and transparency.

In conclusion, bridging the AI skills gap demands a concerted and collaborative effort between educational institutions, industry, and government. By implementing innovative education programs, promoting lifelong learning, investing in research, and fostering a culture of ethical AI development, we can create a workforce equipped to harness the transformative potential of artificial intelligence while mitigating its inherent risks. The need to proactively address this challenge is not merely a matter of economic competitiveness; it's essential for ensuring responsible innovation and shaping a future where AI benefits all of society. The successful integration of AI into our world depends critically on our ability to develop and retain the talent needed to guide its trajectory and to ensure its equitable distribution of benefits. This requires not only the training of specialists, but also the wider dissemination of AI literacy throughout the workforce, empowering everyone to understand, engage with and effectively utilize this transformative technology.

Curriculum Development Integrating AI into Existing Educational Programs

The imperative to integrate AI into education isn't simply about adding a few AI-related courses; it demands a fundamental restructuring of how we approach learning and skill development. This transformation must encompass all levels of education, from kindergarten to postgraduate studies, acknowledging that AI literacy is no longer a niche skill but a fundamental requirement for navigating the modern world. K-12 education, traditionally focused on foundational skills in mathematics, science, and language, must incorporate introductory concepts of AI, fostering computational thinking, problem-solving, and data analysis skills from an early age. This isn't about making every child a coder, but about equipping them with the critical thinking skills to understand the increasingly AI-driven world around them.

One effective approach is to introduce age-appropriate coding exercises and robotics projects. These activities can make abstract concepts like algorithms and data processing more tangible and engaging. Elementary school students can learn the basic principles of programming through visual coding languages like Scratch, which allow them to create interactive stories and games. As they progress, they can delve into more complex languages like Python, learning to analyze simple datasets and build basic AI models.

Incorporating robotics into the curriculum provides a hands-on approach to understanding how AI algorithms control and interact with the physical world. Students can build and program robots to perform tasks, fostering their problem-solving and engineering abilities.

High school curricula can build upon these foundations, introducing more advanced concepts like machine learning, natural language processing, and computer vision. Integrating AI into existing subjects like mathematics, science, and social studies can demonstrate the practical applications of AI across diverse fields. For example, students could use AI tools to analyze historical data, predict weather patterns, or model ecological systems. This interdisciplinary approach not only makes AI learning more relevant and engaging but also strengthens students' skills in critical thinking, data analysis, and problem-solving. The emphasis should be on developing analytical skills, understanding the ethical considerations of AI, and promoting responsible technology use. By fostering a critical and ethical approach, education can equip the next generation to navigate the complex ethical dilemmas inherent in the development and deployment of AI systems.

Higher education institutions face the challenge of keeping pace with the rapid advancements in AI. Traditional computer science programs need to be updated to reflect the current state of the art, including specialized courses on deep learning, reinforcement learning, natural language processing, and computer vision.

However, the need for AI literacy extends far beyond computer science departments. Business schools, for example, should incorporate AI into their curricula to prepare students for the AI-driven business landscape. Students should learn how to use AI tools for market analysis, risk management, and strategic decision-making. Similarly, medical schools should equip future doctors with the skills to interpret AI-powered diagnostics and imaging systems.

Integrating AI across diverse disciplines emphasizes its pervasiveness and ensures that graduates possess the necessary skills for a wide range of careers.

Beyond traditional academic courses, universities can offer a range of AI-related initiatives, such as specialized workshops, hackathons, and student-led research projects. These activities provide students with hands-on experience working with cutting-edge technologies and encourage them to develop their innovative problem-solving skills. Furthermore, universities can establish partnerships with industry to provide students with internships and mentorship opportunities. These collaborations not only expose students to real-world AI applications but also create valuable networking connections that can lead to future employment opportunities. The emphasis on practical experience, coupled with theoretical knowledge, will significantly enhance the employability of graduates and bridge the ever-widening gap between academic training and industrial needs.

To effectively integrate AI into existing educational programs, several key considerations must be addressed. One critical aspect is the need for ongoing professional development for educators. Teachers and professors need access to resources and training to update their skills and effectively teach AI-related concepts. This includes workshops, online courses, and mentorship programs tailored to the needs of educators. The training should focus not only on the technical aspects of AI but also on pedagogical approaches that effectively engage students and foster critical thinking. Creating a supportive and collaborative environment for educators to share their experiences and expertise is crucial for ensuring the successful integration of AI into the curriculum.

Another critical aspect is access to the necessary technology and resources. Schools and universities need to invest in state-of-the-art computing infrastructure, including high-performance computing clusters and advanced software tools. This will allow students to work with complex AI models and datasets, gaining practical experience with the technologies they will encounter in their future careers. Furthermore, ensuring equitable access to these resources is crucial, preventing any disparities in educational opportunities based on socioeconomic status or geographical location. This necessitates a strategic investment in technology infrastructure and digital literacy programs across all educational institutions, regardless of their funding levels or location.

The evaluation of AI integration in education also requires careful consideration. Traditional assessment methods may not be sufficient to evaluate students' understanding and application of AI concepts. New assessment strategies are needed that can effectively measure students' critical thinking skills, problem-solving abilities, and ethical awareness in relation to AI. This could involve project-based assessments, simulations, and case studies that challenge students to apply their knowledge in real-world scenarios. Furthermore, collecting and analyzing data on student outcomes is crucial for refining curricula and improving the effectiveness of AI education programs. This data-driven approach to evaluation will ensure that educational institutions are continuously improving their methods and aligning their offerings with the evolving needs of the AI industry.

Finally, addressing potential biases in AI systems and educational materials is vital. AI algorithms are trained on data, and if that data reflects existing societal biases, the algorithms will perpetuate and even amplify those biases. Educators must be aware of this potential and teach students to identify and mitigate bias in AI systems. This includes educating students on the importance of data diversity, algorithmic transparency, and responsible AI development.

Furthermore, the educational materials themselves should be carefully reviewed to ensure that they are free from bias and accurately represent diverse perspectives. This commitment to inclusivity and equity is essential for ensuring that AI education benefits all students and contributes to a more just and equitable society. By addressing these issues proactively, education can play a vital role in shaping the future of AI, ensuring that it is used responsibly and for the benefit of all humankind. The integration of AI into existing educational programs is not just a matter of technological advancement; it is a critical step in fostering responsible innovation and preparing the next generation to navigate the increasingly AI-driven world.

Chapter 13: Government Policies and Regulations

The Role of Government in Supporting Workforce Transition

The transformative potential of artificial intelligence necessitates a proactive and comprehensive response from governments worldwide. The rapid automation driven by AI is not a distant threat; it's reshaping industries and job markets in real-time. This necessitates a shift in governmental roles, moving beyond passive observation to active intervention in supporting workforce transitions. The crucial question is not whether jobs will be lost—that's practically guaranteed—but how effectively governments can mitigate the negative consequences and foster a smooth transition to an AI-driven economy.

One of the most direct approaches is the implementation of robust retraining and upskilling programs. These programs should be designed not as generic job-training initiatives, but as highly targeted interventions focused on the specific skills in demand in the evolving AI-driven economy. This means a deep understanding of the skills gap analysis, constantly updated to reflect the dynamic nature of AI advancements. Instead of offering blanket training in outdated technologies, these programs should emphasize skills complementary to AI, such as critical thinking, complex problem-solving, creativity, emotional intelligence, and strong communication skills—areas where humans currently retain a significant advantage. Furthermore, these programs should be readily accessible to workers across all socioeconomic backgrounds, ensuring that the benefits of retraining are not limited to those with existing privilege.

The design of these retraining initiatives must also address the practical realities faced by displaced workers. This includes considering factors like age, education level, and previous work experience. A one-size-fits-all approach will inevitably fall short; a flexible and personalized curriculum is crucial. Modular training, allowing workers to acquire new skills incrementally and integrate them into their existing knowledge base, will be more effective than lengthy, intensive programs that may overwhelm and disengage participants. Such programs should ideally incorporate elements of mentorship, allowing experienced professionals to guide and support those undergoing retraining. This personalized support system can significantly increase the likelihood of successful transitions.

Beyond retraining, governments must also strengthen social safety nets to provide a cushion for workers during the transition period. This includes expanding unemployment benefits, providing income support for individuals undergoing retraining, and offering healthcare and childcare subsidies. These measures are not merely acts of charity; they are essential investments in human capital, ensuring that individuals have the financial stability to pursue retraining opportunities without undue hardship. The goal should be to ease the transition, not to exacerbate the existing inequalities that already hinder economic mobility. A robust safety net minimizes the economic anxieties associated with job displacement, allowing individuals to focus on acquiring the skills needed for future employment.

Financial assistance plays a crucial role in enabling access to retraining programs. Many workers, particularly those in lower-paying jobs, lack the financial resources to afford the time and expense associated with retraining. Governments can provide grants, scholarships, and low-interest loans to help cover training costs, childcare expenses, and living expenses during the retraining period. This financial support ensures that socioeconomic status does not determine access to opportunities in the new AI-driven economy, fostering equity and inclusivity. It is crucial that this assistance is not solely focused on the initial cost of the program but also on ongoing support during and after the program's completion.

Government initiatives should also focus on fostering collaboration between educational institutions, industry, and government agencies. This collaboration is crucial for ensuring that retraining programs align with the actual needs of the evolving job market. Industry partnerships can provide valuable insights into the skills employers seek, leading to the development of highly relevant and effective training programs. These partnerships can also create opportunities for internships, apprenticeships, and job placements, bridging the gap between training and employment. Such collaborations create a virtuous cycle, with industry providing feedback that refines training programs, making them more effective and better aligned with market demands.

Furthermore, governments must actively promote the development and adoption of AI-related technologies, creating an environment conducive to innovation and job creation in this sector. This involves strategic investments in research and development, creating incentives for AI-focused businesses to locate and operate within their borders, and providing funding for startups developing cutting-edge AI technologies. This approach is not merely about supporting the AI industry; it's about creating the very jobs that will compensate for those displaced by automation. By actively fostering the AI sector, governments create new opportunities for employment, mitigating the negative impacts of automation.

Successful government initiatives demonstrate the effectiveness of these strategies. Several countries have implemented noteworthy programs: Denmark's focus on lifelong learning has provided retraining opportunities for a significant portion of their workforce, adapting to changes in the job market. Canada has invested heavily in STEM education and AI-specific programs, preparing their population for the demands of a technologically advanced economy.

Singapore's initiatives focus on reskilling workers through government-funded courses and industry partnerships, creating a seamless transition for individuals affected by automation. These examples showcase the importance of a multi-pronged approach, incorporating retraining, social safety nets, financial assistance, and active promotion of the AI sector itself.

Beyond specific programs, government policy must also address the ethical considerations of AI and automation. This includes creating regulations that ensure fair labor practices, protect against algorithmic bias, and address the potential displacement of workers.

Transparency and accountability in the development and deployment of AI systems are critical. Governments have a role in setting the ethical standards and enforcing them to prevent the exacerbation of existing inequalities. Such regulation does not stifle innovation but rather channels it towards beneficial and equitable outcomes.

The role of government in supporting workforce transition is not merely reactive; it's proactive and preventative. By embracing this role, investing in retraining, enhancing safety nets, providing financial assistance, promoting collaboration, and establishing ethical frameworks, governments can not only mitigate the negative consequences of AI but also harness its transformative power to create a more equitable and prosperous future for all. The challenges are substantial, but the opportunity to create a truly inclusive and sustainable economy through intelligent government intervention is immense. Failure to act decisively risks exacerbating existing inequalities and creating societal instability; decisive and well-planned action offers the path to a future where technological advancement benefits all citizens.

Regulations for Ethical AI Development and Deployment

The preceding discussion highlighted the crucial role of governments in mitigating the societal impacts of AI-driven automation through retraining initiatives and robust social safety nets. However, the success of these efforts hinges on another critical element: the ethical development and deployment of AI itself. Without appropriate regulations, the very technologies intended to improve our lives could exacerbate existing inequalities and create new forms of societal harm. This necessitates a comprehensive regulatory framework focused on responsible AI governance.

The core challenge lies in balancing the imperative to foster innovation with the need to protect individuals and society from potential harms. Unfettered AI development risks exacerbating biases present in existing data sets, leading to discriminatory outcomes in areas like loan applications, hiring processes, and even criminal justice. Algorithmic opacity, where the decision-making processes of AI systems are opaque and inexplicable, further compounds these concerns. Citizens deserve transparency and accountability, particularly when AI systems make decisions with significant consequences for their lives.

Data privacy is another crucial area requiring stringent regulation.

AI systems often rely on vast quantities of personal data, raising concerns about potential misuse and breaches. Regulations must ensure that data collection and use are transparent, consensual, and secure, protecting individuals from unauthorized access and exploitation. Existing regulations like GDPR in Europe provide a valuable framework, but a globally harmonized approach is essential to address the transnational nature of AI development and data flows. This requires international cooperation and the establishment of common standards for data privacy and protection.

Algorithmic transparency is closely related to data privacy.

Governments should mandate that developers provide clear explanations of how AI systems make decisions, particularly in high-stakes contexts like healthcare, finance, and criminal justice.

This does not necessarily require the complete disclosure of proprietary algorithms, but rather a requirement to provide understandable summaries of the factors influencing AI decisions. "Explainable AI" (XAI) is an emerging field focusing on developing techniques to make AI's decision-making processes more transparent and understandable, and governments should incentivize and support research in this area. The goal is not to stifle innovation but to make AI systems more accountable and less prone to bias or error.

Bias mitigation is a critical component of responsible AI governance. AI systems inherit the biases present in the data they are trained on, potentially perpetuating and amplifying existing societal inequalities. Regulations should require developers to actively identify and mitigate biases in their systems through various techniques, such as data augmentation, algorithmic adjustments, and rigorous testing. Independent audits of AI systems can also play a vital role in ensuring fairness and accountability.

These audits should be conducted by qualified experts and made publicly available, fostering trust and transparency in AI development.

Beyond data privacy, algorithmic transparency, and bias mitigation, government regulations should also address issues related to AI safety and security. The potential for AI systems to be misused for malicious purposes, such as creating deepfakes or deploying autonomous weapons, requires proactive measures to prevent harm.

Regulations should mandate security standards for AI systems, including rigorous testing and vulnerability assessments.

International cooperation is crucial to address the global nature of these threats, ensuring that regulations are effective across borders.

Enforcement of AI regulations is crucial for their effectiveness.

Governments need to establish clear mechanisms for monitoring compliance, investigating violations, and imposing penalties for non-compliance. This requires a dedicated regulatory body with the expertise and resources to oversee the development and deployment of AI systems.

Furthermore, effective enforcement requires collaboration between different government agencies, ensuring a coordinated approach to regulating AI across various sectors.

The development of AI regulations requires a delicate balance between promoting innovation and protecting against potential harms. Overly restrictive regulations can stifle innovation, while insufficient regulations can lead to widespread harm. A collaborative approach, involving government agencies, industry stakeholders, and civil society organizations, is crucial to find this optimal balance. This collaborative dialogue should aim to establish clear guidelines and standards while fostering a culture of responsible innovation.

The challenge of regulating AI is not unique to any one nation; it's a global issue requiring international cooperation. While individual nations may have their own specific regulatory frameworks, the transnational nature of AI development necessitates harmonization of standards and mutual recognition of certifications. This requires international forums for dialogue and collaboration, allowing nations to share best practices and develop common standards for AI safety, security, and ethics.

The long-term success of AI regulations depends on public awareness and engagement. Citizens need to understand the implications of AI for their lives and have a voice in shaping the regulatory landscape.

Government initiatives should promote AI literacy and public education, empowering citizens to participate meaningfully in the policy-making process. This public engagement is crucial for building trust and ensuring that AI regulations are both effective and legitimate.

Finally, the regulatory landscape around AI is likely to evolve rapidly as the technology advances. Regulations must be flexible and adaptable, allowing for adjustments as new challenges and opportunities emerge. This necessitates ongoing monitoring and evaluation, with regular reviews and updates to existing regulations to ensure their continued relevance and effectiveness. The goal is not to create a static set of rules but a dynamic framework capable of adapting to the rapid pace of technological change. By embracing this adaptive approach, governments can effectively guide the development and deployment of AI while safeguarding the interests of society.

In conclusion, the ethical development and deployment of AI necessitates a comprehensive and evolving regulatory framework.

This framework should encompass data privacy, algorithmic transparency, bias mitigation, AI safety and security, and effective enforcement mechanisms. International cooperation, public engagement, and adaptive governance are crucial for ensuring that AI benefits society while mitigating potential risks. The ultimate goal is not merely to regulate AI but to harness its transformative power to create a more equitable, prosperous, and secure future for all. The path forward requires a collective effort, blending innovation with a deep commitment to ethical considerations and societal well-being. The future of work, indeed the future of society, depends on it.

Investment in AI Research and Infrastructure

The preceding discussion focused on the crucial regulatory aspects needed to guide the responsible development and deployment of artificial intelligence. However, robust regulation alone is insufficient to unlock the full potential of AI for societal benefit. Equally critical is significant government investment in AI research and the underlying digital infrastructure. This investment acts as the bedrock upon which innovation flourishes, ensuring that AI technologies are not only ethically sound but also readily accessible and beneficial to a broad range of industries and citizens.

Public funding plays a pivotal role in fostering AI innovation. Private sector investment, while substantial, often focuses on short-term returns, potentially neglecting high-risk, high-reward research areas with long-term societal benefits. Governments, with their capacity for long-term strategic planning and risk tolerance, can fill this crucial gap, supporting fundamental research that lays the groundwork for future breakthroughs. This includes funding research into areas such as explainable AI (XAI), which tackles the "black box" problem by making AI decision-making processes more transparent and understandable. Public investment in XAI is vital for building public trust and ensuring the accountability of AI systems, especially in sensitive sectors like healthcare and finance.

Furthermore, government funding can accelerate the development of AI technologies specifically designed to address societal challenges. This might involve supporting research into AI applications for improving healthcare outcomes, enhancing educational opportunities, or developing sustainable solutions for climate change. By strategically directing research funds towards areas of national priority, governments can harness AI's potential to address pressing societal needs and drive positive social change. For example, governments could fund research into AI-powered diagnostic tools for early disease detection, personalized learning platforms tailored to individual student needs, or AI-driven systems for optimizing energy consumption and reducing carbon emissions.

Such investments are not merely altruistic; they represent a strategic investment in a more prosperous and sustainable future.

Beyond supporting research, government investment must extend to developing and upgrading the digital infrastructure necessary for widespread AI adoption. AI applications rely heavily on robust computing power, high-speed internet access, and vast datasets. Investing in these foundational elements is crucial for ensuring that the benefits of AI are not limited to a select few but are broadly accessible across different sectors and geographical locations. This includes investing in high-performance computing facilities, expanding broadband access to underserved communities, and developing secure data storage and management systems. Without this foundational infrastructure, the transformative potential of AI will remain unrealized.

Several nations have already demonstrated the effectiveness of strategic government investment in AI. For example, China's national AI strategy, launched in 2017, outlines ambitious plans for AI development, including substantial investments in research and infrastructure. This proactive approach has led to rapid advancements in several AI-related fields, establishing China as a global leader in AI innovation. Similarly, the European Union's AI strategy focuses on promoting ethical and trustworthy AI, with significant investments in research, development, and infrastructure. The EU's commitment to responsible AI development sets a crucial precedent for other nations, emphasizing the importance of aligning technological progress with ethical considerations.

The United States has also invested heavily in AI through various government agencies, including the National Science Foundation (NSF) and the Defense Advanced Research Projects Agency (DARPA). The NSF supports fundamental research across a range of disciplines, including AI, while DARPA undertakes more applied research aimed at solving specific technological challenges. These initiatives, while significant, could be further expanded to ensure that the U.S. maintains its competitiveness in the global AI race while prioritizing ethical development and inclusive access.

However, effective government investment in AI requires more than simply allocating funds. It demands careful planning, strategic prioritization, and effective collaboration between government agencies, research institutions, and the private sector. This collaborative approach ensures that research efforts align with national priorities, that infrastructure development is efficient and cost-effective, and that the benefits of AI are shared broadly across society. Moreover, continuous monitoring and evaluation are crucial to ensure that investments are producing the desired outcomes and are adaptable to the rapidly evolving nature of AI technology.

Furthermore, consideration must be given to the potential societal impacts of AI, including the risk of job displacement and the exacerbation of existing inequalities. Government investment should incorporate initiatives to mitigate these risks, such as retraining and upskilling programs for workers whose jobs may be affected by AI-driven automation, alongside efforts to ensure equitable access to AI technologies and their benefits. Failing to address these issues risks undermining public support for AI development and hindering its positive societal impact.

Another critical aspect of government investment lies in supporting the education and training of the next generation of AI researchers, developers, and users. This requires significant investment in STEM education at all levels, from primary school to postgraduate studies, emphasizing the importance of AI literacy and promoting interest in AI-related careers. A highly skilled workforce is crucial for ensuring that a nation can effectively develop, deploy, and utilize AI technologies, reaping the associated economic and societal benefits. Investment in education should also include programs for retraining and upskilling existing workers, equipping them with the skills needed to thrive in an AI-driven economy.

Finally, responsible government investment in AI necessitates careful consideration of ethical implications. This involves prioritizing the development of AI systems that are fair, transparent, and accountable. Funding research in ethical AI is crucial, and government policies should promote the development and adoption of ethical guidelines and standards for AI development and deployment. This includes considering the potential for bias in AI systems, the importance of data privacy, and the need for mechanisms for accountability and redress when AI systems cause harm.

In conclusion, government investment in AI research and infrastructure is not merely a financial commitment; it is a strategic imperative. It is a vital component of ensuring that AI technologies are developed responsibly, are accessible to all, and are used to address pressing societal challenges. By strategically investing in research, infrastructure, education, and ethical considerations, governments can unlock the transformative potential of AI and create a more prosperous and equitable future for all. A forward-looking approach, integrating technological innovation with a commitment to social justice and responsible governance, will be crucial in shaping the beneficial societal transformation that AI promises. The stakes are high, and proactive, well-considered investment is the key to realizing a future where AI serves humanity to its fullest potential.

International Collaboration on AI Governance

The preceding discussion highlighted the critical role of individual nations in shaping the future of AI through strategic investment and robust regulation. However, the inherently global nature of artificial intelligence necessitates a move beyond national boundaries toward a framework of international collaboration on AI governance. The rapid proliferation of AI technologies across borders, coupled with their potential to impact global economies and societies, underscores the urgent need for harmonized standards and regulations. Without such collaboration, a fragmented and inconsistent regulatory landscape risks hindering innovation, creating unfair competitive advantages, and potentially exacerbating existing global inequalities.

The development of global AI governance presents a unique set of challenges. Unlike traditional areas of international cooperation, AI is characterized by its rapid evolution, its multifaceted applications across various sectors, and its inherent complexity. This presents considerable obstacles in forging consensus among nations with diverse technological capabilities, economic interests, and cultural perspectives. Establishing common definitions and standards for AI systems, particularly regarding ethical considerations, data privacy, and algorithmic transparency, requires a sophisticated diplomatic process capable of navigating differing national priorities.

One of the primary hurdles to international collaboration lies in the inherent tension between the need for regulatory harmonization and the preservation of national sovereignty. Nations are naturally protective of their own regulatory frameworks and technological advancements, often wary of relinquishing control to international bodies. This tension is particularly acute in areas where AI intersects with national security, economic competitiveness, and social values. Finding a balance that respects national autonomy while promoting global cooperation remains a delicate balancing act.

The diversity of national approaches to AI regulation further complicates matters. Some countries favor a more permissive regulatory approach, prioritizing innovation and market growth.

Others adopt a more cautious stance, emphasizing ethical considerations and the potential societal risks associated with AI. These differing philosophies can make it difficult to reach consensus on common standards and regulations. Furthermore, the rapidly evolving nature of AI technology renders any agreed-upon framework potentially obsolete within a short period, necessitating ongoing dialogue and adaptation.

Despite these challenges, international collaboration on AI governance is not merely desirable but essential for several critical reasons. First, a harmonized regulatory framework can facilitate the global flow of data and AI technologies, fostering innovation and economic growth.

Inconsistent regulations across borders can create significant barriers to trade and investment, hindering the development and deployment of AI applications. Secondly, a collaborative approach can help address the global ethical challenges posed by AI, including algorithmic bias, job displacement, and the potential misuse of AI for malicious purposes.

By establishing common ethical principles and standards, the international community can strive toward a more equitable and responsible use of AI technologies.

Several existing international organizations and initiatives are attempting to facilitate collaboration on AI governance. The Organization for Economic Co-operation and Development (OECD) has played a significant role in promoting the development of AI principles and guidelines. The OECD Principles on AI, adopted in 2019, provide a framework for the responsible stewardship of AI, emphasizing human-centered values, transparency, and accountability. However, these principles remain largely non-binding, and their practical implementation varies significantly across nations.

The G20, a group of the world's major economies, has also recognized the importance of international cooperation on AI. G20 discussions have focused on issues such as data governance, AI ethics, and the need for international standards. However, the G20's diverse membership and varying national priorities can often hinder the development of concrete agreements.

The United Nations (UN) is another important player in the field of international AI governance. The UN's focus on human rights and sustainable development offers a valuable framework for considering the broader societal implications of AI. Various UN agencies are involved in discussions on AI ethics, with a growing recognition of the need for international cooperation to address the potential risks and benefits of AI. Efforts are underway to develop international norms and guidelines for AI, potentially leading to the creation of a binding international instrument.

Beyond these formal organizations, numerous informal collaborations exist between individual governments, research institutions, and private sector companies. These collaborations often involve the sharing of best practices, the development of common technical standards, and the fostering of mutual understanding regarding the challenges and opportunities presented by AI. Such initiatives can complement formal international efforts, creating a more comprehensive approach to global AI governance.

A key aspect of successful international collaboration lies in fostering a culture of trust and mutual respect among nations. This requires open communication, transparency, and a willingness to compromise.

Regular dialogues between government officials, AI experts, and civil society representatives are essential to build consensus and address concerns. Furthermore, inclusive participation is crucial, ensuring that all stakeholders, including developing countries and marginalized communities, have a voice in shaping the future of AI governance.

Looking ahead, several strategies could facilitate increased international collaboration on AI governance. These include the development of a global AI observatory to monitor and assess AI technologies and their impact across borders, strengthening existing international organizations' capacity to address AI-related issues, and creating incentives for nations to adopt common standards and regulations. Furthermore, promoting the development and adoption of common technical standards for AI systems can simplify cross-border data flows and facilitate the interoperability of AI applications. Establishing clear mechanisms for addressing disputes and resolving conflicts related to AI is crucial, potentially involving the creation of international arbitration bodies.

In conclusion, international collaboration on AI governance is not simply a desirable objective; it's a necessity for navigating the complexities and maximizing the benefits of this transformative technology. The challenges are significant, but the potential rewards – a more equitable, responsible, and innovative global AI ecosystem – make the pursuit of international cooperation a vital endeavor. The path forward demands sustained dialogue, compromise, and a commitment to building a global governance framework that prioritizes both technological progress and human well-being. Failure to achieve this could lead to a fragmented, unpredictable, and potentially harmful global AI landscape, jeopardizing the potential benefits for all. The collaborative effort needed requires patience, persistent diplomacy, and a shared vision for a future where AI serves humanity's best interests on a global scale.

Addressing the Societal Impacts of AI Automation

The preceding discussion focused on the crucial role of international cooperation in regulating AI. However, the implications of AI automation extend far beyond international borders, reaching into the very fabric of our societies. The transformative potential of AI, while offering unprecedented opportunities for economic growth and societal advancement, also presents significant challenges, particularly concerning its impact on employment, income inequality, and social welfare. Addressing these societal impacts requires proactive policy interventions that go beyond technical regulations and delve into the realm of social and economic justice.

One of the most pressing concerns surrounding AI automation is its potential impact on employment. While the narrative often focuses on the displacement of low-skilled workers, the reality is far more nuanced. AI-driven automation is increasingly impacting jobs across all skill levels, from factory workers to white-collar professionals.

The rapid advancement of machine learning, natural language processing, and computer vision is leading to the automation of tasks previously considered the exclusive domain of human intelligence. This necessitates a significant shift in how we approach workforce development and education. Simply retraining displaced workers in traditional skills may prove insufficient, as the nature of work itself is undergoing a fundamental transformation. We must instead focus on cultivating skills that are uniquely human—creativity, critical thinking, complex problem-solving, emotional intelligence, and adaptability—skills that are less susceptible to automation.

The potential for increased income inequality is another major societal challenge posed by AI automation. The benefits of AI-driven productivity gains are not always evenly distributed. Often, the owners of capital—the companies that develop and deploy AI technologies—reap the lion's share of the rewards, while workers, especially those in sectors most affected by automation, may experience wage stagnation or job losses. This widening gap between the rich and the poor can exacerbate social tensions and undermine social cohesion. Addressing this issue requires policies that promote equitable distribution of AI's benefits, such as progressive taxation, robust social safety nets, and investments in education and training programs that equip workers with the skills needed to compete in an AI-driven economy. This could involve exploring models like universal basic income (UBI), which could provide a safety net for those displaced by automation while stimulating demand and fostering economic innovation. The design and implementation of UBI, however, would require careful consideration of various factors, including funding mechanisms and potential unintended consequences.

Beyond employment and income inequality, the societal impacts of AI automation extend to issues of social welfare and access to opportunities. AI systems, if not carefully designed and implemented, can perpetuate and even amplify existing societal biases. Algorithmic bias, often embedded in training data, can lead to discriminatory outcomes in areas like hiring, loan applications, and even criminal justice. This necessitates the development of ethical guidelines and regulations for AI development and deployment, ensuring fairness, transparency, and accountability.

Furthermore, access to the benefits of AI technology is not uniformly distributed across the globe or even within nations. A digital divide, both in terms of access to technology and digital literacy, could exacerbate existing inequalities, creating a two-tiered society where those with access to AI-powered tools and services thrive while others are left behind. Bridging this digital divide is crucial for ensuring equitable access to the benefits of AI and preventing further marginalization. This could involve targeted investments in infrastructure, education, and training programs, particularly in underserved communities.

To mitigate the negative societal impacts of AI automation and ensure equitable distribution of benefits, proactive policy interventions are necessary. These interventions must encompass a multi-faceted approach, addressing various dimensions of the problem. Firstly, governments need to invest heavily in education and retraining programs that focus on developing uniquely human skills. These programs should not simply be remedial measures for those displaced by automation but should be forward-looking, anticipating the skills required in an AI-driven future. Secondly, social safety nets need to be strengthened to provide support for those affected by automation, including unemployment benefits, healthcare access, and affordable housing. This might involve exploring innovative approaches like UBI, which could serve as a cushion against job displacement and promote economic security.

Thirdly, regulations are needed to address algorithmic bias and ensure fairness and accountability in the design and deployment of AI systems. This might involve establishing independent auditing bodies to review algorithms for bias, mandating transparency in algorithmic decision-making, and implementing mechanisms for redress in cases of algorithmic discrimination.

Furthermore, fostering collaboration between government, industry, and academia is vital for navigating the societal impacts of AI. Open dialogue and knowledge sharing can lead to more effective policy design and implementation. This collaborative effort could involve establishing task forces and expert panels to study the impacts of AI on various sectors and develop evidence-based policy recommendations. Industry participation is essential in ensuring that regulations are practical and do not stifle innovation. Academic research can provide valuable insights into the long-term societal impacts of AI, informing policy decisions and ensuring that policies are grounded in robust evidence.

Beyond national policies, international collaboration is crucial in addressing the global societal impacts of AI. As AI technologies are increasingly interconnected across borders, a fragmented and inconsistent regulatory landscape could create challenges for both businesses and individuals. Harmonized standards and regulations across nations are essential for ensuring a fair and equitable global AI ecosystem. International cooperation on issues like data privacy, algorithmic transparency, and ethical guidelines for AI development can help prevent a race to the bottom, where countries compete to attract AI-related businesses by lowering regulatory standards.

In conclusion, the societal impacts of AI automation are profound and multifaceted, requiring a comprehensive and proactive approach to policy-making. Addressing these impacts necessitates a combination of investment in education and retraining programs, strengthening social safety nets, regulating against algorithmic bias, and fostering collaboration between government, industry, and academia. The path forward requires a long-term vision that prioritizes not only economic growth but also social equity and human well-being. Failure to address these societal challenges could exacerbate existing inequalities, leading to social unrest and undermining the potential benefits of AI for all members of society.

A collaborative, forward-thinking approach is essential for harnessing the transformative potential of AI while mitigating its potential risks and ensuring a future where technology serves humanity's best interests. The proactive adoption of sensible and ethical policies will be the key determinant in ensuring a future shaped by AI that benefits all members of society, not just a select few.

Chapter 14: The Future of Human-AI Collaboration

Augmenting Human Capabilities with AI A New Era of Productivity

The previous sections highlighted the considerable anxieties surrounding AI's impact on employment and societal structures. However, the narrative shouldn't solely focus on displacement and disruption. AI also presents a powerful opportunity to augment human capabilities, leading to a new era of unprecedented productivity and innovation. This augmentation isn't about replacing humans; it's about empowering them with tools that amplify their inherent strengths, creating a synergistic partnership where the combined output far surpasses the sum of its parts.

Consider the realm of design. Architects, for instance, traditionally relied on manual drafting and iterative physical models to visualize and refine their creations. Now, AI-powered tools can analyze vast datasets of architectural styles, building codes, and environmental factors, offering architects intelligent suggestions and alternative design options instantaneously. This doesn't eliminate the architect's creative vision; rather, it accelerates the design process, allowing for more iterations, greater exploration of possibilities, and ultimately, more innovative and sustainable structures. The human element—the artistic vision, the intuitive understanding of space and functionality—remains crucial, but AI acts as a powerful collaborator, enhancing speed, efficiency, and potentially, even the quality of the end result.

The same principle applies to fields like medicine. AI algorithms can analyze medical images with extraordinary speed and accuracy, identifying subtle anomalies that might escape the human eye.

Radiologists, armed with these AI-powered diagnostic tools, can interpret scans more efficiently, reducing diagnostic errors and improving patient outcomes. This isn't a question of replacing radiologists; it's about equipping them with tools that enhance their expertise, allowing them to focus on the more complex aspects of diagnosis and patient care. The human touch—the empathy, the personalized approach to treatment—remains irreplaceable, while AI handles the more computationally intensive aspects of the workflow.

The synergy extends beyond diagnosis. In drug discovery, AI is accelerating the identification of potential drug candidates by analyzing vast molecular databases and predicting their efficacy. While AI can identify promising molecules, the human expertise of chemists and biologists is still essential for understanding the intricacies of biological processes and ensuring the safety and efficacy of new drugs. The collaboration between human ingenuity and AI's computational power promises a revolutionary acceleration in the pace of medical advancements.

In manufacturing, AI-powered robots are transforming production lines. These robots aren't simply performing repetitive tasks; they're learning, adapting, and optimizing processes in real time. Human workers, instead of being replaced, are shifting their roles towards overseeing and managing these sophisticated systems, focusing on higher-level tasks like programming, maintenance, and quality control. This allows for greater efficiency, reduced error rates, and improved overall productivity. The human element, however, is still crucial—the expertise to maintain the robotic systems, troubleshoot problems, and adapt the production lines to changing demands.

The financial sector also benefits significantly from AI-driven augmentation. AI algorithms are analyzing market trends, predicting risks, and managing portfolios with greater efficiency than traditional methods. Financial analysts, instead of being replaced, are leveraging these tools to enhance their insights, develop more sophisticated investment strategies, and provide personalized financial advice to their clients. AI handles the computationally intensive tasks, allowing human analysts to focus on strategic planning, client relationships, and the interpretation of complex market dynamics.

Furthermore, AI is transforming the realm of education.

Personalized learning platforms, powered by AI, adapt to individual student needs, providing tailored content and feedback. This allows educators to focus on individualized instruction, mentoring, and fostering critical thinking skills—tasks that require the uniquely human capacity for empathy and understanding. AI handles the task of content delivery and assessment, while human educators focus on the crucial aspects of shaping young minds.

The examples are numerous and span across various sectors. In customer service, AI-powered chatbots provide immediate support, freeing human agents to handle more complex inquiries. In agriculture, AI-driven systems optimize crop yields and manage resources efficiently. In transportation, AI is improving traffic flow and enhancing logistics. In every instance, the pattern remains consistent: AI handles repetitive, computationally intensive tasks, freeing human workers to focus on higher-level functions requiring creativity, critical thinking, emotional intelligence, and complex problem-solving—skills that are uniquely human.

The key to successfully integrating AI into the workplace lies in understanding this symbiotic relationship. It's not about a human-versus-machine competition; it's about a human-machine collaboration. This collaboration demands a shift in mindset, both on the part of employees and employers. Employees must embrace AI as a tool to enhance their capabilities, learning how to effectively leverage these new technologies to improve their productivity and performance. Employers must invest in training and development programs to equip their workforce with the necessary skills to work alongside AI, fostering a culture of continuous learning and adaptation.

The successful integration of AI requires not only technological advancements but also a robust societal infrastructure. This includes access to quality education and training, social safety nets to support workers during transitions, and ethical guidelines to ensure responsible AI development and deployment. Addressing these societal considerations is critical to realizing the full potential of AI augmentation and ensuring that the benefits are shared broadly across society.

However, the implementation is not without its challenges. The transition to an AI-augmented workforce requires careful planning and execution. Companies need to develop strategies for reskilling and upskilling their employees, ensuring a smooth transition to new roles and responsibilities. This might involve providing training programs, mentorship opportunities, and career counseling to help workers adapt to the changing landscape of work.

Furthermore, the ethical implications of AI augmentation must be carefully considered. Concerns around data privacy, algorithmic bias, and job displacement need to be addressed proactively.

Transparent and accountable AI systems are crucial to ensure fairness and prevent unintended consequences. Establishing clear ethical guidelines and regulations is essential to guide the development and deployment of AI in the workplace.

In conclusion, the future of work isn't about humans versus AI; it's about humans *with* AI. This partnership holds the potential to unlock unprecedented levels of productivity and innovation, creating a more efficient, effective, and ultimately, more fulfilling work environment. By embracing AI as a tool to augment human capabilities, we can create a future where technology empowers individuals, fostering economic growth and societal progress. The key lies in proactively addressing the societal implications of this technological revolution, ensuring a just and equitable transition to an AI-augmented world where humans and machines work together to achieve shared goals. The potential rewards are immense, but the path requires careful navigation and a commitment to fostering a collaborative and ethical approach to AI integration. This necessitates a concerted effort from governments, businesses, and individuals alike to build a future where technology serves humanity's best interests.

Redefining Work Roles and Responsibilities in the Age of AI

The integration of AI into the workplace is not merely a technological shift; it's a profound societal transformation that necessitates a re-evaluation of work roles and responsibilities. The narrative often centers on job displacement, but a more nuanced perspective reveals the emergence of a symbiotic relationship between human expertise and artificial intelligence capabilities. This collaboration is fostering the creation of new job roles and the evolution of existing ones, reshaping the very fabric of the professional landscape.

Instead of a simple replacement of human workers, we are witnessing a profound augmentation of human capabilities. AI is handling the repetitive, data-heavy tasks, freeing human workers to focus on tasks that require uniquely human skills – critical thinking, creativity, emotional intelligence, complex problem-solving, and strategic decision-making. This shift demands a reassessment of traditional job descriptions and the creation of roles designed specifically to leverage this human-AI synergy.

One clear consequence is the emergence of entirely new job titles.

The demand for AI trainers, for example, is rapidly escalating. These professionals are responsible for teaching AI systems, fine-tuning their algorithms, and ensuring they function accurately and ethically. Their expertise lies not just in technical programming but also in understanding the nuances of human behavior and the potential for bias in algorithms. Similarly, the role of prompt engineers, individuals who craft effective prompts to elicit desired outputs from AI models, has gained immense importance, underscoring the human element required even in the most technologically advanced processes.

Data scientists, already a vital profession, are gaining even more significance in the age of AI. Their responsibility extends beyond simple data analysis; they are now tasked with managing vast datasets, ensuring data integrity, and interpreting the results of AI-driven analyses to inform strategic decisions. This requires not only technical expertise but also a deep understanding of the business context and the ability to communicate complex findings to non-technical audiences.

The evolution of existing roles is equally significant. Consider the role of a marketing manager. While AI can automate many aspects of marketing campaigns, such as targeted advertising and social media management, the human manager's role is shifting towards strategic planning, creative campaign development, and interpreting the insights generated by AI-powered analytics. They are no longer simply executing campaigns but leveraging AI to optimize their strategy and enhance the effectiveness of their marketing efforts. This requires a significant shift in skillset, emphasizing strategic thinking, creativity, and the ability to work effectively with AI tools.

Similarly, the role of a financial analyst is undergoing a transformation. AI-powered tools can analyze market trends and predict risks with remarkable speed and accuracy, but the human analyst's expertise remains vital in interpreting these predictions, developing sophisticated investment strategies, and providing personalized financial advice to clients. Their role is becoming more focused on strategic planning, risk management, and client relationships, while AI handles the more computationally intensive aspects of the job.

The legal profession is also experiencing a significant shift. AI-powered tools can now assist in legal research, document review, and contract analysis, freeing up lawyers to focus on more complex tasks, such as strategic litigation, client negotiation, and courtroom advocacy. This requires lawyers to develop proficiency in using AI tools, alongside maintaining their traditional legal expertise and ethical considerations.

Healthcare is another sector experiencing a dramatic reshaping of roles. AI-powered diagnostic tools are augmenting the capabilities of radiologists and other medical professionals, leading to more efficient diagnoses and improved patient outcomes. However, the human element—the empathy, the ability to build rapport with patients, and the nuanced understanding of individual medical histories—remains irreplaceable. The role of healthcare professionals is evolving to become more patient-focused, allowing AI to handle the more data-intensive aspects of their work.

Beyond these specific examples, the broader trend is the increasing demand for professionals with hybrid skillsets. Individuals who possess both strong technical expertise and a deep understanding of human-centered design, ethical considerations, and the intricacies of specific industries will be in high demand. This necessitates a shift in educational priorities, emphasizing interdisciplinary learning and the development of skills that complement AI capabilities.

Furthermore, the rise of AI necessitates a focus on continuous learning and adaptation. The rapid pace of technological change demands that professionals constantly update their skills and knowledge to remain relevant in the evolving workplace. This requires a cultural shift within organizations, fostering a culture of lifelong learning and providing employees with access to training and development opportunities.

The redefinition of work roles and responsibilities in the age of AI presents both challenges and opportunities. While some roles may be displaced, many more will be created or transformed, demanding a proactive approach to upskilling and reskilling the workforce.

Governments, businesses, and educational institutions must work together to ensure a smooth transition, providing the necessary support and resources for individuals to adapt to the changing landscape of work. This includes investing in education and training programs that equip individuals with the skills needed to thrive in an AI-augmented world.

Moreover, social safety nets must be strengthened to support those displaced by automation, ensuring a just and equitable transition.

The successful navigation of this transformation hinges on fostering a collaborative relationship between humans and AI, understanding that AI is not a replacement for human ingenuity but rather a tool to amplify it. By embracing this symbiotic relationship and proactively addressing the challenges, we can create a future where AI empowers individuals, fostering economic growth, societal progress, and a more fulfilling work environment for all. The key is to harness the power of AI not as a replacement, but as a catalyst for human potential, creating a future where humans and machines work in harmony to achieve shared goals and prosperity. This requires strategic foresight, collaborative effort, and a commitment to responsible innovation. The future of work is not a competition, but a partnership – a partnership between human ingenuity and artificial intelligence. And it's a partnership we must nurture and cultivate if we are to fully realize the transformative potential of this technological revolution.

The Changing Nature of Leadership in Human-AI Teams

The rise of AI necessitates a fundamental shift in leadership paradigms. No longer are leaders solely responsible for directing human teams; they now must effectively manage collaborations between humans and artificial intelligence. This requires a new skillset, a different approach to decision-making, and a profound understanding of the strengths and limitations of both human and AI collaborators. The traditional command-and-control leadership style is largely inadequate in this new environment; instead, leaders must embrace a more collaborative, adaptive, and even facilitative approach.

One of the most critical shifts is the need for leaders to become proficient in understanding and utilizing AI technologies. This doesn't require every leader to become a programmer, but a fundamental grasp of AI's capabilities, limitations, and ethical implications is crucial. Leaders need to understand how AI systems function, what types of tasks they excel at, and where human intervention is still necessary. This includes familiarity with different AI models, their strengths and weaknesses, and the potential for biases in algorithms. Furthermore, leaders need to be able to interpret the output generated by AI systems, recognizing the need for human oversight and validation.

Beyond technical proficiency, effective leadership in human-AI teams requires a deep understanding of human-AI interaction. Leaders must foster a collaborative environment where humans and AI work together seamlessly. This includes establishing clear communication channels, defining roles and responsibilities for both human and AI team members, and ensuring that the AI system is integrated appropriately into the workflow. It's critical to avoid the perception of AI as a threat, but rather to position it as a tool to enhance human capabilities. This means emphasizing the value of human intuition, creativity, and critical thinking, while simultaneously leveraging AI's ability to process vast amounts of data and automate repetitive tasks.

Emotional intelligence becomes even more crucial in this new context. Leaders must be adept at navigating the potential emotional responses of team members to the integration of AI.

Some individuals may feel threatened by the prospect of automation, while others may be excited by the possibilities.

Leaders must be able to address these concerns, foster trust and transparency, and ensure that the transition is managed effectively. Open communication, empathy, and active listening are critical in building a team that embraces AI as a partner, not a competitor.

Furthermore, the role of a leader shifts from primarily directing tasks to fostering a collaborative problem-solving environment. The leader's primary function is to set the strategic direction, define the overall goals, and ensure that the human-AI team is working towards a shared vision. However, the actual execution of tasks is increasingly shared between humans and AI, requiring the leader to act as a facilitator, guiding the collaborative process and ensuring that the contributions of both human and AI team members are effectively integrated.

Effective leadership in this context also entails a strong emphasis on continuous learning and adaptation. The rapid pace of technological advancement necessitates a constant reassessment of strategies and approaches. Leaders must encourage a culture of experimentation, learning from both successes and failures, and adapting to the evolving capabilities of AI systems. This includes providing opportunities for team members to develop new skills, acquire knowledge about AI technologies, and understand the implications of these technologies for their work.

Training programs, workshops, and access to relevant resources are essential in fostering a culture of continuous learning and adaptation.

Another critical aspect of leading human-AI teams is establishing clear ethical guidelines and protocols. Leaders must ensure that the AI system is used responsibly and ethically, avoiding biases and ensuring that it aligns with the organization's values and principles.

This includes considering the potential societal impact of the AI system, addressing issues of privacy and data security, and ensuring that the system is used in a way that is fair and equitable. A leader's responsibility extends beyond the immediate team; they must consider the broader societal ramifications of their AI deployments.

Illustrative examples of successful AI-augmented leadership are emerging across various industries. In healthcare, leaders are leveraging AI-powered diagnostic tools to improve the accuracy and efficiency of medical diagnoses, while still maintaining the crucial human element of patient care and personalized treatment plans. This requires leaders to not only select and implement the AI tools but also to train their teams on the effective use of these tools, ensuring that the human-AI collaboration enhances, not replaces, the expertise of medical professionals. The focus here is on augmentation, not replacement.

In finance, AI is revolutionizing risk management and investment strategies. However, successful leaders recognize that human judgment and expertise remain vital in interpreting AI-generated insights and making crucial investment decisions. They are not simply relying on AI algorithms; they are using AI to augment their own judgment and experience, leading to more informed and effective decisions. This underscores the importance of not just selecting appropriate AI tools, but also integrating them appropriately into existing workflows and decision-making processes.

Similarly, in the manufacturing sector, AI-powered robots are automating many tasks on the factory floor, but human workers are still essential for overseeing the robots, maintaining them, and ensuring the overall smooth operation of the production line.

Effective leaders in this context are focusing on creating a harmonious human-robot collaboration, leveraging the strengths of both humans and robots to optimize productivity and efficiency.

They are actively involved in managing the transition, providing training to workers, and addressing any concerns or anxieties surrounding the introduction of robots into the workspace.

However, challenges persist. One significant hurdle is the potential for bias in AI systems. If the data used to train an AI system is biased, the system itself will likely perpetuate those biases. This can lead to unfair or discriminatory outcomes, particularly in areas like hiring, loan applications, and criminal justice. Leaders must be aware of this potential and take steps to mitigate it. This includes carefully examining the data used to train AI systems, employing techniques to identify and correct biases, and implementing processes to ensure fairness and equity in the application of AI.

Another challenge is the potential for job displacement. While AI can augment human capabilities, it can also automate tasks previously performed by humans. Leaders must carefully manage this transition, providing support and retraining opportunities for employees whose roles may be affected. This requires a proactive approach to workforce planning, investing in employee training and development, and ensuring that employees have the skills they need to succeed in a changing workplace. Ethical considerations necessitate that leaders prioritize the well-being of their workforce.

Furthermore, ensuring the security and privacy of data used by AI systems is paramount. Leaders must implement robust security measures to protect sensitive information and comply with relevant regulations. This includes adopting appropriate data encryption techniques, implementing access control mechanisms, and establishing clear protocols for data handling and storage.

In conclusion, the leadership landscape is being radically transformed by the integration of AI. Successful leaders are those who embrace a collaborative, adaptive, and ethically-minded approach, recognizing the strengths and limitations of both human and AI collaborators. They are not simply managers of human teams, but architects of human-AI partnerships, fostering a culture of continuous learning, collaboration, and ethical responsibility.

The future of work is a human-AI collaboration, and the leaders who can successfully navigate this new terrain will be instrumental in shaping the future of work and driving progress in the 21st century. The shift requires proactive leadership, a commitment to lifelong learning, and a deep understanding of both technology and human dynamics. The future belongs to those who can forge this new partnership effectively and ethically.

Managing the Human-AI Relationship Fostering Trust and Collaboration

Building trust between humans and AI is paramount for successful collaboration. This isn't simply about accepting AI as a tool; it's about fostering a genuine partnership where human strengths complement AI's capabilities. Transparency is key. Employees need to understand how the AI system works, what data it uses, and how its decisions are made. This transparency fosters a sense of control and reduces anxieties about job security or the perception of AI as a mysterious, potentially adversarial entity. Openly sharing information about the AI's limitations and the areas where human judgment is still essential builds trust and validates the human role in the process.

One effective strategy is to involve employees in the AI implementation process. Seeking their input on how AI can best support their work, addressing their concerns, and incorporating their feedback into the system's design helps build ownership and buy-in. This participatory approach ensures the AI system is not imposed upon employees but rather integrated as a collaborative partner, designed to enhance, not replace, their contributions.

Regular feedback sessions, where employees can share their experiences and suggest improvements, are crucial for maintaining open communication and building trust.

Furthermore, training programs focused not just on the technical aspects of AI but also on its ethical and societal implications are vital. These programs should equip employees with the skills to understand and critically evaluate AI's output, identify potential biases, and raise ethical concerns when necessary. Such education empowers employees, reducing their fear of the unknown and providing them with the tools to actively participate in the human-AI partnership. This collaborative approach to training fosters a shared understanding of the technology and its role within the organization, solidifying trust and facilitating successful integration.

Effective communication is crucial for navigating the human-AI relationship. Clear communication protocols should be established, specifying how humans will interact with the AI system, how data will be shared, and how feedback will be provided. This structured approach prevents misunderstandings and ensures that everyone is on the same page. The communication channels must be easily accessible, allowing for seamless information exchange and quick resolution of any issues that might arise. This could involve dedicated communication platforms, regular meetings, or even integrating AI feedback directly into existing workflow systems.

Another crucial aspect of fostering collaboration is defining clear roles and responsibilities for both human and AI team members. This ensures that there is no overlap or ambiguity in tasks and that everyone understands their contribution to the overall objective. The AI should be viewed as a tool augmenting human capabilities, not replacing them. For instance, AI might handle data analysis and pattern recognition, while humans focus on strategic decision-making, creativity, and complex problem-solving that require nuanced human judgment and intuition. By clearly delineating these responsibilities, conflicts are minimized, and collaboration becomes more efficient.

However, managing the human-AI relationship also requires anticipating and addressing potential conflicts. One common concern is job displacement. Open communication about potential automation and the implementation of retraining programs that prepare employees for new roles is crucial in mitigating anxieties and fostering a sense of security. Leaders should emphasize the transformative nature of AI, highlighting its potential to create new opportunities and roles within the organization rather than solely focusing on job displacement. This requires a long-term perspective on workforce development, with continuous investment in employee skill enhancement and adaptation.

Another potential conflict arises from the limitations of AI. AI systems are not infallible; they can make mistakes, and their decisions might not always align with human intuition or judgment.

Establishing mechanisms for human oversight and validation is crucial. This includes creating systems where human employees can review and approve AI-generated outputs, ensuring accuracy and correcting errors before final decisions are made. This dual-check system safeguards against potential negative consequences while reinforcing the importance of human expertise.

Furthermore, managing biases in AI systems is critical. AI systems trained on biased data will produce biased outcomes, leading to unfair or discriminatory results. Leaders must implement rigorous processes for detecting and mitigating these biases, including regular audits of AI decision-making processes and careful selection of training data to ensure fairness and equity. Transparency in these processes is crucial for building and maintaining trust within the workforce. This involves not just technological solutions but also the implementation of robust ethical guidelines that guide AI development and deployment.

Addressing the challenges associated with data privacy and security is also essential for building trust. Employees need to be assured that their data is being handled responsibly and securely, in compliance with relevant regulations. This requires transparent data handling policies, robust security measures to protect sensitive information, and mechanisms for addressing data breaches if they occur. Establishing clear protocols and demonstrating a commitment to data security instills confidence among employees and minimizes concerns about potential misuse of their personal information.

Finally, fostering a culture of continuous learning and adaptation is crucial. The rapid pace of technological advancement necessitates ongoing training and development for both human and AI systems.

This includes providing employees with opportunities to learn about new AI technologies, understand their implications for their work, and acquire new skills to thrive in the evolving workplace.

This continuous learning process strengthens the human-AI partnership, allowing employees to adapt to new technologies and contribute effectively to a dynamic and increasingly automated environment. A culture of continuous improvement benefits both the employees and the organization, ensuring that the collaboration remains efficient and effective.

In conclusion, managing the human-AI relationship requires a proactive, multifaceted approach. It's not enough to simply introduce AI into the workplace; it requires a strategic effort to build trust, foster collaboration, and address potential challenges proactively. By focusing on transparency, communication, role clarity, conflict resolution, bias mitigation, data security, and continuous learning, organizations can create a successful human-AI partnership that drives innovation, efficiency, and overall success in the age of artificial intelligence. This integrated approach is not just about utilizing AI; it's about building a resilient and adaptable workforce that can thrive in an increasingly AI-driven world.

Embracing a Human-Centered Approach to AI Integration

The successful integration of AI isn't solely about technological prowess; it's profoundly about people. A human-centered approach places human well-being, ethical considerations, and the broader social impact of AI at the forefront of every decision, from initial design to ongoing implementation. This isn't a peripheral concern; it's the foundational principle upon which successful and sustainable AI integration rests. Ignoring this crucial aspect can lead to resistance, resentment, and ultimately, failure to realize the full potential of AI within the organization.

A human-centered approach begins with recognizing the anxieties and uncertainties surrounding AI adoption. The fear of job displacement is a legitimate concern, and addressing it head-on is crucial. Instead of viewing AI as a replacement for human workers, we must reframe it as a tool to augment human capabilities, freeing up individuals to focus on higher-level tasks that require creativity, critical thinking, and emotional intelligence – areas where humans currently excel and are unlikely to be easily replaced by AI. This requires a strategic shift in workforce development, investing in reskilling and upskilling initiatives to equip employees with the skills necessary to thrive in this evolving landscape. Transparency in this process is critical. Openly communicating potential changes, outlining plans for retraining, and offering support systems to ease the transition will build trust and alleviate anxiety. This proactive approach fosters a sense of security and collaboration rather than fostering a climate of fear and uncertainty.

Ethical considerations are paramount. Bias in algorithms, a prevalent issue in AI systems, can perpetuate and even amplify existing societal inequalities. A human-centered approach necessitates a rigorous commitment to fairness and accountability.

This includes scrutinizing the data used to train AI systems, ensuring it is representative and free from biases, and implementing mechanisms to identify and mitigate bias in AI outputs. Regular audits of AI decision-making processes and ongoing monitoring are critical for maintaining ethical standards. Furthermore, ethical guidelines need to be clearly defined and communicated, ensuring that everyone involved understands their responsibilities in promoting ethical AI practices. The development and deployment of AI should not simply be driven by technological advancement; it should be guided by a strong ethical compass.

The social impact of AI integration extends beyond the immediate workforce. It affects the community, the industry, and even broader society. A human-centered approach requires considering the potential implications of AI on various stakeholders, including customers, suppliers, and the wider community. This might involve assessing the impact of AI-driven automation on employment in related industries or analyzing the potential consequences of AI-powered decision-making on social equity. Proactive engagement with stakeholders, fostering open dialogue, and establishing mechanisms for feedback and collaboration are essential for addressing potential societal impacts and building a shared understanding of the benefits and challenges of AI integration.

Central to a human-centered approach are several key principles.

First, **prioritize human well-being**: The design and implementation of AI systems should always prioritize the well-being of human workers, promoting a safe, supportive, and fulfilling work environment. This includes promoting work-life balance, addressing potential stress associated with AI integration, and ensuring that AI tools are designed to support, rather than overburden, human employees. Second, **embrace collaboration** : View AI as a collaborative partner, not a replacement for human intelligence. Foster a culture of collaboration between humans and AI, leveraging the strengths of both to achieve common goals. This involves designing systems that support seamless human-AI interaction, facilitating a smooth workflow and clear communication channels. Third,

promote transparency and explainability: Ensure that AI systems are transparent and explainable, allowing humans to understand how decisions are made and why. This fosters trust and accountability and helps to address concerns about the "black box" nature of some AI systems. Fourth, **ensure fairness and equity**: Implement rigorous measures to prevent bias and ensure that AI systems treat all individuals fairly, regardless of their background or characteristics. This includes rigorous testing and monitoring of algorithms to identify and mitigate potential biases. Fifth, **focus on continuous learning and adaptation**: AI is constantly evolving. Invest in ongoing training and development for employees, equipping them with the skills to work effectively alongside AI systems and adapt to the changing nature of their roles. This includes not just technical training but also training on ethical considerations, critical thinking, and problem-solving.

Implementing these principles necessitates a structured approach. It begins with a thorough needs assessment to identify specific areas where AI can enhance productivity and efficiency without compromising human well-being or ethical principles. This assessment should involve input from employees at all levels, gathering their perspectives and addressing concerns proactively.

The development process itself should be iterative, involving ongoing feedback loops to ensure the AI system aligns with human needs and expectations. Regular evaluations of the system's performance, focusing not just on efficiency but also on its impact on employee well-being and ethical considerations, are critical for continuous improvement. Finally, it's crucial to establish clear communication channels to facilitate ongoing dialogue between employees and management, fostering a culture of open communication and feedback.

The adoption of a human-centered approach to AI integration is not merely a matter of best practice; it is a strategic imperative for long-term success. It fosters a workforce that is not only efficient and productive but also engaged, empowered, and committed to the organization's success. By prioritizing human well-being, embracing collaboration, promoting transparency, ensuring fairness, and focusing on continuous learning, organizations can harness the transformative power of AI while preserving the essential human element that drives innovation and fuels organizational growth. The future of work is not about humans versus AI; it is about humans *with* AI, a powerful partnership built on mutual respect, collaboration, and a shared commitment to a future where technology empowers, rather than replaces, human potential. This approach will not only ensure the successful integration of AI but also pave the way for a more equitable, sustainable, and fulfilling future of work for all. The human element is not just a crucial part of the equation, it's the key to unlocking the true potential of artificial intelligence. Ignoring this fundamental truth would be a grave strategic error.

Chapter 15: Conclusion: Thriving in the Age of AI

Recap of Key Strategies for FutureProofing Your Career

We've journeyed through the transformative landscape of AI's impact on the workplace, examining its rapid integration across various sectors and levels of expertise. We've debunked the misconception that only low-skilled jobs are vulnerable, showcasing how AI's automation capabilities are reshaping roles from entry-level positions to executive suites. This journey has not been about fear-mongering but about equipping you with the knowledge and tools to navigate this new era successfully. The central message, repeatedly emphasized throughout this book, is that proactive adaptation, not passive acceptance, is the key to thriving in the age of AI. This isn't merely about survival; it's about securing promotions, accessing high-paying opportunities, and shaping a fulfilling and successful career trajectory in an evolving job market.

The core of our proactive strategy rests on three interconnected pillars: embracing AI tools, cultivating uniquely human skills, and establishing yourself as an AI-literate leader. Let's revisit each of these, solidifying their importance and translating them into actionable steps you can implement immediately.

Embracing AI Tools: From User to Collaborator

The first step is not about fearing AI but about understanding it, becoming comfortable with its capabilities, and strategically integrating it into your daily workflow. This goes beyond merely using AI-powered tools; it's about understanding their underlying mechanisms and limitations. Start by identifying the specific AI tools relevant to your industry and profession. This might involve exploring AI-powered writing assistants, data analysis software, project management platforms, or specialized applications within your field. Don't simply use these tools passively; actively seek opportunities to master them. Explore their advanced functionalities, experiment with different techniques, and actively seek feedback on the quality and efficiency of your work.

The key is to move beyond being a mere user and become a collaborator with AI. This means leveraging AI's capabilities to augment your own skills, not to replace them. For instance, a marketing professional might use AI to analyze large datasets of consumer behavior, identifying trends and patterns that would be impossible to discern manually. This allows them to focus their time and energy on the creative and strategic aspects of their role, developing innovative campaigns and crafting compelling narratives. Similarly, a financial analyst might use AI-powered tools to automate routine tasks, such as data entry and report generation, freeing up time for more complex analysis and strategic decision-making. The goal isn't to become an AI engineer, but to become proficient enough in using AI tools to significantly enhance your efficiency and productivity.

Consider this: a lawyer might use AI to sift through vast volumes of legal documents, identifying relevant precedents and clauses far more efficiently than manual review. This frees them to dedicate more time to strategic legal argumentation and client interaction—tasks that demand uniquely human skills. A doctor might use AI for preliminary diagnosis, leading to more rapid and accurate initial assessments, allowing more time for personalized patient care and complex case management. The effectiveness of these examples isn't about replacing the professionals; instead, they're about creating space for them to perform their critical human roles more effectively.

Developing proficiency with these tools requires a commitment to continuous learning. Stay updated on the latest advancements in AI technology and the emergence of new tools relevant to your field. Participate in online courses, workshops, and industry conferences to expand your knowledge and skillset. Follow relevant industry blogs and publications to stay informed about best practices and emerging trends. This ongoing commitment to learning will not only make you a more valuable asset to your employer but also open up new career opportunities.

Cultivating Uniquely Human Skills: The Irreplaceable Edge

While AI excels at automating tasks based on patterns and data, it significantly lags in areas requiring uniquely human skills. These are the capabilities that will become increasingly valuable in an AI-driven workplace. These skills include:

Emotional Intelligence: The ability to understand and manage emotions, both your own and those of others, is crucial in building relationships, resolving conflicts, and navigating complex social dynamics. This is an area where AI currently falls short. Invest in developing your emotional intelligence through self-reflection, mindfulness practices, and interpersonal skills training.

Critical Thinking and Problem-Solving: AI can process vast amounts of data, but it still struggles with complex, ambiguous problems that demand creative solutions and critical evaluation of information. Sharpen your critical thinking skills by engaging in debates, analyzing complex issues, and developing your ability to identify biases and assumptions.

Creativity and Innovation: AI can generate creative outputs, but it lacks the originality, imagination, and emotional depth that fuels truly innovative ideas. Cultivate your creativity by engaging in activities that spark your imagination, experimenting with new approaches, and embracing risk-taking.

Complex Communication and Storytelling: AI can generate text and translate languages, but it lacks the nuance, empathy, and persuasive power of human communication. Develop your communication skills by practicing clear and concise writing, honing your public speaking abilities, and mastering the art of storytelling.

Adaptability and Lifelong Learning: The pace of technological change is accelerating, demanding a commitment to continuous learning and adaptation. Embrace new technologies and methodologies, be open to feedback, and actively seek opportunities to expand your skillset.

Developing these uniquely human skills requires a deliberate and ongoing effort. Consider enrolling in courses focusing on emotional intelligence, critical thinking, or creative problem-solving. Seek out mentors who can guide your development and provide valuable feedback. Actively engage in projects that challenge you to apply these skills in practical situations. This continuous investment in your personal and professional growth will differentiate you from the competition and make you an indispensable asset in an AI-driven workplace.

Positioning Yourself as an AI-Literate Leader: Shaping the Future of Work

The final pillar of our strategy involves not just mastering AI tools and human skills but also positioning yourself as a leader who understands and can effectively leverage AI within your organization. This means developing a deep understanding of AI's capabilities and limitations, its ethical implications, and its potential impact on your industry. It also involves fostering a collaborative environment where humans and AI work together to achieve shared goals.

This leadership role necessitates:

Strategic Foresight: Anticipate how AI will affect your organization and your industry. Identify potential opportunities and challenges, and develop strategies to leverage AI to improve efficiency and competitiveness.

Ethical Awareness: Understand the ethical considerations surrounding AI, including bias, privacy, and accountability. Develop policies and procedures to ensure the ethical and responsible use of AI within your organization.

Change Management: Effectively manage the transition to an AI-driven workplace. Communicate openly with employees, addressing their concerns and providing support during the change process.

Collaboration and Teamwork: Foster a collaborative environment where humans and AI work together effectively. Develop workflows and processes that optimize the contributions of both human workers and AI systems.

Developing your leadership capabilities in the age of AI is not simply about acquiring technical knowledge. It is about cultivating the strategic thinking, ethical awareness, and emotional intelligence needed to navigate the complexities of this rapidly changing landscape. Seek opportunities to lead projects involving AI implementation. Actively participate in discussions about the ethical and societal implications of AI. Mentor junior colleagues, sharing your knowledge and experience to help them succeed in this new era. Building these leadership qualities will position you for advancement and influence in your organization.

In conclusion, the future of work in the age of AI is not about fear or resignation. It's about embracing the opportunities presented by this transformative technology while simultaneously cultivating the uniquely human skills that will continue to be in high demand. By actively embracing AI tools, developing irreplaceable human skills, and positioning yourself as an AI-literate leader, you will not only navigate the changes successfully, but you will also thrive in this new era, achieving your professional aspirations and creating a fulfilling and impactful career. The proactive steps outlined in this book are not just recommendations; they are your roadmap to success in the age of artificial intelligence. The path forward is clear: adapt, learn, lead. The future of your career is in your hands.

The Importance of Continuous Learning and Adaptation

The journey through this book has underscored the profound and multifaceted impact of artificial intelligence on the modern workplace. We've explored how AI is reshaping roles across all sectors and skill levels, dispelling the myth that only low-skilled jobs are at risk. But the narrative isn't one of impending doom; it's a roadmap for navigating this transformation, not just surviving but thriving. This final section emphasizes a crucial element underpinning that success: the unwavering commitment to continuous learning and adaptation.

In the rapidly evolving landscape of AI, complacency is a luxury we cannot afford. The skills and knowledge that are highly valued today might become obsolete tomorrow. This isn't a pessimistic outlook; it's a call to action – a recognition that lifelong learning is no longer a desirable attribute but a fundamental necessity for career resilience in the age of AI. The ability to adapt, to learn new skills, and to embrace emerging technologies is the key differentiator between those who simply weather the storm and those who seize the opportunities presented by this technological revolution.

This necessitates a paradigm shift in our approach to professional development. The traditional model of acquiring a skill set and then relying on that expertise for an entire career is no longer sustainable. The speed of technological advancement, particularly within the AI sector, demands a more dynamic and agile approach to learning. We must move from a mindset of static skill acquisition to one of continuous learning and iterative skill enhancement.

This continuous learning isn't about haphazardly pursuing every new trend; it's a strategic and focused endeavor. It requires a careful analysis of emerging technologies, an understanding of the evolving demands of your industry, and a proactive identification of skills that will be valuable in the future. This involves several key elements:

Staying Informed: This goes beyond simply reading industry news.

It means actively engaging with the field, participating in discussions, and seeking diverse perspectives. Subscribe to relevant journals and newsletters. Attend webinars and conferences. Engage with online communities dedicated to AI and its applications within your field. This constant intake of information keeps you at the forefront of innovation, allowing you to anticipate changes and adapt proactively.

Targeted Skill Development: Identifying specific skills gaps is crucial. Analyze your current skill set and compare it to the projected demands of your field. Are there specific AI tools or techniques that you need to master? Are there areas where human skills are becoming increasingly valuable? Once you've identified these areas, you can actively seek out learning opportunities, such as online courses, workshops, boot camps, or even mentorship programs.

Embracing New Technologies: Don't shy away from new tools and platforms. Many are designed to simplify tasks and enhance productivity. Explore AI-powered tools that are relevant to your profession – whether it's data analysis software, project management platforms, or specialized applications within your industry. Experiment with these tools, learn their capabilities, and find ways to integrate them into your workflow to boost efficiency and improve your output.

The impact of continuous learning extends beyond simply maintaining one's current position. It's a catalyst for career advancement and unlocking new opportunities. By developing a reputation as a quick learner, adaptable professional, and someone who actively seeks to improve their skills, you position yourself for greater responsibility and higher-level roles within your organization. This commitment to lifelong learning becomes a significant differentiator in the job market, making you a more attractive candidate for future opportunities.

Consider the case of a marketing professional. Just a few years ago, digital marketing involved a relatively straightforward set of skills. Today, it's inextricably linked with AI. This professional needs to not only understand the fundamentals of SEO, social media, and content marketing, but also have a working knowledge of AI-powered tools for ad targeting, customer segmentation, and content creation. Those who fail to adapt will find themselves outpaced by colleagues who embrace continuous learning.

Similarly, a financial analyst must master AI-driven tools for predictive modeling, risk assessment, and algorithmic trading. The ability to effectively use these tools, not merely as users, but as collaborators capable of interpreting the outputs and making informed decisions, will define success in this field. This requires ongoing training and exploration of new methodologies within the rapidly evolving landscape of financial technology.

Even roles traditionally perceived as immune to automation require ongoing adaptation. A surgeon, for instance, benefits from continuous learning in utilizing AI-powered diagnostic tools and robotic surgical systems. While the core surgical skills remain paramount, the integration of AI tools enhances precision, minimizes invasiveness, and facilitates faster recovery times.

Staying abreast of these technological advancements is not optional; it is essential for maintaining the highest standards of care and professional expertise.

Moreover, continuous learning cultivates a mindset of growth and resilience. The ability to embrace change, adapt to new situations, and continuously learn is not only valuable in a professional context but also crucial for personal fulfillment. It fosters a sense of agency and control amidst the rapid pace of technological change, preventing a sense of being overwhelmed and powerless.

However, continuous learning is not just about acquiring technical skills. It also necessitates a deep understanding of the ethical and societal implications of AI. We must grapple with issues of bias, fairness, transparency, and accountability as AI systems become increasingly integrated into our lives. Understanding these ethical considerations is crucial for ensuring that AI is used responsibly and for the benefit of society.

In essence, continuous learning and adaptation is not merely a component of success in the AI-driven workplace; it is the bedrock upon which long-term career viability is built. It's the compass guiding us through the uncharted waters of technological advancement, equipping us not just to survive, but to flourish in a world increasingly shaped by artificial intelligence. Embracing this principle is not simply a professional imperative; it's a pathway to a more rewarding and fulfilling career journey. The future of work belongs to those who continually learn, adapt, and lead.

Embracing the Opportunities Presented by AI

The preceding chapters have detailed the significant shifts AI is bringing to the workplace, dispelling the misconception that only low-skill jobs are at risk. We've examined the pervasive influence of AI across various sectors, from finance and marketing to leadership roles. However, the overarching message isn't one of impending obsolescence, but rather of immense opportunity. The key to thriving in this new era isn't resisting change, but proactively embracing it, viewing AI not as a threat, but as a powerful tool for growth and advancement.

This transformation requires a shift in mindset. Instead of fearing AI's capabilities, we must leverage them to enhance our own productivity and potential. AI is not intended to replace human ingenuity; rather, it's designed to augment it, freeing us from repetitive tasks and allowing us to focus on higher-level strategic thinking, creative problem-solving, and complex decision-making—tasks that currently remain uniquely human.

Consider the example of a data analyst. While AI can automate data cleaning and basic statistical analysis, the analyst's role evolves to become more strategic. Instead of spending hours sifting through spreadsheets, they can use AI tools to identify trends and patterns, allowing them to focus on interpreting the data, formulating insights, and providing actionable recommendations. The human element remains crucial in understanding the context of the data, formulating insightful narratives, and translating complex information into digestible insights for stakeholders.

This shift towards higher-level thinking and strategic decision-making extends to other roles as well. In marketing, AI-powered tools can automate campaign optimization, but the human strategist remains vital in determining campaign goals, crafting compelling narratives, and understanding the nuances of consumer behavior. In finance, AI algorithms can analyze market trends and predict potential risks, but the human financial advisor is still essential in providing personalized guidance, building client relationships, and managing complex portfolios.

The opportunities presented by AI extend beyond enhanced efficiency and productivity. It also opens doors to entirely new roles and industries. The development, implementation, and maintenance of AI systems require a skilled workforce capable of designing, training, and managing these complex technologies. This creates a burgeoning demand for AI specialists, data scientists, machine learning engineers, and AI ethicists. These are high-demand, high-paying jobs that simply didn't exist a few years ago.

Moreover, AI fosters innovation and creativity. By automating mundane tasks, AI frees up human resources to focus on more creative endeavors. This could lead to breakthroughs in various fields, including medicine, engineering, and the arts. Imagine a composer using AI to generate unique melodies, then building upon these to create entirely new musical compositions. Or a physician using AI to diagnose diseases more efficiently, freeing up more time for direct patient care and personalized treatment. These are just a few examples of how AI can empower human creativity and lead to groundbreaking innovations.

Furthermore, AI is not only transforming individual roles, but also reshaping entire industries. Consider the rise of personalized medicine, where AI algorithms analyze patient data to tailor treatment plans. Or the emergence of smart cities, where AI manages traffic flow, optimizes energy consumption, and improves public safety. These advancements necessitate a workforce that is not only AI-literate but also capable of collaborating effectively with AI systems.

The key to leveraging these opportunities lies in proactive adaptation. We need to constantly upskill and reskill ourselves to remain relevant in a rapidly changing job market. This means actively seeking out opportunities to learn new technologies, develop our human skills, and network with professionals in related fields. Investing in continuous learning is not merely a suggestion; it is a necessity for survival and thriving in the age of AI.

This continuous learning isn't a passive process. It demands a proactive approach, encompassing several key strategies. First, it's vital to identify the skills gap between your existing capabilities and the future needs of your profession. This requires careful self-assessment and diligent research, analyzing the latest industry trends and the capabilities of emerging AI tools. Are there specific AI tools or techniques that could enhance your productivity? Are there emerging areas where human expertise will be particularly valuable?

Second, having identified these areas, the next step is to actively seek out learning opportunities. This could involve enrolling in online courses, attending workshops, pursuing formal education, or engaging in mentorship programs. Numerous online platforms offer high-quality courses in AI-related fields, from basic programming to advanced machine learning techniques. Industry conferences and workshops provide opportunities to network with peers and stay abreast of the latest advancements. Mentorship programs can offer invaluable guidance from experienced professionals, offering personalized insights and support.

Third, it's crucial to embrace new technologies and actively experiment with AI-powered tools. Many of these tools are designed to streamline workflows and boost efficiency. Don't be afraid to explore new software, platforms, and applications that are relevant to your profession.

Experiment with different tools, learn their functionalities, and identify ways to integrate them into your work processes to improve your productivity and output. The learning curve might be steep initially, but the long-term benefits far outweigh the initial effort.

Fourth, proactively cultivate uniquely human skills that are difficult for AI to replicate. These include emotional intelligence, critical thinking, complex problem-solving, creativity, and adaptability.

These skills are increasingly valuable in the age of AI, as they enable us to collaborate effectively with AI systems, to make insightful judgments, and to navigate complex and uncertain situations. Developing and honing these human skills differentiates us from AI and positions us for success in the future.

Fifth, foster a growth mindset. View challenges as opportunities for learning and growth. Embrace change as a catalyst for innovation and self-improvement. This mindset allows individuals to adapt readily to new technologies and evolving job requirements, ensuring continued relevance and competitiveness in a dynamic job market.

Finally, embrace lifelong learning as a continuous process. The rapid pace of technological advancement requires constant upskilling and reskilling. Commit to ongoing professional development, actively seeking new knowledge and skills throughout your career. This continuous learning is not merely a professional imperative but also a key to personal growth and fulfillment.

In conclusion, the advent of AI presents not a threat, but a remarkable opportunity. By embracing change, proactively adapting to new technologies, and cultivating uniquely human skills, we can not only navigate the evolving landscape of the workplace, but also seize the considerable advantages AI offers. The future of work belongs to those who are agile, adaptive, and committed to continuous learning. AI is not a replacement for human ingenuity; it is a powerful tool that, when harnessed effectively, can elevate our capabilities and usher in a new era of unprecedented professional growth and fulfillment. The future is not about resisting AI, but about collaborating with it, innovating with it, and thriving alongside it. Embrace the change, and unlock your full potential in the age of artificial intelligence.

Building a Resilient and Fulfilling Career in the Age of AI

The previous discussion highlighted the transformative power of AI across various industries and job roles. However, the true impact of this technological revolution isn't simply about surviving the changes—it's about thriving amidst them. This necessitates a proactive and strategic approach to career development, one that embraces continuous learning, cultivates uniquely human skills, and navigates the evolving job market with resilience and foresight.

Building a fulfilling career in the age of AI isn't about clinging to outdated skills or fearing automation. Instead, it's about recognizing AI as a powerful tool that can augment human capabilities, creating new opportunities and enhancing productivity. This requires a shift in mindset, from viewing AI as a threat to recognizing it as a collaborator.

One crucial element in this transformation is the cultivation of uniquely human skills—attributes that AI, at least for the foreseeable future, cannot replicate. These are not merely soft skills; they are the essential qualities that define human ingenuity, creativity, and adaptability. Emotional intelligence, for instance, plays a critical role in building strong relationships, understanding diverse perspectives, and navigating complex interpersonal dynamics. In a world increasingly reliant on AI-driven systems, the capacity for empathy, understanding, and nuanced communication becomes even more valuable.

Similarly, critical thinking remains paramount. While AI can process vast quantities of data and identify patterns, it lacks the inherent human capacity for independent thought, critical analysis, and the ability to make nuanced judgments within a broader context. The ability to evaluate information objectively, identify biases, and formulate well-reasoned conclusions is indispensable in an era of information overload. This requires developing the skill to question assumptions, analyze data critically, and form independent, well-supported conclusions.

Problem-solving, too, transcends simple algorithmic solutions.

While AI can excel at tackling structured problems, many real-world challenges are complex, multifaceted, and require creative, out-of-the-box thinking. The human ability to connect seemingly disparate ideas, identify innovative solutions, and adapt to unexpected circumstances remains invaluable. This involves the ability to not only solve problems, but also anticipate them, identify potential obstacles, and devise preventative measures. This adaptability is a critical skill, allowing professionals to navigate uncertainty and capitalize on unforeseen opportunities.

Furthermore, creativity remains a distinctly human trait. While AI can generate content and designs based on patterns, it lacks the imagination and originality that drives true innovation. The ability to envision new possibilities, conceive original ideas, and translate them into tangible outcomes is increasingly valuable in an AI-driven world. This creative thinking is essential for both innovation and problem-solving, driving the development of novel solutions and contributing to breakthroughs in various fields.

Adaptability, the capacity to adjust to change and thrive in dynamic environments, is another vital skill. The rapid pace of technological advancement requires professionals to continuously acquire new skills and adapt to evolving job requirements. This necessitates a mindset of lifelong learning, a commitment to continuous professional development, and a willingness to embrace new technologies and methodologies. This adaptability will prove essential not only in the immediate future but also in the longer term, as the landscape of work continues to evolve around us.

Beyond cultivating these uniquely human skills, building a resilient and fulfilling career necessitates embracing continuous learning. The rapid pace of technological advancement means that the skills valued today might be obsolete tomorrow. Therefore, committing to lifelong learning is not merely a professional advantage; it's a necessity for survival and advancement.

This commitment requires more than passively absorbing information; it demands a proactive approach to skill development.

Individuals must regularly assess their skill sets, identify areas needing improvement, and proactively seek out learning opportunities. This could involve pursuing online courses, attending workshops and conferences, engaging in mentorship programs, or pursuing formal education. Numerous online platforms offer high-quality courses in various fields, allowing individuals to acquire new skills at their own pace. Industry conferences and workshops provide opportunities for networking and keeping abreast of current trends. Mentorship programs offer invaluable insights from experienced professionals, offering personalized guidance and support.

Furthermore, it's crucial to embrace experimentation with new technologies. AI-powered tools are constantly emerging, and familiarity with these tools can significantly enhance productivity and efficiency. Experimenting with different software, platforms, and applications allows individuals to understand their functionalities and identify ways to integrate them into their work processes. The initial learning curve may be steep, but the long-term benefits far outweigh the initial investment of time and effort.

Networking also plays a crucial role. Building strong relationships with colleagues, mentors, and industry professionals can open doors to new opportunities, facilitate knowledge sharing, and provide support during challenging times. Participating in industry events, joining professional organizations, and actively engaging in online communities can broaden one's network and enhance career prospects. Networking is not simply about accumulating contacts; it's about cultivating meaningful relationships that can enhance professional development and future opportunities.

Finally, building a resilient and fulfilling career necessitates a growth mindset. This involves viewing challenges as opportunities for learning and growth, embracing change as a catalyst for innovation, and maintaining a positive attitude towards continuous improvement. A growth mindset empowers individuals to adapt readily to new technologies and evolving job requirements, fostering a sense of agency and control over their career trajectory. This proactive attitude is essential for navigating the dynamic world of work and achieving lasting professional success and fulfillment.

In conclusion, thriving in the age of AI demands a proactive and strategic approach to career development. By cultivating uniquely human skills, embracing continuous learning, proactively engaging with new technologies, building a strong network, and fostering a growth mindset, individuals can not only navigate the evolving job market but also seize the significant opportunities presented by this transformative technological revolution. The future of work belongs to those who are agile, adaptive, and committed to lifelong learning– those who view AI not as a threat, but as a powerful catalyst for growth, innovation, and ultimately, a more fulfilling and resilient career. The key is not to fear the change, but to embrace it, learn from it, and leverage it to achieve lasting professional success and fulfillment.

Looking Ahead The Long-Term Vision for Human-AI Collaboration

Looking beyond the immediate challenges and opportunities presented by AI, we can envision a future workplace characterized by seamless human-AI collaboration. This isn't a utopian fantasy; it's a realistic projection based on current trends and the inherent potential of this powerful technology. The long-term vision is not one of human replacement, but of human augmentation – a partnership where AI handles repetitive, data-intensive tasks, freeing up human workers to focus on creative problem-solving, strategic decision-making, and the uniquely human aspects of work that require empathy, critical thinking, and nuanced judgment.

This collaborative model will redefine job roles and responsibilities.

Instead of simply automating existing tasks, AI will enable the creation of entirely new roles and industries. Imagine, for instance, AI-assisted healthcare professionals capable of diagnosing illnesses with unprecedented accuracy, freeing doctors and nurses to focus on patient care and relationship building. Similarly, AI could power personalized education systems, adapting to individual learning styles and optimizing teaching methods, allowing educators to dedicate more time to mentoring and inspiring students. The possibilities are vast and span across numerous sectors.

The key to realizing this vision lies in fostering a culture of continuous learning and adaptability. Individuals will need to acquire new skills not just once, but continuously throughout their careers. This necessitates a shift in educational paradigms, moving away from traditional, rigid curricula to more flexible, lifelong learning models that emphasize adaptability, critical thinking, and problem-solving. Educational institutions and companies alike will play a crucial role in creating training programs that prepare workers for the constantly evolving demands of the human-AI workplace.

This includes a focus on cultivating skills that complement AI's capabilities. While AI excels at data analysis and pattern recognition, humans bring emotional intelligence, critical thinking, creativity, and ethical reasoning to the table. These are not simply "soft skills" to be tacked on; they are the foundational elements of effective human-AI collaboration. Training programs should prioritize developing these uniquely human attributes, preparing workers to leverage AI's strengths while contributing their own irreplaceable skills.

The role of leadership will also undergo a transformation. Leaders of the future will need to be AI-literate, understanding both the capabilities and limitations of this technology. This doesn't mean they need to be AI programmers; rather, they need to be able to effectively manage and leverage AI tools within their organizations, fostering a collaborative environment where humans and AI work in synergy. This requires a deep understanding of how AI can augment human capabilities, optimize workflows, and enhance productivity, coupled with the ability to lead and inspire teams in this new context.

Moreover, ethical considerations will be paramount. As AI becomes increasingly integrated into the workplace, questions of bias, fairness, accountability, and transparency will need to be addressed.

This necessitates the development of ethical guidelines and regulations for the development and deployment of AI systems, ensuring that these technologies are used responsibly and ethically, minimizing potential risks and maximizing their benefits. Leaders will play a critical role in implementing and enforcing these ethical guidelines, ensuring that AI is used to enhance, not undermine, human well-being.

The long-term impact of AI on the workplace will extend beyond individual job roles and organizational structures. It will reshape entire industries and economies, potentially leading to a more efficient, productive, and innovative world. However, this transformation also presents challenges. The potential for job displacement, the need for workforce retraining, and the ethical considerations surrounding AI deployment all require careful consideration and proactive planning.

Governments and policymakers will have a crucial role to play in navigating these challenges. Investing in education and retraining programs, creating social safety nets to support workers affected by automation, and developing ethical guidelines for AI development and deployment are all essential steps. International collaboration will also be vital, ensuring consistent standards and regulations for the responsible use of AI across borders.

The long-term vision for human-AI collaboration extends beyond the purely economic and professional spheres. It touches upon fundamental questions about the nature of work, the meaning of human contribution, and the future of society. As AI takes over more routine and repetitive tasks, it opens up the possibility for humans to engage in more meaningful, fulfilling work that taps into their creativity, empathy, and problem-solving abilities. This could lead to a more balanced and enriching work-life integration, with individuals having more time and autonomy to pursue personal interests and passions.

However, the transition to this future will not be seamless. It will require significant investment in education, retraining, and infrastructure, along with careful consideration of ethical and societal implications. Addressing the potential for job displacement, ensuring equitable access to opportunities in the AI-driven economy, and mitigating potential biases in AI systems are all critical challenges that must be tackled proactively.

The future of work is not a predetermined outcome; it is a shared responsibility. Individuals, organizations, governments, and the broader global community must work together to shape a future where human and AI work in harmony, maximizing the benefits of this transformative technology while mitigating its potential risks.

This requires a long-term vision, a commitment to continuous learning and adaptation, and a shared understanding of the ethical principles that should guide the development and deployment of AI.

The journey towards a future of seamless human-AI collaboration will undoubtedly involve complexities and unforeseen challenges.

Yet, the potential rewards – a more efficient, innovative, and equitable workplace that allows humans to flourish – make this endeavor a worthy pursuit. By embracing a proactive and collaborative approach, we can ensure that AI serves as a powerful tool for human advancement, leading to a future where technology empowers us to achieve unprecedented levels of productivity, innovation, and human well-being. This is not a future to be feared, but a future to be shaped, a future where technology and humanity work together to create a more prosperous and fulfilling world for all. The path forward requires foresight, adaptability, and a steadfast commitment to building a future where the human element remains central to our progress and prosperity. The challenge lies not in resisting change, but in harnessing its potential for the betterment of humanity.

Glossary

A

Adaptability

The ability to adjust to new conditions, technologies, or changes in the workplace, especially as AI transforms job roles and industries.

Algorithm

A step-by-step set of instructions used by AI systems to process data, make predictions, or automate tasks.

Artificial Intelligence (AI)

The simulation of human intelligence by machines, enabling them to learn, reason, and perform tasks that typically require human cognition.

Automation

The use of technology, including AI and robotics, to perform tasks previously done by humans, reducing manual effort and increasing efficiency.

B

Bias in AI

The presence of unfair or discriminatory patterns in AI decision-making, often due to biased training data or flawed algorithms.

Big Data

Extremely large datasets that AI systems analyze to identify patterns, trends, and insights for decision-making.

Blockchain

A decentralized and secure digital ledger technology that records transactions, often used in industries like finance, supply chain, and digital contracts.

C

Chatbot

An AI-powered virtual assistant that interacts with users via text or voice, commonly used in customer service and business automation.

Cognitive Computing

AI systems designed to mimic human thought processes, including understanding language, recognizing patterns, and making decisions.

Critical Thinking

A crucial human skill involving analysis, reasoning, and problem-solving, which remains essential in an AI-driven workplace.

D

Data Science

The field of study that uses algorithms, statistics, and AI to extract insights and knowledge from structured and unstructured data.

Deep Learning

A subset of machine learning that uses neural networks with multiple layers to analyze complex data and improve AI performance.

Digital Transformation

The process of integrating digital technology, including AI, into business operations to enhance efficiency and innovation.

E

Emotional Intelligence (EQ)

The ability to understand, manage, and express emotions effectively, a critical skill in leadership and human-AI collaboration.

Ethics in AI

A framework for responsible AI development, ensuring fairness, transparency, accountability, and minimizing harm to individuals and society.

Exponential Growth in AI

The rapid acceleration of AI capabilities and adoption, leading to significant changes in the workforce and business operations.

F

Future-Proofing

The process of preparing for future changes by developing adaptable skills, staying updated with trends, and leveraging AI tools.

Fourth Industrial Revolution

The current era of rapid technological advancements, driven by AI, automation, robotics, and the Internet of Things (IoT).

G

Gig Economy

A labor market characterized by short-term, freelance, or contract-based work, often influenced by AI-driven platforms like Uber and Upwork.

Generative AI

AI systems that create new content, such as text, images, music, and code, based on training data (e.g., ChatGPT, DALL·E, Midjourney).

H

Headhunting

A specialized recruitment process where recruiters identify and attract top talent, often for high-level executive positions.

Human-AI Collaboration

A work model where AI assists humans rather than replacing them, enabling increased efficiency and innovation.

I

Internet of Things (IoT)

A network of interconnected devices that collect and exchange data, impacting industries like healthcare, manufacturing, and smart cities.

Innovation Economy

A knowledge-driven economy where creativity, problem-solving, and technology drive economic growth and job creation.

J

Job Automation Risk

The likelihood of a job being replaced or transformed by AI and automation, influencing workforce trends and reskilling needs.

Job Displacement

The reduction or elimination of certain job roles due to AI and technological advancements.

K

Key Performance Indicators (KPIs)

Metrics used to measure success in a job role, often evolving due to AI's ability to analyze and track productivity in new ways.

Knowledge Work

Professional work that relies on intellectual skills, problem-solving, and critical thinking, often enhanced by AI tools.

L

Lifelong Learning

The continuous process of acquiring new skills and knowledge, essential for staying relevant in the AI-driven job market.

Low-Code/No-Code AI

AI-powered tools that allow users to create applications or automate tasks without advanced programming skills.

M

Machine Learning (ML)

A subset of AI where algorithms learn from data to improve their performance without explicit programming.

Metaverse

A virtual, AI-driven digital space where people interact using avatars, with potential implications for remote work and online business.

Mindset Shift

The necessary change in perspective for workers adapting to AI and automation, emphasizing flexibility, growth, and lifelong learning.

N

Natural Language Processing (NLP)

A branch of AI that enables machines to understand, interpret, and respond to human language (e.g., Siri, Alexa, ChatGPT).

Neural Networks

AI models inspired by the human brain, used in deep learning to recognize patterns and improve decision-making.

O

On-Demand Workforce

A flexible labor market where companies hire temporary workers or freelancers based on short-term needs, often enabled by AI platforms.

Overfitting

A machine learning issue where an AI model learns patterns too specifically from training data, leading to poor generalization in real-world tasks.

P

Predictive Analytics

AI-driven analysis that forecasts future trends based on past data, commonly used in finance, marketing, and hiring.

Professional Reskilling

The process of learning new skills to transition into a different career path as AI reshapes industries.

Q

Quantum Computing

A futuristic computing model that leverages quantum mechanics to solve complex problems faster than traditional computers, with potential impacts on AI.

R

Remote Work & AI

The increasing use of AI tools to enhance virtual collaboration, productivity, and task automation in remote jobs.

Reskilling vs. Upskilling

- **Reskilling**: Learning new skills for a completely different job.

- **Upskilling**: Enhancing existing skills to stay relevant in a current profession.

S

Soft Skills

Human abilities like communication, emotional intelligence, and teamwork that remain valuable despite AI automation.

Surveillance AI

The use of AI-powered monitoring systems in workplaces, raising ethical concerns about privacy and productivity tracking.

T

Talent Acquisition & AI

The use of AI-driven tools for hiring, screening resumes, and predicting candidate success.

Transferable Skills

Skills applicable across different jobs and industries, crucial for career adaptability.

U

Universal Basic Income (UBI)

A proposed economic policy where governments provide a guaranteed income to citizens, often debated as a solution for job displacement due to AI.

Unsupervised Learning

A machine learning method where AI models analyze data without predefined labels, discovering hidden patterns on their own.

V

Virtual Assistants

AI-powered tools that assist users with tasks like scheduling, reminders, and information retrieval (e.g., Siri, Google Assistant).

Voice Recognition AI

Technology that enables machines to interpret and process spoken language, used in applications like speech-to-text and customer service bots.

W-Z

Workforce Automation

The increasing use of AI-driven software and robotics to handle tasks traditionally performed by human workers.

Zero Trust AI Security

A cybersecurity approach ensuring AI systems operate securely, preventing data breaches and unauthorized access.

References

Books on AI & the Future of Work

1. **"The Future of Work: Robots, AI, and Automation"** – Darrell M. West (Brookings Institution Press, 2018)

     o   Explores how AI and robotics are transforming jobs, politics, and the economy.

2. **"Human + Machine: Reimagining Work in the Age of AI"** – Paul R. Daugherty & H. James Wilson (Harvard Business Review Press, 2018)

     o   Discusses how AI augments human capabilities rather than replacing them.

3. **"The Big Nine: How the Tech Titans and Their Thinking Machines Could Warp Humanity"** – Amy Webb (PublicAffairs, 2019)

     o   Examines how global AI powerhouses shape the future of AI and automation.

4. **"The Second Machine Age: Work, Progress, and Prosperity in a Time of Brilliant Technologies"** – Erik Brynjolfsson & Andrew McAfee (W.W. Norton, 2014)

     o   A deep dive into how AI and digital technologies impact business and society.

5. **"AI Superpowers: China, Silicon Valley, and the New World Order"** – Kai-Fu Lee (Houghton Mifflin Harcourt, 2018)

     o   Explores AI advancements in China vs. the U.S. and their impact on jobs.

6. **"Futureproof: 9 Rules for Humans in the Age of Automation"** – Kevin Roose (Random House, 2021)

- o A practical guide on how to stay relevant in an AI-driven world.

7. **"The Age of AI: And Our Human Future"** – Henry Kissinger, Eric Schmidt & Daniel Huttenlocher (Little, Brown and Company, 2021)

   - o Explores AI's role in shaping society, politics, and careers.

Articles & Reports on AI and the Workforce

1. **World Economic Forum – "The Future of Jobs Report 2023"**

   - o Available at: www.weforum.org

   - o A comprehensive report on job displacement, reskilling, and AI's impact on careers.

2. **Harvard Business Review – "How AI is Changing the Way We Work" (2023)**

   - o Available at: hbr.org

   - o Discusses AI's role in augmenting human decision-making and creativity.

3. **MIT Technology Review – "AI at Work: The Rise of Intelligent Automation" (2022)**

   - o Available at: www.technologyreview.com

   - o Analyzes AI's role in automating white-collar jobs.

4. **McKinsey & Company – "Jobs Lost, Jobs Gained: Workforce Transitions in a Time of Automation" (2023)**

   - o Available at: www.mckinsey.com

- A research-based assessment of automation and job shifts.

5. **The Guardian – "AI and the Future of Work: How Will It Change Your Job?" (2023)**

   - Available at: www.theguardian.com

6. **Forbes – "How AI Will Impact the Job Market in the Next Decade" (2023)**

   - Available at: www.forbes.com

Thought Leaders & Experts on AI & Careers

1. **Dr. Andrew Ng** – AI researcher, co-founder of Coursera, former Chief Scientist at Baidu

   - His work on AI education is crucial for career development in AI fields.

   - Website: www.andrewng.org

2. **Kai-Fu Lee** – AI investor & author of *AI Superpowers*

   - A leading expert on AI's impact on jobs.

   - Website: www.sinovationventures.com

3. **Fei-Fei Li** – AI Ethics & Computer Science Professor at Stanford University

   - Specializes in AI's impact on ethics, education, and the workforce.

4. **Yann LeCun** – Chief AI Scientist at Meta, co-founder of deep learning

   - Provides insights into AI's capabilities and limitations.

5. **Erik Brynjolfsson** – Director at the MIT Initiative on the Digital Economy

    o   Researches AI's effect on productivity and employment.

6. **Kevin Roose** – *Futureproof* author & NYT journalist covering AI in careers

    o   Writes extensively on human skills needed in an AI-driven world.

AI Tools & Platforms for Career Growth

1. **ChatGPT & OpenAI** – www.openai.com

    o   AI-powered assistant for automation and career productivity.

2. **Google's Bard AI** – bard.google.com

    o   AI-powered research and writing assistant.

3. **LinkedIn Learning AI Courses** – www.linkedin.com/learning

    o   Online courses on AI, automation, and future-proof skills.

4. **Coursera AI & Machine Learning Courses** – www.coursera.org

    o   Free & paid AI courses from universities like Stanford & MIT.

5. **IBM Watson AI Career Tools** – www.ibm.com/watson

    o   AI-powered tools for job search and career insights.

Podcasts & Video Content on AI & Jobs

1. **"AI Alignment Podcast"** – **Future of Life Institute**

   o   Explores the ethics and long-term impact of AI on work.

2. **"The A16Z Podcast"** – **Andreessen Horowitz**

   o   Covers AI advancements in the workplace.

3. **TED Talks on AI & Work:**

   o   "The Workforce of the Future" by Daniel Susskind

   o   "The Future of AI: Why Human Skills Still Matter" by Kai-Fu Lee

4. **YouTube Channels on AI & Careers:**

   o   **DeepLearning.AI** – AI career guidance by Andrew Ng

   o   **MIT Artificial Intelligence Lab** – Research on AI & automation

---

Academic Papers on AI & Employment

1. **"Artificial Intelligence and the Future of Work"** – MIT Work of the Future Initiative (2023)

   o   Available at: https://workofthefuture.mit.edu

2. **"The Impact of AI on Jobs and the Economy"** – National Bureau of Economic Research (2022)

   o   Examines job creation vs. displacement due to AI.

3. **"The Skill Shift: Automation and the Future of the Workforce"** – McKinsey Global Institute (2021)

   o   Discusses which skills will remain valuable in an AI-driven economy.

AI Ethics & Regulation

1. **EU AI Act** – The European Union's approach to regulating AI's use in employment.

   o Available at: https://digital-strategy.ec.europa.eu

2. **U.S. AI Bill of Rights** – The White House's framework for AI ethics.

   o Available at: www.whitehouse.gov

3. **UNESCO AI & Human Rights Report (2023)**

   o Covers the risks and ethics of AI in hiring & employment.

About the Author

*Get a Free Bonus Book! See below...

****

Bradford M. Smith, born 1967 and raised in Lancaster County, PA, has been a polymath when it comes to life. Brad's interests range widely across business, philosophy, science, cooking, travel, magic, the arts, spirituality, engineering, mystery, fantasy, writing, psychology, wellness, sports and history.

After attending Shippensburg University for Accounting and Marketing, Brad started several independent businesses and organizations in the construction and advertising industries prior to focusing on the global franchise industry over 25 years ago with a love of small business and entrepreneurship.

When not writing, speaking, awarding franchises, consulting or just dwelling in thought, Brad enjoys the outdoors, nature, gardening, family, and the occasional cigar, while living with his wife, Judy, in West Palm Beach, FL.

****

*Claim Your Free Book!

Thank you for reading! Your thoughts matter, and I'd love to hear your feedback. Leave an honest review on Amazon of any of my books you've read, and as a thank-you, I'd love to send you a FREE copy of another of my books.

How It Works:
- Post an honest review on Amazon.
- Then, just click to FOLLOW me on the Amazon Author Page, and we will match up the Review Name with the Follower Name from the review.
- Finally, I'll send you a FREE digital promo code for another book as a thank-you!

Thank you for your support — I appreciate you being part of this journey!

Printed in Great Britain
by Amazon